AD
WHAT

MW01005999

"Sebastian Stuart's dazzling memoir held me in its thrall like the best kind of novel. His mastery of suspense and his inherent humanity make for one electrifying read. And, like all good memoirists, he made me reexamine my own life along the way."
—Armistead Maupin

"A gripping read—as sad and sweet as life itself." —Edmund White

"Reading this rowdy and seductive memoir is like meeting the most fascinating person at the party and having him all to yourself. With both humor and pathos, Sebastian Stuart whispers all the juiciest gossip in your ear while examining the consequences of privilege and the shockwaves of intergenerational trauma, sparing no one in his sights—especially himself. At the heart of this story, though, is a love: a transformational friendship between two members of an utterly unforgettable family, and a journey of self-discovery that becomes a moving tale of survival."
—Christopher Castellani, author of *Leading Men*

"*What Wasn't I Thinking?* is a sexy joyride of a memoir. It takes readers from a privileged upbringing in glamorous post-war New York to a wild San Francisco in the '70s and then back again. You can't help but cheer for Sebastian Stuart as he makes his way into the world and watches helplessly as his best friend and soulmate, an emotionally fragile cousin named Tina, starts to lose her grip on reality. An affecting and addictive read." —Alysia Abbott, author of *Fairyland*

"*What Wasn't I Thinking?* focuses on the bond between two devoted, precocious cousins and their unfolding lives. With its shifting scenes of Bohemian Greenwich Village and European cruises and modeling agencies and sexual frankness and complicated mothers and ever-clinking glasses, it balances being both madcap and a captivating, deeply moving chronicle of madness—a combination of *The Marvelous Mrs. Maisel, Franny and Zooey*, and *The Bell Jar*. Or, more precisely, imagine Scout and Dill running away from home down in Alabama and being rescued by John Cheever. And yet know this: Sebastian Stuart has being queer in his writer's quiver and a voice all his own—plaintive and funny with the cadence of kindness running through it." —Kevin Sessums, author of *Mississippi Sissy*

"A very fine memoir about a brilliant, kind, scared, lonely gay boy becoming a man." —Meredith Hall, author of the *New York Times* bestselling memoir *Without a Map*

"I had to take an Ambien because I was lying in bed and couldn't stop thinking about this book. And when I did fall asleep, I dreamed all night about this book! *What Wasn't I Thinking?* goes from the world of John Cheever to Graham Greene to Joan Didion. I'm just amazed at Stuart's story and how well he tells it. Wow-ee!"
—Tom Judson, composer and entertainer

"Told with both child-like wonder and keen-eyed wisdom, *What Wasn't I Thinking?* is a captivating glimpse into a reckless, heartbreaking, and ultimately redeeming life. It's also sex-fueled, celebrity-ridden, and binge-worthy. A wild ride." —Stewart Lewis, author of *Happily Whatever After*

"Sebastian Stuart's compulsively readable new book is that rare thing: a very personal memoir that reflects upon fascinating times and far-flung places with empathy and delight rather than bitterness and blame. *What Wasn't I Thinking?* vividly captures how it felt to be in the most happening of places in late 20th-century America: San Francisco in the 70s, and New York City in the surrounding decades. It's a tender and funny account of a life well, and generously, lived."
—Peter Cameron, author of *The City of Your Final Destination*

"Nobody who enjoys a good comic mystery will be able to put this book down. It's fast and fun and laced with vivid human nature in all its contradictions and moral ambiguity ... As vividly as John D. MacDonald captured Florida in Travis McGree's adventures, Stuart immortalizes our dear, messy valley." —*Chronogram Magazine*

"Mystery-loving Valleyites would do well to pick up this fast-paced thriller ... Stuart's description of small-town Valley life—as seen through he eyes of an acerbic but sympathetic heroine—dead-on (no pun intended)." —*Hudson Valley Magazine*

THE HOUR BETWEEN

"A cross between *A Separate Peace* and *Breakfast at Tiffany's*, *The Hour Between* is charming, hilarious, effervescent, and dead serious. I read it in one sitting and adored it." —Anita Shreve

"Novelist-playwright Stuart sets his fully drawn character loose in a familiar era, but there's nothing quaint or retro about his '60s set; the ubiquitous drugs, the war, the new sense of sexual freedom and the fight against the establishment are pervasive and essential elements. This simple but wholly moving coming-of-age story features a worthy successor to Holden Caulfield coming to grips with what (and who) he cannot change." —*Publishers Weekly*

"I love stories about friendship, particularly those in which friendship is recalled under a nostalgic haze ... I found the whole thing quite lovely ... Stuart knows how to cut the pathos with some sharp wit." —Daniel Goldin of Boswell Book Company for *National Public Radio*

WHAT WASN'T I THINKING?

A Story of Rebellion, Madness, and My Mother

Also by Sebastian Stuart

WHAT WASN'T I THINKING?

A Story of Rebellion, Madness, and My Mother

Sebastian Stuart

Querelle Press
New York, NY

Published by Querelle Press LLC
www.querellepress.com

ISBN 978-1-63760-363-5, paper edition
ISBN 978-1-63760-355-0, e-book edition

Printed in the United States
Cover design by Linda Kosarin/The Art Department
Typeset by Raymond Luczak

In memory of

Christina Montemora
and
Elsie Masson Malinowski

"Give sorrow words; the grief that does not speak knits up the o-er wrought heart and bids it break."

—William Shakespeare, *Macbeth*

PROLOGUE

It was a Saturday morning in the early spring of 1967. I raced down the long drive of my Connecticut prep school and flagged down the bus to the city.

The night before I'd been in my dorm room reading when the hall pay phone rang. Someone answered it and called, "Sebastian, it's for you."

I went out into the hall and picked up the dangling receiver. "Hello."

"Hello, darling," Mom said in her English accent, which she held onto all her life, a calling card that announced her superiority. "I'm afraid I have some dreadful news ..." Her tone was hushed and grave. She paused to milk my anxious curiosity.

"Well, what is it?"

I heard her light a cigarette and take a deep pull. "Tina has had a full-blown psychotic break."

"*What?*" I froze and my pulse started racing. "What happened?"

"She was found wandering around Central Park screaming at people to leave her alone, not to kidnap her. Someone called the police, and she gave them our number. They were going to take her to Bellevue, but your father and I put her in Gracie Square. It's the city's *best* mental hospital."

"I want to see her."

"I would strongly advise against that, Sebastian. We saw her this afternoon. She's in terrible shape. It will distress you to see her. You have to look out for yourself."

"What's that supposed to mean?"

"Well, darling, you *have* been arrested for drugs, and expelled from two schools. I'm not sure seeing Tina would enhance your own ... *emotional stability*." My shoulders went up and I felt myself start to sweat. Mom knew how to go right for the jugular. "You seem awfully upset."

1

"*Of course I'm upset!* Tina is my best friend."

Mom sighed. "Calm down, for Christ's sake. Your father and I will go see her again on Monday and I'll call with a full report. Until then, I forbid you to visit her."

I hung up and went to find a copy of the bus schedule.

On the two-hour ride into the city I couldn't sit still, obsessively replaying Mom's phone call in my head. I had a vague sense that my life was about to change in a serious way. From the bus window I saw two black horses galloping across a field, manes and tails flying.

Maybe I shouldn't have been so shocked by Tina's psychotic episode. Over the last year or so she'd had bouts of acting remote and strange, clamming up, a faraway look in her eyes. Sometimes she lay on her bed like a corpse for hours at a time, staring up at the ceiling. My powers of denial kicked in early, though, and I hadn't dwelled on these episodes. Everybody gets moody. She would sort it out.

Tina was my cousin—and so much more. She was my best friend all through my childhood, a fellow seeker of all-day adventures, we finished each other's sentences and were both fascinated by the macabre and exotic, by outsiders and misfits. Our friendship was rock-strong, the great article of faith in my life. And now this? Screaming paranoid rants at strangers in Central Park?

When the bus finally pulled into the Port Authority bus station, I raced outside and hopped into a cab uptown. Gracie Square Hospital is a modern building on far East 76th Street, between First and York Avenues. After signing in I took the elevator up to Tina's floor, where a nurse showed me to her room. It was sparse and immaculate with two neatly made beds, two dressers, and a framed Matisse print on the wall. It smelled like clean linens and floor wax, with a slight Pine-Sol tang. No snake pit this.

Tina was sitting on a straight-back chair, hands clasped in her lap, looking straight ahead. Her mouth was open, and her eyes were wide, as if she were in shock and had seen something so terrifying and grotesque that it had frozen her in place. She was wearing a hospital-issue nightgown and backless slippers with socks.

I felt an urge to recoil, to run away.

"Tina," I said.

She looked at me and it took her a moment to register who I was. They had her seriously medicated.

"... Sebastian ...," she said wistfully, as if I was someone visiting from another lifetime. Maybe I was.

"How are you feeling?"

She raised her eyebrows in thought and said, "Crazy." She smiled a tiny wan smile.

"This place ain't too shabby," I said, trying to lighten the mood.

"I guess rich people go crazy, too." Her speech was slow and deliberate.

There was a silence, and I said, "You'll get better."

"Will I?"

I didn't know how to answer. Glib optimism seemed insulting and hollow. But I didn't want to hear any details about the hospital or her breakdown. I could barely handle the gist—that she went psychotic in Central Park. I wanted to push away the discomfort, so I started blathering about school and hearing from colleges. Tina frowned and I realized she wasn't in school anymore and might never go to college.

There we were, two friends who never ran out of things to talk about, stunned into silence. Finally, Tina said, "I want to lie down now."

She shuffled over to the bed and lay down, arms at her sides, staring up at the ceiling. This was the position I'd discovered her in several times over the last year. I walked over and smoothed her hair.

"I love you," I said.

Her head stayed immobile, but her eyes moved to me. She looked at me for a moment, and then her eyes began to well with tears. She looked back at the ceiling.

"I'll come visit again soon. You hang in there." I leaned down and kissed her on the forehead. She didn't respond.

I walked outside feeling gutted but oddly hopeful, which may just be another word for denial. At least her illness had come to a head. Mom had assured me she was in the city's best mental hospital. The doctors and nurses were trained to help people like Tina. She'd get better. Right?

It was a bright mild day with a hint of a loamy spring smell in the air, but as I walked past families on weekend outings, my hope evaporated. Mom was right—Tina was in bad shape. Something was seriously wrong with her.

My breath grew short as my anxiety spiked. New York City was my hometown, but it suddenly felt like a forbidding foreign land. The streets I loved to roam looked unsettling and unwelcoming, off kilter, with a hint of menace. The ugly post-war white-brick apartment houses that lined the avenue looked grimy and cheap, the curbs filled with litter, a city in decline.

Tina and I, inseparable, joking, knocking about, having deep discussions, taking epic bike rides—would we ever have that back? Or were we in Tina's "after"—no, *our* "after"—where everything had come unglued, and the roadmap to our future was suddenly written in Sanskrit? Would I be left to navigate on my own, without my best friend?

I remembered Tina's stunned expression as she sat on that straight-back chair. She'd looked so vulnerable. I felt a wave of sympathy and sadness.

I also felt the first stirrings of survivor guilt. Yes, I was glad it wasn't me in that hospital room, but why had Tina gotten sick and not me? Was it genetic? If so, did I also carry that gene? Was she sick because of her unstable childhood? Her detached and undermining mother, and absent father? Maybe it was simply bad luck, the wheel of a bitter fortune landing on her name.

It would take me years to untangle the answers to these questions about my family. The quest hasn't always been pretty. In fact, it's gotten seriously ugly at times. But I needed to figure it out.

For Tina.

And for me.

1

I was born uptown, at Doctors Hospital on East End Avenue, near the end of 1949, as the country was roaring into post-war prosperity. Hitler and Hirohito had been defeated, good had triumphed over evil, and a giddy optimism swept across the nation. Babies were booming.

We lived downtown, in Greenwich Village, in a house on the MacDougal-Sullivan Gardens, two rows of identical townhouses, each with a private yard that opened onto a common garden in the center. The houses were charming and homey, with a London feel, but they weren't grand like their uptown cousins.

There were lots of other kids around and for us the Garden was a hidden world of trees and lawns and stone walls, of ivy and turtles and roll-out awnings in striped canvas, of hide-and-seek and splashing in the rain that gushed out of the gutter spouts. The adults sat on flagstone terraces clinking the ice cubes in their drinks. Nobody paid a whole lot of attention to us kids. That was fine with me.

My dad, Walker, was the heir to some Albany banking money, and the Garden was the perfect place for him and my mom, Jozefa, who went by "Zef." It was filled with sophisticated, well-educated, and well-heeled young couples. All the grownups smoked constantly and drank quite a bit—cocktails for the women, Scotch for the men, wine for everyone. I remember hovering at the edges of the patios, listening to lively and intense conversations full of laughter, dropped names, talk of trips and books and politics. Everyone was a leftie. The women were pretty and chic in capri pants and string sandals, silk blouses and red lipstick. The men favored chinos and well-worn denim shirts.

Mom was a star, even in that starry crowd. She was nimble, quick-witted, vivacious, stylish. With her thick brown hair and great smile, she looked like Ingrid

Bergman. Then there was her intellectual pedigree, which carried some coinage at the time (more on that shortly).

I had a sister, Diana, four years older, and a brother, David, two years older. Rebecca came along four years after me. You won't be hearing a lot about them in these pages. The only story I can tell with any certainty is my own.

There was great excitement the day Diana, David, and I cabbed up to Richard Avedon's studio—he was a friend of my parents—to shoot a *New Yorker* print ad for a furniture maker. We were dressed in pajamas and hung over the back of a midcentury chair in front of a white backdrop. Avedon worked fast, mercurial, and we each got a candy-bar reward. Getting out of the cab back on MacDougal Street, I remember thinking, *We're a special family.*

When it came to parenting, my folks were hands-off types influenced by the progressive ideas of pediatrician and author Dr. Benjamin Spock. I used to wander the neighborhood alone at age six, which might seem shocking today, but back then you'd see kids bopping around the Village streets all the time. City kids, with our Spaldeen pink rubber balls that we squeezed and tossed and played handball with against playground walls.

I loved the streets. New York still had a post-war feel back then—the cars were fat, the men wore hats, and everything looked like a black-and-white movie. Music blared from windowsills and car radios, there were shouts across alleyways strung with clotheslines, the air smelled of fresh-roasted coffee and car exhaust, and sometimes you'd see a horse-drawn vendor cart clip-clopping by with its proud display of fresh fruits and vegetables. It was Fellini, the dance of life.

The Garden was magical at Christmas. A huge tree was put up in the center oval and on Christmas Eve we all gathered around it and sang carols. Then a wooden Santa appeared in the sky above us, riding a zip wire that had been strung across from one rooftop to another. Midway, Santa dropped down a blizzard of candy and we kids all turned into little terrors. Who cares about some holy night when there are Tootsie Rolls to be had?

I was fascinated by our urbane Garden neighbors. There were Cass and Joe. He was a high-school principal, and she was right out of a Dorothy Parker short story—an insecure girl from Wisconsin in over her head. Joe drank and—I found out years later from my folks—was closeted. When Cass found out Joe was queer, she had what was then called a "nervous breakdown" and moved back to the Midwest. According to Mom, she was "a broken woman." It was a New York story. Years later, when I was about thirteen and we lived on Central Park West, I ran into Joe early one morning in front of our building. He'd clearly been up all night, sunken-eyed, disheveled, unshaven. He eyed me knowingly. Gay boys start to pick up signals at an early age. (That's another New York story. I'll get to it.)

Then there was Mom's great chum, beautiful irresistible Jemmy Hammond, first wife of legendary music producer John Hammond. Jemmy had a romance with the then-famous actor Gary Merrill. (I bring this up because their affair figures in later.) The Garden was a starry place back then and still is—more recent residents include Anna Wintour, Richard Gere, and Bob Dylan.

My very first memory is of being in my crib at night. Dad comes in, turns out the lights, and waves his cigarette through the air, the burning tip tracing incandescent swirls against the blackness. I'm enchanted—it's just me and Dad and magic.

I beg him for "more-more-more", but he gets bored. He turns and leaves, and I miss him with an ache. My first word is "paper" because I see Dad reading the *New York Times* every day and I want to copy him. I still read the *Times* and sometimes when I'm reading it, I think of Dad and the swirling tip of his cigarette.

In 1953, when I was three years old, Ruby Turner became our housekeeper. She would stay for more than twenty years.

I took to Ruby like snap to crackle. I loved her dark skin and would run my hand down her arm and hold my arm next to hers in comparison. I began to spend a lot of time in the kitchen, we would talk and talk for hours, often about Black celebrities she'd read about in the gossip columns or in *Jet* magazine. Calypso was the rage, and we were both in love with Harry Belafonte (if you had a pulse you were in love with Harry Belafonte). Or I would sit and watch her cook. Every month or so she'd bake a cake from scratch and let me lick the last of the buttery batter from the bowl. Then the kitchen would fill with rich moist baking smells.

Ruby's cakes were frosted nirvana.

I loved to ask Ruby questions about her life. She lived in the Bronx, in the projects, with her daughter and grandson. One day after school when I was sitting at our kitchen table eating a plate of Ritz crackers with peanut butter and cheddar cheese that she'd made for me, I asked, "How come you only had one baby?"

Ruby was at the sink rinsing vegetables and she stopped what she was doing. Then she said, "I had another one."

"You did? A boy or a girl?"

She turned to me, wiping her hands on her apron. "He was a boy. His name was James."

"What happened to him?"

Ruby hesitated. "He was born dead. He was strangled by his umbilical cord."

Her eyes filled with tears. And so did mine. Then she turned back to the sink and said, "You run along now. I have work to do."

I slowly fell in love with Ruby. She gave me attention and concern and affection, and she was a buffer against Mom's volatile moods. She was a proud woman and once flexed her bicep and said to me, "Feel this. I'm strong. Not like you Stuarts."

Years later, when we kids had grown and my folks had moved to an apartment on Central Park West, Ruby was let go. She quickly found a new gig–her "employment office" was the grapevine of maids and housekeepers that wound through the basement laundry rooms of the grand old buildings. Of course I know now that Ruby wasn't part of our family. She worked for us. And when she was no longer needed, she was let go. But when I was a kid, I didn't understand that. Ruby lived in the house with us. She and I spent easy, even intimate, hours together. In my mind (and heart) the lines blurred.

2

The really big day came in the spring of 1954. That's when my Aunt Wanda and her three children—my cousins Michael, Nicola, and Christina—returned to New York City after living in Italy for four years. They were staying at a borrowed apartment on Washington Square and Mom and I walked up to meet them.

The apartment was graceful and high-ceilinged with windows overlooking the park. When we entered, Wanda was pacing the room, and there was a feeling of restlessness, transition, uncertainty. Michael and Nicky stood nearby looking anxious on this unfamiliar turf.

I was immediately fascinated by my Aunt Wanda. She looked like a movie star, blonde and beautiful, tall and glamorous. At one point she held her palm to her chest and got a faraway look in her eyes. When she smiled the room filled with warmth and charm.

Wanda knelt down to my level. "How lovely to see you, Sebastian."

"It's nice to see you."

She kissed the top of my head. Then she stood and shook her hair. She seemed so much looser and more fun than Mom, who shot me a cold look.

"Where are the children going to go to school?" Mom asked.

"I just arrived, Jozefa, I haven't figured that out yet. Don is talking about getting a house in Westport. Then they can just go to public school." Don Allen was Wanda's latest paramour and soon-to-be second husband.

"All well and good, but until then the children need to be in school. And Nicky's dress is too small. And look at that stain on Michael's shirt. Don't they have other clothes?"

"I need to get my bearings," Wanda said. Then she walked over to the liquor cart and poured herself a glass of red wine.

"Wanda, it's eleven in the morning," Mom said.

"It's dinner time in Italy," Wanda replied.

"And you have three children to look after."

Wanda ignored this comment and Mom clenched her teeth.

I knew from dinner-table discussions that Mom, Wanda, and their younger sister Helena had moved from London to the States in 1939. Mom and Helena had gone off to Vassar, and Wanda had stayed in the city and modeled under the name Wanda Delafield. During these years she had affairs with a number of men, including William Styron, but she married Vincent "Monty" Montemora, a restaurateur with a gambling problem who lost Wanda's $40,000 in savings (a hefty sum at the time) at the track.

The marriage fell apart. Wanda, with no income and three young children, moved to the family house in the Dolomite Mountains of northern Italy, bought by my grandparents—both long dead—in 1923. They could live there for free. They'd ended up staying for four years.

Now they were back.

And my life was about to take a profound turn.

While Mom and Wanda bickered, I wondered where Tina was. Since we were the cousins closest in age, I was especially eager to meet her. Then she appeared in the doorway to a bedroom. She was about my height, with auburn hair, olive skin, and bright, curious, amber eyes. Our eyes locked and she looked down, shy, holding back.

"Hi," I said.

"Sebastian?" she asked. I nodded.

Then she smiled and I was gone. We just had this immediate and instinctive simpatico, platonic love at first sight.

We retreated into the bedroom where we could be alone.

"You lived in Italy?" I asked. Tina nodded. "Do you speak Italian?"

"No, but I speak German. That's what they speak in Oberbozen."

"But it's in Italy."

"I know, but it *was* part of Austria, where they speak German."

"That's history. Are you coming to the Grace Church School? That's where I go to school."

"Maybe. I hope so. My father lives in New York."

"Will you be staying with him?"

"He doesn't even know we're here. Mommy doesn't want to tell him. She hates him."

"That's strange."

"I think grownups are strange, don't you?" Tina said.

"My dad is nice. You'll meet him. I can show you around the Village a little, if you want," I said.

"That would be fun. Mom says we're cousins."

"Do you like cake?"

"Yes."

"Because Ruby makes delicious cakes. I'll ask her to make one for you. The Tina Cake."

"Who's Ruby?"

"She lives with us."

"Can she make a chocolate cake?"

"Yes."

The words just poured out of us. It was as if we'd skipped the early steps of a budding friendship and went right to being best pals. It was alchemy.

"Do you want to come over tomorrow after I get home from school?"

Tina nodded and sat on the edge of the bed and started bouncing. I joined her and we bounced together. Then we started to laugh.

"What are you children up to in there?" Mom called.

She sounded like she was a thousand miles away.

3

The grown-up parties on the Garden were always fun. We kids would get cooed over and could raid the kitchen for special goodies like fancy cheese on little round crackers and melon-wrapped prosciutto stabbed through with a toothpick. When I was around eight years old Jemmy Hammond had a lively bash. The Modern Jazz Quartet was on the record player, accompanied by the cozy din of clinking ice cubes and throaty laughter.

At one point I wandered upstairs. Jemmy's bedroom door was ajar and I peered in. She and Gary Merrill were on her bed going at it. They were clothed, but Jemmy's breasts were out, pale and full, and he was partaking of their charms. This was my first look at sex, real sex, and I was riveted for the split second it took before Merrill growled, "Scram!" But that second was enough to sear the image into my brain, where it remains to this day.

The next day I was dying to call Tina up in Westport—where Wanda and Don had moved after getting married—and give her a full report on my brush with sex. Of course, in those days phones were fixed in place and our house had only one downstairs, on a drop-leaf table in the foyer, across from the staircase. I waited until Mom and Dad were out and Ruby and my sibs were upstairs. I dialed and scooted under the table for extra soundproofing.

"Hello?" Wanda answered.

"Oh, hi, this is Sebastian."

"Hello, lovey."

"Can I talk to Tina?"

I heard the receiver drop on a table, followed by footfalls on the stairs and then, "Hi, Sebby."

"I saw Jemmy having sex last night!"

"Wow! With who? What were they doing? Were they naked?"

"Gary Merrill. He was on top of her, kissing her breasts, but they weren't naked."

"What were *you* doing there?" Tina asked.

"It was at a party at Jemmy's, I went upstairs to explore and saw them. Then he told me to get lost."

"I don't blame him. Did you see his penis?"

"No."

"Well, what was it like?"

"I just said I didn't see his penis."

"No, I mean the sex, what was that like?"

"They were in another world; it was really intense."

"I've seen dogs having sex," Tina said. "That's intense, too."

"I guess sex is intense."

"Maybe that's why they call it sex."

"That makes no sense."

There was a pause as we both basked in our brush with this thrilling new world.

"Are we going to have sex someday? I mean with other people?" I asked.

"Probably. Most likely. Yes, of course we are."

"It kind of scares me."

"I wish you had seen his penis."

"Me too."

"Really?"

There was a pause. I felt myself blush. "I mean ... "

"It doesn't matter, Sebby."

Tina, at age eight, had instinctively thrown me a life preserver. Then I saw Ruby's feet as she descended the staircase.

"I should get going," I said.

"Okay, see you soon."

"What are you doing under that table?" Ruby asked.

"Just calling Tina."

"That must have been a top-secret conversation," she said, and we laughed.

I hated school from day one. My first school, Grace Church School, was up on Fourth Avenue and Tenth Street. It had enormous front doors and I dreaded going through them. My favorite activity—and the only one I was any good at—was nap. We'd grab our blankets from their cubbyholes, lay them out the floor and curl up. Naps are still kind of my favorite thing in life. I guess good habits start young.

Sometimes Mom would walk me to school. I remember holding her hand as she strode in front of me, pulling me along. She had this driving energy, and I was just trying to keep up. When we reached school, she would shoo me up the front steps. I'd turn and see her hurrying away, lighting a cigarette. Once in a while she'd kneel down, straighten my collar, kiss me on the forehead and say, "I hope school is fun today." I wanted her to be like that every day and I found the contrast confusing. I never knew what to expect. I was already starting to feel wary of her.

4

The Village was full of skinny effeminate men in pastel t-shirts and tight pants. They often travelled in small packs, exuberant, laughing, swishing a little. I was fascinated, sensing even then that this was my tribe. And that it made me an outsider. And that I liked being an outsider.

One afternoon on the patio Mom and two friends lowered their voices.

"They're fags and fairies," Mom said.

"Brilliant with flowers and hair."

"But useless when we really need them."

They laughed.

Indignity was everywhere during those years. Queers were the butt of jokes, shown as mincing, lisping queens in our few cameos in pop culture, vilified by religion, especially the then all-powerful Catholic Church, ignored by politicians and exiled from families. The mocking laughter of Mom and her friends echoed in my ears and made me ashamed and uncertain.

I know now that in the larger gay community surrounding the Garden, rage and rebellion were percolating under the fear and shame. The nascent gay liberation movement was fomenting, inspired by the civil rights movement, which taught us that while nobody is going to give you your rights, if you fight hard enough there will be progress. Even sitting in the sylvan cocoon of the Garden, if you listened carefully, you could hear the low rumble of distant thunder.

But all that was years away. Back then I was just a kid growing up in Greenwich Village.

Half a block north of the Garden, across Bleecker, was the heart of the jazzy beatnik world of MacDougal Street, with its clubs, bars, and coffee houses. Copies of Ginsburg's *Howl* were strewn on tabletops, everyone wore black, couples kissed in cafes, the girls favored berets, black tights and ballet flats, poetry and sex were in the air.

On the corner of Bleecker and MacDougal there was a stand that sold fresh oysters and clams. Dad loved to stop there and get a dozen, watching as the man deftly opened them and arrayed them in a circle on a paper plate, squeezing on lemon, which made them squirm in their shells. We shared them. They tasted like a salty burst of a lemony sea.

Dad, an aspiring filmmaker, had style, with his black knit ties and his Pall Malls, which he smoked in a black cigarette holder with a tiny handle you pushed to eject the butt. We would walk around the neighborhood holding hands. An Italian man with a camera and a palomino pony plied the streets. Dad put me up on the pony and the man took my picture. I still have it. When I look at it today, I think of our long-ago excursions.

Dad loved to walk around and look—especially at people. He just loved people. I never felt like I was getting his full attention, but I was happy to be tagging along. He once said to me, "Look around you, Sebastian, it's the humanity, the sheer beautiful *humanity* of it all."

Dad was so different from Mom, in some ways her opposite. He was calm, kind, and funny, while she was high-strung, unpredictable, and waspish. Ironically, I think this contrast is part of what kept them together. Dad tempered Mom's anger and outbursts, and he loved her drive and charisma.

One night at dinner when I was about ten, Rebecca asked Dad, "What's a homosexual?"

"It's someone who loves a person of the same sex," Dad answered.

While I sensed I was gay I was a long way from admitting it, even to myself. When I was older and fully out, I realized how powerful his words were—how thoughtful and empathetic he was. No wonder I loved him so much. He died in 2006 but more than anyone else in my life his example guides me today.

In the other direction from the beatnik scene, just to the south across Houston Street, was Little Italy. It was filled with squat women in widow's weeds, Italian

16

bakeries, burly men, and skinny boys. I loved the Italian boys. They were rough and cool and had panache, a sexy contrast to the upper-middle-class kids who lived on the Garden or who I went to school with.

A highlight of the year in Little Italy was the Feast of St. Anthony one block over on Sullivan Street. The street was lined with games where you could toss a beanbag into a hole or shoot a mechanical duck and go home with a stuffed pink elephant the size of a small refrigerator. There were food stalls selling sausage heroes piled high with fragrant sautéed onions and peppers, there was fried dough and Italian ice, Italian music blaring, beer flowing, people dancing, amusement rides in the parking lot, yelling and laughing, and finally the procession of men carrying a statue of St. Anthony—with hundreds of crisp green bills pinned to it— up the street and into the church.

I would wander wide-eyed though all the excitement, swept up, feeling like I'd been dropped into another world, raucous, carnal, and delicious. And while it may have been a feast for a saint, I'm convinced the devil sent that fried dough, to which I quickly got—and remain—addicted. It's basically heroin with a little flour tossed in.

A few blocks north and west from the Garden, on the corner of Sixth and Greenwich, sat the Women's House of Detention. Nothing grabbed my imagination like this towering brooding Art Deco prison. The street below was always filled with the girlfriends pining for the incarcerated bull dykes and they would scream steamy and explicit endearments back and forth. It was wild and primal, nasty and moist. I didn't fully understand what was happening, but I found it enthralling. If I walked by with a grown-up, they would hurry their pace, but I just wanted to linger, listen, and watch.

One day, not long after *l'affaire de Gary Merrill*, Tina was visiting.

"I want to show you something," I told her. We slipped out of the house and I led her up Sixth Avenue.

"What is it?"

"A prison for women."

"Murderers and stuff?"

"Yeah, probably," I said. Talking about crime, being this close to prisoners, upped our excitement level—these were the outcasts we were so fascinated by. We lowered our voices and leaned into each other. "It's called the Women's House of Detention," I added.

"I love that name."

"So do I."

"Women should be allowed to be criminals, too."

"And I don't think stealing to feed your family should be a crime even."

We reached Greenwich Avenue. Sure enough there was a group of girlfriends out on the street. In the windows above, the prisoners pressed their faces against the bars, and there was lots of shouting back and forth.

"I MISS YOU SO BAD!"

"YOU WET, BABY, YOU WET?"

"I'M SO LONESOME, GEORGIE!"

We stood soaking it up. "I can feel their heartache," Tina said.

One young Black woman was cradling a baby and looking up mournfully, searching for her beloved's face. I wondered what her story was, where the baby had come from. A couple of the girlfriends were femme to the max with high lacquered hair, Cleopatra eye makeup, and low-cut tops that showed plenty of cleavage. They all seemed so brave and proud, screaming their love, defiant in the face of the stares of passersby.

"WHEN I GET THE FUCK OUTTA HERE I'M GONNA MAKE LOVE TO YOU FOR TWO WEEKS!" echoed down from a high floor.

"OHHH, BABY!"

"MY CLIT IS ROCK HARD FOR YOU, HONEYDOLL!"

"What's a clit?" I asked Tina.

"I'm pretty sure it's part of the vagina."

"I wish they had guided tours of the prison," I said.

"That might be kinda sad."

"Yeah, I guess you're right. It's not exactly an amusement park."

One of the femmes noticed us and smiled. "You kids are nice." She pulled out a pack of Juicy Fruit gum and offered us each a stick. We took it. She went back to screaming.

"We better get home," I said.

"Do we have to?"

As we walked back to the Garden—and the city swirled around us—I felt an intimacy with Tina. Our shoulders touched, we walked in the same rhythm, the same step. The cacophony of the city fell away, morphed into a soothing din, a soundtrack for our adventure.

"We'll always be friends, don't you think?" I said.

Tina mussed my hair. "I guess you're stuck with me."

5

I don't know when I first learned the word *Malinowski*, but I suspect I heard it so often in the womb that I was born with it on my lips. My maternal grandfather, Bronislaw Malinowski (who died in 1942), was a well-known Polish anthropologist whose fieldwork was centered on the Trobriand Islands, a ring of coral atolls off the east coast of New Guinea. His method, which entailed living with his subjects day-to-day for an extended time, was called "participatory observation." It went against then-accepted anthropology methods, which called for studying subjects at a remove. Malinowski's 1922 book, *Argonauts of the Western Pacific*, and his 1929 book, *The Sexual Lives of Savages* (okay, *that* goes into the Title Hall of Fame), had both been influential bestsellers and remain read and taught. After his death his face was put on New Guinean and Polish stamps and a Polish coin.

Mom talked about "Daddy" *all the time*. He was "a member of the intellectual aristocracy" and "a frightfully complex and driven man." She dealt with his book contracts and interviews by scholars writing about his work. Tablemates at dinner parties were eager to hear stories and gossip. In the family he was exalted and revered, but he was also, according to Mom, "an arrogant shit" who could be "cold and cutting as ice" and "had little time for his daughters. He desperately wanted a son."

Still, Mom wrapped herself in his reflected glory. Her identity was dependent on his. He gave her—and by extension the whole family—cachet, entrée, an aura of intellectual superiority, and we wrung every ounce of juice we could out of the mythic Malinowski. But this heritage also brought pretension and condescension that I believe has had a deeply corrosive effect on the family. Just thinking or saying you're smart doesn't make you smart, especially when there's no common sense attached and lurking under all that puffery is profound insecurity.

Tina and I were hardly immune to the myth of Malinowski. One weekend I was visiting her in Westport. She had a small wagon and we decided to name it Malinowski.

"Let's paint it his favorite color," Tina said.

"Great idea! What *was* his favorite color?"

"Let's go ask."

Wanda and a small group of friends were on the patio, having drinks.

"Mom, what was Malinowski's favorite color?" Tina asked.

Wanda said, "Don't ask me, I barely knew the man." Her friends laughed. "Go with black."

As Tina and I were painting the wagon black, she asked, "Who was Malinowski married to?"

"You mean who was our grandmother?"

"Yes."

"I don't know. My mom has never mentioned her," I said.

"Neither has mine. That's kind of strange, isn't it, when you think about it?"

"It *is* odd. To never mention your own mother to your children."

We stopped painting and looked at each other, sensing that we had lifted a dark rock. We loved dark rocks. They held mystery and secrets and brought us closer together.

"We'll have to look into this," Tina said.

6

In the mid-1950s, when I was six or seven, Mom got a job as a researcher at the cooperative photo agency Magnum. Founded in 1947 by the legendary photographers Robert Capa, David "Chim" Seymour, and Henri Cartier Bresson, Magnum was an exciting place to be. Mom brought me into the office a few times. I remember the steel mullioned windows and wooden cabinets with thin deep horizontal drawers, and the radiant, bristling energy of all the bright young things. Mom was at an epicenter of post-war culture with famous members of the Greatest Generation.

The annual Christmas party captivated me. One year it was held in an enormous loft and a trapeze was set up because one of the photographers had been taking lessons. He was wearing a sparkly one-piece costume and there was mounting excitement as he climbed up to one of the two small platforms. A young woman near me, pretty, vivacious, wearing jeans, a white oxford shirt, and a colorful scarf leaned down and said, "He's the daring young man on the flying trapeze." I was in heaven.

The photographer grabbed the bar and took off, indeed flying through the air, before deftly landing on the opposite platform. We all cheered—then moaned when his midair somersault fell short and he tumbled into the safety net.

Presents wrapped in multicolored tissue paper were handed out to us kids. Everything was colorful and fun, everyone was exuberant and kind, there was delicious food, I saw young couples, including Mom and Dad, kissing and laughing.

Yet no one was frivolous. These were people who believed in photography as a means of bettering the world, exposing the truth, bending that arc of history toward justice. This was life or death stuff. World War II was over, but it was followed by the Korean War and the Indochina War in Vietnam. The world remained full of brutal dictators and rank injustice. I remember passionate talk about the power of photography and a free press to act as weapons against fascism. (My brother David continues this tradition today. He and his wife, noted Bulgarian photographer Svetlana Bachenova, founded and run FotoEvidence, which publishes photography books that highlight social injustices around the world.)

I was too young to grasp these truths. But I knew that my family was surrounded by exciting, driven people who had open hearts and a just cause. Their fervor was palpable, their kindness abundant, even to a quiet little kid.

One Sunday morning I walked into Mom and Dad's bedroom and Mom was sitting up in bed, sunlight streaming in the large windows that overlooked the Garden. Smiling blissfully, she threw open her arms and cried, "Come to me, my darling!"

That never happened again.

Mom had a lot of word rules: "Never say drapes, say *curtains*." "Never say gift, say *present*." "Never say home, say *house*." She stated these like moral imperatives. Even as a kid I thought they were ridiculous and delighted in teasing her: "Mom, should I bring a gift of drapes to Judy's home for her birthday party?"

"Sarcasm is unbecoming in the young," she'd fling back.

And Mom laughed and charmed, she was lively and fun, but she brooked no argument. Her opinions were facts. She was always dropping names and judging people, proud and unrepentant: "*Of course* I'm a snob."

During the week Mom was busy with her nascent career, first at Magnum and then at *Fortune* magazine, where she was hired as a researcher. Rushing out the door with a quick kiss in the morning, rushing in after work, changing clothes, putting on lipstick, rushing back out, in the kitchen talking to Ruby about meals and cleaning and schedules, welcoming friends for drinks, always with a determined look on her face, her jaw tight, smoking, always and forever, holding her cigarette between her first and second fingers, tracing circles on her thumbnail with the tip of her ring finger.

Like so many New Yorkers, like the city itself, Mom was always racing off to the next *thing*—show, concert, dinner party, art opening, museum exhibit, benefit—going-going, running, running.

It would be many years before I understood that she was also running away from something.

7

In 1958, when I was eight, my folks made a fateful move—one that haunts the family still.

They sold the house on the Garden and moved to Westchester County, just north of the city.

They did it for us kids—to give us space to play, fresh air, and a pool. But they realized it was a mistake almost immediately. Shortly before he died Dad said to me, "I regret selling the house on the Garden. I don't have a lot of regrets, and that's probably the biggest one." The sale of the house took on enormous meaning in the later, lean years, as both a symbol of our lost privilege and as a guilt-cudgel we kids used to batter Mom and Dad.

The suburban Colonial they bought was large, located in a nice section of un-chic Yonkers. We had the pool, an acre of land on one side and a large playing field on the other, and a garage with an apartment above it. All in all, the place was a mini-estate, grander than any of its neighbors, which were a mix of Colonials, Tudors, and split-levels.

The family next door had moved from Queens and had a son my age. One day we were playing on his lawn and I asked him why they'd moved. "Because the coloreds moved in," he said. I asked him what he meant, and he didn't elaborate but just repeated, "The coloreds moved in." I had no idea what he was talking about. All I could think of were the stained-glass windows beside his Tudor's front door; they were colored.

I later learned that a lot of the families around us were part of "white flight"— those years in the 1950s and 1960s when close to a million white middle- and working-class families fled to the suburbs in response to the Great Migration of Black families from the South to the job-rich North.

An Italian American doctor and his family lived nearby. There were two sexy and exciting sons, nice kids who were already cool in fourth grade. One night when I was about ten, the son who was my age—he had a chipped front tooth that I found so sexy—took me behind a tree, told me to drop my pants and dry humped my butt cheeks from behind.

That was my initiation into sex. It was thrilling that he wanted me—his need, his thrusts were so urgent. We made a pact not to tell anyone. When we were around other kids, we would sometimes exchange a glance that held our secret. The secret was as exciting as the sex. I developed a stunted crush on him. In my mind I didn't grasp what was happening, that I was taking a step into queerdom. In my body I didn't care, I just wished he would take me behind the tree again. He did.

We lived at the top of a steep hill and at the bottom the road curved sharply. One fall day I sat on my bike and looked down the hill and thought: *Wouldn't it be exciting to race down there?* Part of me sensed it was dangerous but that added to the thrill—my impulsive nature was leading the charge. I took off. The ride down was exhilarating but when I got to the bottom, I tried to make the turn and lost control. The bike flew out from under me, and I flew into the curb, face first. I got up with blood spouting from my left temple, dizzy, lights and colors flashing in front of my eyes.

I wobbled up the hill, and the kids who saw me started to scream. Mom came rushing out of the house in a panic. "WALKER! WALKER! SEBASTIAN'S HURT! COME QUICKLY!" We drove to the nearest hospital ER, my battered, bleeding head in Mom's lap. I had a concussion and spent several weeks in bed.

Tina came to visit me a few days after the accident. She walked into my bedroom with a look of concern on her face. When she saw I was in one piece, she said, "That was a stupid thing to do."

"It was fun while it lasted." She didn't crack a smile. Her gravity made me feel cared for. "Yeah, you're right, it was stupid."

"We probably should try not to be stupid in general."

"But sometimes we don't know something is stupid until we try it."

"That's called being stupid."

She smiled and then we ate Fig Newtons and played Parcheesi on my bed.

I was sent to public school for third grade. It was one of those low-slung suburban schools with lots of windows. The teachers were blonde and perky and reminded me of stewardesses. We were always making, giving, or getting greeting cards—the whole school year was structured around holiday cards. I was shy and quiet and on Valentine's Day I got very few valentines.

One girl in my class was a miniature bohemian already. She wore her hair in a black bob like the old movie star Louise Brooks, and was droll and worldly. "My folks walk around the house naked," she told me one day. She was my favorite thing about school.

There was one Black kid in my class or maybe in the whole school: Jerome. We became friends. I walked home for lunch every day and one day I brought Jerome along. When he and Ruby saw each other they both looked surprised. The truth was I wanted to show Ruby that I had a Black friend. I guess I didn't stop to think how Jerome would feel about the fact that we had a Black housekeeper. This was the 1950s and Dad had drilled into us that "Negroes are every bit as good as Caucasians and deserve all the same respect and rights." Still, it would be decades before I understood the extent of my white privilege.

"Can we visit your house?" I asked Jerome one day.

He grew uncomfortable and said vaguely, "I don't know."

A few days later I asked him again. Again, his face had a pained expression.

"Come on. Why not?"

There was a pause. "Oh, okay."

After school we walked to a large pillared old white house. When we walked in the front door, I was surprised to see that there wasn't a stick of furniture in the whole place, just lots of drop-cloths and cans of paint. We walked through the large rooms and in one of them we came upon a Black man up on a ladder, painting the ceiling.

"This is my dad."

"Hi," I said.

Jerome's dad looked down at me warily and then got back to work. Jerome led me into the kitchen.

"Want a cookie?" he said, holding out a bag.

We stood eating chocolate chip cookies for a few minutes. The house was quiet, empty and echoing.

"Where do you sleep?"

He led me into two rooms off the kitchen: the pantry and the maid's room. They were cluttered with clothes and shoes and school supplies and a few toys. The huge empty house, the tiny lived-in rooms, how transitory it all was—I found it romantic. And Jerome was so smart and sweet. I wanted to touch him, to run my hand down his chest ... to kiss him.

"Where's your mom?"

"She works at the Burry Biscuit factory. It's down in New Jersey so she sleeps down there at her sister's most nights. When Dad's done here, we'll move," Jerome said. Sure enough, he disappeared a few weeks later.

Ruby moved out to Westchester with us and I spent more time than ever with her. I loved baseball back then, not playing it—I had a morbid fear of any team sport—but watching it on TV. On Saturday afternoons Ruby and I would retreat to the upstairs TV room, its thick blue curtains filtering out the sunlight, and root for the Yankees to lose. We hated the Yankees because they always won, year in, year out. Give somebody else a chance! Ruby was from Detroit and so we rooted for the Tigers. She sat on the couch, and I sat on the floor. I was an excitable fan and would jump up and scream when the Yankees messed up. Ruby would laugh or applaud along with me. A lot of the time we just sat and watched. I felt so much more comfortable with her than I did with Mom.

Dad had a company called Stuart Productions, with an office in the city, and he owned the rights to some Betty Boop cartoons. It was always fun when they were on TV and "Stuart Productions" appeared at the end. But Dad had bigger dreams. He wanted to direct movies. He began producing a short film that he hoped to use as his calling card.

In 1959, Mom got a contract to write a biography of Robert Capa, one of Magnum's co-founders and a friend of the family. I have a faint memory of Capa—exuberant, large and burly with thick black hair. His most famous works are the shots he took on D-Day when, on assignment for *Life* magazine, he swam ashore with the second assault wave on Omaha Beach. He took rolls of pictures in the first couple of hours, but someone set the dryer too high in the London darkroom and melted the emulsion in the negatives. Only eight pictures were recovered; though blurry, they have become iconic.

In 1954, Capa and two *Life* reporters were covering the Indochina War, traveling with a French regiment. Capa got out of the Jeep and walked ahead so that he could photograph the troops' advance. About five minutes later the reporters heard an explosion. Capa had stepped on a landmine. When they reached him, he was still alive, but his left leg had been blown to pieces and he had a wound in his chest. He died within minutes, his camera in his hand.

We were still living on the Garden then and I remember hearing the news of his death, how serious all the grownups became, and the quiet in the house.

Mom worked on her Capa biography for months. Her papers covered the dining room table and we tiptoed around her. Then one day the piles of papers disappeared. Nothing was said. I asked her, "What happened to the book you were working on?"

She lit a cigarette and poured herself another cup of coffee. "I'm going into the city today. *Time* magazine wants me to come onboard as an editor."

"But what about the book?"

"Let's discuss it another time." She ground out her cigarette and walked out of the kitchen.

It nagged at me. A few days later I asked Dad, "How come Mom stopped writing that book?"

He was quiet for a moment, then said, "She's very excited to be working at *Time*."

I gave up, sensing the topic was off-limits. It was never mentioned again. I still wonder why she quit and how she squared it with her merciless judgment of other people's failings.

8

The place my grandparents had bought in the Dolomite Mountains was in a village called Oberbozen (OB to the family), which hugs the side of the Ritten plateau above the prosperous city of Bozen. When I was about six, after Tina and her family had moved back to the States, we started to visit at least every other summer. The region had been part of the Austro-Hungarian Empire before World War I and was annexed by Italy in 1919. Today there's a road up the mountain, but when I was a kid the only way up was by a rickety cog railway.

When you got off the tram you were in a world of horse-drawn carts, cows in fields, men wearing lederhosen and women in long skirts. The houses looked like cuckoo clocks with balconies and shutters with heart-shaped cutouts. There were a couple of fancy hotels, a butcher, a baker, and a gift shop that we called the Nifty Gifty, run by a tense woman who wore a lot of make-up and was sort of chic by mountain standards —she always had a silk scarf around her neck. Nifty Gifty loved to see us coming—*cha-ching!*

The whole vibe was very Germanic and wiener schnitzel-y. Everyone spoke German and there were a few Austrian secessionists hiding in the hills. Small bombs went off now and then. Nowadays the region is a semiautonomous Italian state and some schools still teach in German.

I loved to walk on the mountain, following winding trails through mossy woods that seemed right out of a fairy tale, collecting wild blueberries by the fistfuls and devouring them until my whole lower face was stained blue. Sometimes I'd come across fairs set deep in the forest—peasants eating fat sausages, drinking and dancing to a small oompah band, bosomy women laughing as they pushed away the groping men, booths and games, all lit by a string of lanterns. It was time travel back to the Middle Ages.

I felt close to Tina when I was in OB. Many villagers remembered her and asked after her. And Tina loved to talk about her time there. One summer I decided to mail her a postcard from the mountain every day. Some of the cards recounted hikes or day trips but others were just a single word, like "Wowie!" Others were informational, like "Ant invasion!" Still others were nonsensical, like "Alice married an alligator. Then he ate her. More cake for me." Tina saved these cards for many years and sometimes we'd look at them and laugh wistfully. Eventually, after she had moved one too many times, they fell through the cracks in her life.

Tina had forewarned me about Hilda, the housekeeper who ran the place in OB. She was stout and stalwart and stern, her ink-black hair pulled into a tight bun. Clomping around and rarely smiling, she looked like she boiled naughty children alive. She lived on the third floor, where I never went because it was spooky and she lived there.

Old Penguin paperbacks filled the bookshelves in OB, and I devoured *Three Men in a Boat*, Kipling, and Agatha Christie. There was also an old record player and I listened to Little Richard and the Platters over and over again. "Twilight Time" was my favorite song:

Each day I pray for evening

Just to be with you

Together

At last

At twilight time

Mom would calm down when we were in OB. She would sit on the long veranda reading and smoking and declaiming and making plans, but in a more relaxed way than she did back home. Malinowski's spirit was ever-present and "Daddy-this, Daddy-that" was a continual chorus, but Mom never mentioned her Australian mother, Elsie Masson Malinowski. One day I asked Dad about Elsie. His face grew grave and he lowered his voice.

"She had multiple sclerosis."

"She did?"

"Yes. It's a terrible disease."

"What happens?"

"Communication between the brain and the nerves and muscles goes out of whack. There's a slow and painful wasting."

"When did she die?"

"When your mother was fifteen."

"That must have been very sad for Mommy"

"Yes, it no doubt was," Dad said. Then he paused and his face grew troubled, "Don't bring Elsie up to your mother."

One night at dinner in OB, Elsie's name did come up. Mom said, "She was a very nice woman," in a casual tone, as if she'd been a distant cousin. Then she changed the subject.

I was a kid and didn't think much of it at the time. After all, Elsie had died years before I was born. It was only when I was researching this book that I learned how my doomed grandmother shaped, and continues to shape, the family, perhaps more than anyone else. I also learned how deeply Elsie loved OB. In the early 1930s, as she grew more ill, it became her refuge. Mom must have felt close to her, sitting on the veranda in the evening, in the same spot her mother had sat, remembering their long-ago times together in OB, before Elsie got too sick to come up the mountain. But Mom never said a word to us. There were no photographs of Elsie in the house. Or copies of the two books she wrote.

My grandmother was a ghost.

9

Airedales were the fashionable dog back then, and ours was named Skipper. I was crazy about her. But while I loved running and playing with Skipper, I considered myself to be very unathletic and had a terror of gym class. Mom insisted that I go to the Catholic Youth Organization swimming pool in Yonkers with some of the neighborhood boys. We were assigned to teams—competition was another thing that freaked me out—and I shivered in my wet trunks next to the clammy pool.

The next week, just before I was due to leave for the pool, I found Mom reading in the living room and said, "I don't want to go back to the CYO."

She put down the book. "Why not?"

"I don't like it."

Mom's face darkened and she grew strangely agitated. "I think you should go back, darling. I really do."

"I don't want to."

"Why not?"

"Because I don't."

"I think it's good for you. *Please.*"

"It's too cold."

She reached for her purse. "I'll give you five dollars if you go."

I shook my head. Mom tilted her head and looked at me. Then she sighed. "All right." She picked up her book and went back to reading. I've always wondered why she got so worked up and why she acquiesced so quickly. Was it because she sensed I was queer and wanted to try and nip it in the bud? Or was it simply because she'd reached the limit of her available energy for dealing with me?

My folks basically never forced us to do anything. Part of me yearned for them to be stricter, to set rules and check my homework and forbid me to sneak candy bars into the house. But they never did. There were no consequences, just a mild scolding when we egged a neighbor's car or skipped school and spent the day roaming the neighboring town of Tuckahoe. I think Dad was so lenient because he wanted our love even if it came at the cost of our respect. As for Mom, she had better things to do than police her kids.

I know now that kids, like dogs, do better with limits.

Sports may not have been my thing, but I loved to redecorate my bedroom. One time I went all out, moving the furniture into what I felt was a pleasing configuration, pinning comic book covers and other "works of art" to the walls. I found a few toss pillows and just totally tarted the place up. I dragged my folks up to the third floor and proudly showed it off. They were taken aback by their clearly queer son's efforts.

"It looks nice," Dad said mildly.

"Yes, well ..." Mom added as she walked out the door.

One of my favorite days was Dad's birthday. We'd sit around the dining room table and Ruby would bring out one of her amazing cakes, blazing with candles. Dad would make an exaggerated show of blowing them out. Then, before he opened his own presents, he gave each of us one. They were small novelties, usually picked up at a joke store, but he seemed to take more delight in giving them than he did in opening his own. I found it so charming and I remember thinking Dad was the greatest guy, with his generosity and his mischievous sense of humor.

Later on, that generosity cost him dearly.

10

Mom said the public schools in Westchester were "simply appalling." So David, Rebecca and I started commuting into the city, to the excellent United Nations International School, UNIS. The school was set up for the kids of UN employees and I had classmates from Burma, Peru, Liberia, you name it. Many of the teachers were English, all crisp and fervent, and they drilled learning into you. I recited the multiplication tables a million times, practiced penmanship until my fingers were sore, and conjugated every goddamn verb in the French language.

Our English teacher, Miss Mendelson, would stride into the classroom, plant herself in front of the blackboard, clap her hands—*chop-chop!*—and launch into the day's lesson. She was fond of sayings and mottos, like "There's no use crying over spilt milk," and "Good-better-best, you should never rest, until your good is better, and your better best."

I liked UNIS well enough, but I wasn't into studying. Before tests I spent hours preparing to cheat, writing out whole paragraphs on the inside of my wrist in tiny handwriting. I was always slipping girls notes during the tests, asking if I could crib their answers. I put more effort into cheating than I would have had to into studying. I felt I was taking a principled stand against homework. My teachers didn't see it that way.

Despite having friends at UNIS, I was considered a "problem" by the administration because of my poor study habits and bad attitude. When I was elected class president, the headmaster practically asked for a recount. He called my parents in for a talk. The boom was about to fall.

11

My most vivid Westchester memory is of the afternoon Mom read *Charlotte's Web* to my younger sister, Rebecca. They were lying on Becky's bed, and I was under it looking up at the bedsprings. I don't know how I got there or if Mom knew I was there. It was late afternoon, that quiet time of day, and the light slanting through the windows was a cottony yellow. Mom read slowly, with such feeling, her voice a world of tenderness, a tone I had never heard before and never heard after.

I wept and wept at the book's end, as Charlotte dies, sending her children off into the world. Mom closed the book and let out a choked cry of her own.

It may have been Charlotte saying goodbye, but I know now that's not who Mom was mourning.

12

My folks hated the suburbs. Mom couldn't believe she'd landed in this dull 'hood surrounded by middle-class refugees from the city who to her horror, "cover their sofas in *plastic!*" They were a far cry from their smart friends in town. They often went into the city for dinners, shows, and openings, and never made any local friends. Soon they began plotting their return.

When I heard that a move was imminent, I asked Mom, "Is Skipper coming with us?"

Mom knelt down and said, "The city is a terrible place for a dog. She'd be miserable."

"I don't think so, I would walk her."

"We'll see."

Skipper disappeared. No announcements. No goodbyes. I was hurt and angry and confused that I hadn't been told beforehand. "Where did Skipper go?" I asked Mom.

"We found a nice home for her. On a farm."

A farm? Even I knew there weren't any farms left in Westchester. Why did Mom feel the need to lie to me?

The apartment search began in earnest. Mom took me to see one on Beekman Place, a chic enclave overlooking the East River just north of the UN. She mentioned that someone named Frances Ann had a townhouse across the street. I could tell by the tone of her voice that she was a bit obsessed with this Frances Ann. The Beekman Place apartment was gorgeous, with views of the East River, but too small for our family. In 1962, when I was twelve, my folks bought a co-op at 101 Central Park West.

In the 1960s Central Park West was a decent enough address, but it had nothing like the cachet it has today. Some of the buildings, especially the rentals, were more than a little shabby. But ours, between 70th and 71st Streets, was one of the best addresses. The block-long lobby was furnished like a fancy funeral parlor—lots of sink-in sofas, Oriental rugs, and framed landscape prints. Our apartment was large with a vast living room overlooking the park.

The place was big but not quite big enough. My folks had a wall built down the middle of the enormous master bedroom so my brother and I could each have our own room. They took the library for their bedroom. They also split the dining room to create a bedroom for my sister Diana, who was off at High Mowing, a boarding school in Wilton, New Hampshire.

Visiting Diana at High Mowing was spooky fun. The school sat on a hill overlooking one of those dank narrow New England valleys, all dark and woodsy, with a stony river running through it. The school was dank and clammy too, and woodsy, since all the buildings were made of wood and smelled like wood and were drafty and uncozy, but the place was filled with artistic types and I think Diana liked it there. I loved visiting because we always stayed at this dank tragic motel in the valley. There was nowhere else to stay for miles around, it was a creepy, lonely area. The motel rooms were dank and smelled like mold. From the outside it looked like a real motel, modern and clean with a tiny coffee shop with a Formica counter and about five stools and one of those displays of the miniature cans of Heinz soup. The cans were adorable.

A strange woman with lank hair ran the motel. I'd see her darting around corners, exhausted but chug-chugging along. She was so busy because she did *everything* at the motel plus she had a passel of kids, urchin-like kids, who were also furtive and darting. If you went into the coffee shop, the woman, who never talked, would stop making up the beds and run into the coffee shop and look at you in terror. If someone pulled up to check in, she'd tear out of the coffee shop and into the office. I wonder if she was popping No-Doz or something. One day I snuck into the coffee shop kitchen—it was huge and bare and there was a sheet strung across the middle and behind the sheet were cots and mounds of clothes and stuff. I think the woman and her kids lived behind the sheet. I hope they slept in the rooms when there were no guests, but they probably didn't because that would have meant more work for the rushing woman. And her life seemed hard enough.

13

Our apartment at 101 CPW may have been in a grand old prewar building but the neighborhood was dicey. The side streets off the park were lined with brownstones that had been chopped up into rooming houses filled with queens, junkies, hookers, and meek gay clerks who had moved to the big city from the provinces and looked forlorn and furtive as they rushed off to work in their cheap suits.

Needle Park, the infamous heroin bazaar, was around the corner at Broadway and 72nd Street. Walking by the park you'd always see skinny skanky junkies in full nod. I was fascinated by these sad-eyed addicts. I didn't understand addiction or the need to escape this cruel world, but I found it achingly romantic.

In 1967 the Warhol house-band, the Velvet Underground & Nico, released their first album, which turned inchoate junkie yearning and nameless lurking sorrow into such classic songs as "Waiting for My Man," "Sunday Morning" and "Heroin." I listened to the album a thousand times on my little record player. It made me want to be a junkie. I got pretty close.

On Saturday nights after dinner, Dad and I would sometimes head over to a donut shop on Amsterdam and 73rd Street to pick up dessert. One weekend when Tina was in town the three of us went on the donut run. It was a hot sticky night in early June and the city had that acrid concrete smell that seems to leach out of the sidewalks, cut with a trace of the sea.

"Wait until you see the queens," I told Tina.

"Queens?"

"Yeah, boys who want to be girls."

"Do they dress like girls?"

"You'll see."

Stepping into the donut shop was like stepping onto another planet, one exploding with color and verve. Fluorescent-lit with a horseshoe counter, it smelled like cigarettes, cold coffee, cheap perfume, and deep-fry oil, and it was *jammed* with Puerto Rican drag queens and hormone-pumping semi-transsexuals, chattering and laughing. Because of laws against being in full drag—you had to be wearing at least three items of clothing of the "appropriate sex" or face arrest—they had made-up faces, but no wigs. They wore pegged pants and shirts tied above the navel. They were vamping and laughing like all get out, beyond swishy, beyond dishy.

Dad ordered a dozen donuts while Tina and I gaped in wonder. The queens loved an audience—one looked at me and ran her hands down her breasts and made an exaggerated kissy face.

"Aren't they fabulous?" I said to Tina.

"They're amazing. I love them."

"Where do you think they live? And what do they do for a living?"

"Some have real breasts," Tina said.

"I want to be their friend. Should we invite one home?"

"Would that be weird?"

"Mom would have a nervous breakdown."

Dad got the donuts, and we went outside. There was a small clutch of queens on the sidewalk. "They're just being who they are," Dad said. I could tell he was fascinated, too.

Two rough-looking teenagers walked by and started to taunt the queens.

"Fairy Mary Jane!"

"Sick bitch!"

"I'm going to kick the shit out of your sissy ass."

The queens *instantly* turned into righteous furies, threw back their shoulders, raised their chins and took menacing steps towards the boys, screeching invective in Spanish. The boys were shocked and cowed, and they split pronto.

Who's the sissy now?

I was just captivated by queens. I remember seeing a young Black queen on the 42nd Street subway platform, carrying on like it was a Paris runway, strutting and swaying and swishing and jiving, loving the shocked stares of the straights. She was with a skinny shy white queen who was blonde and looked like a farm-boy queen. He was hiding behind a pillar, abashed but smiling at his friend's antics. Even then I knew the queens were brave and I loved them for their honesty and their courage. And their outfits.

They proved their moxie seven years later. During the historic Stonewall riots it was the queens who led the charge. The cops were harassing them, and they weren't going to fucking take it anymore. The streets erupted with faggots and bull dykes starting fires, breaking car windows, taunting the cops, and demanding their basic human rights. Ironically, they were also fighting for the rights of the closeted and uptight homos who shunned them—in those days a lot of gay bars banned drag queens. After hours of rioting the cops retreated. We won. Those brave queens and dykes are my heroes.

In recent years RuPaul and social media have taken drag queens mainstream. The shame and hiding have gone way down and talented queens can make a nice living. But what's lost is that sense of being an outcast, an outlaw, a rebel, gritty and girly and proud. I miss it.

You are not forgotten, fierce flaming creatures.

14

Moving back to the city was exciting. These days when I tell people just how down-on-its heels New York was—filthy erratic subways, overflowing trash cans, air you could see, soaring crime rates, crumbling bridges and tunnels—they give me a "Yeah, sure it was" look. But it's true. The middle class had fled to the suburbs, tourism was down, and a terrible malaise, a sense of defeat, hung over the town.

Central Park became my playground, and I explored every cranny—the lakes and fountains and fields, the zoo, the skating rink, the carousel. Like the Upper West Side and the whole declining city, Central Park was funky in those days. But I still loved the ratty old park, with its chipped playgrounds, spotty lawns, overgrown paths. It was usually deserted, which added to its faded charm.

The museums were also empty. I had the Met practically to myself. And the Museum of Natural History, just a few blocks up from 101, was a mausoleum, a labyrinth of empty echoing corridors and gloomy chambers. One day I was there in a gallery of cases filled with insects pinned on boards, the wings were crumbling off the moths. A lone Latino man who was lurking around took out his *huge* cock and waved it at me. I was too surprised to do anything but look. But I was learning that if you were a gay kid in the city, especially if you weren't, well, hyper-masculine, you got a fair amount of attention. It was exciting.

I had a palm-sized transistor radio that I kept next to my pillow and at night it played a tinny lullaby. I was thrilled when a new song from girl groups like the Shirelles or the Marvelettes or the Crystals came out: "Soldier Boy," "Please Mr. Postman," "Beachwood 4-5789," "Will You Still Love Me Tomorrow?," "He's a Rebel." I turned Tina on to my fave groups, and even though she was more of a folkie, she loved them too. On Saturday nights we'd watch *American Bandstand* and call each other right after it ended to relive it.

Going to see my idols in person at one of DJ Murray the K's live shows at the Fox Theatre in Brooklyn was a dream fulfilled. Tina came down one weekend and on Saturday afternoon we took the subway out to the Fox, a sumptuous old movie palace.

"I've never been to Brooklyn before," Tina said.

"Mom says *no one* goes to Brooklyn. But I do. In the summer we'll go to Coney Island."

"Do you think our moms hate each other?"

I was surprised by her question. It came out of the blue. But we were obsessed with our mothers and talking about them bonded us.

"I kind of do," I said, "They always say mean things to each other."

"And about each other behind their backs. My mom is jealous that you have a maid. We can't afford one."

"They're so competitive."

"I wonder how it all started," Tina asked.

In earlier talks I'd filled her on what scant information I had on Elsie. "I think their mom getting sick must have been totally traumatic."

Tina drew inward, her eyes got distant and sad, and she looked down at her hands. "Poor Mom."

"Are you okay?"

Tina blinked and raised her head, as if she was willing herself back to the here and now, away from something dark and lurking.

Our ongoing conversation would have to wait for another time. We'd arrived at our station and show time was coming up fast.

We climbed up to the street. The first thing we saw was a mom and dad gently leading their blind son across Flatbush Avenue toward the theater. It was Little Stevie Wonder.

Inside we sat on the edge of our red velvet seats, waiting for the girl groups to appear, luscious in their chiffon gowns or tight satin dresses, the whole place screamed and cheered, bouncing in our seats. They were goddesses and we were their worshippers, transported to a land where beautiful Black girls rule. Where they led, I would follow.

When the show ended, I looked at Tina in pure joy.
"I still love Joan Baez," she said.

15

Mom was a live wire. Sometimes sparks flew and people got burned.

The Frances Ann with the townhouse on Beekman Place turned out to be Frances Ann Cannon Dougherty—Cannon towel heiress, Broadway producer, and ex-wife of writer John Hersey, a woman who famously spurned the advances of JFK. She and Mom became great chums, especially after my folks bought a place in Amagansett, near Frances Ann's oceanfront "cottage" in East Hampton. Frances Ann was a pistol—great looking, with swept-back shimmery silver hair, sharp and witty, up on everything, thoughtful and sincere in her liberal politics—though it was hard not to see the irony in the copy of *The Autobiography of Malcolm X* placed on the hall table in her house one summer. Malcolm and the ocean view were the first things that greeted you.

I was crazy about Frances Ann. She treated kids with a wry no-bullshit attitude, never talked down to us, and always had something interesting to say. My favorite thing about her was the way she'd put on enormous movie-star sunglasses, head into the ocean and bob around for a while, all silver hair and shades. Although she and Mom got along like a house on fire, I think underneath Mom was jealous of Frances Ann's money and her aristocratic pedigree. Mom had to find a way to feel superior. At a dinner party years into their friendship she insulted Frances Ann, belittling her intelligence and contradicting something she said. I heard from a reluctant Dad that they'd been discussing colonialism when Mom corrected Frances Ann, and added, "You're poorly educated."

We never saw Frances Ann again.

The photographer Inge Morath was an old friend of Mom's from her Magnum days. Once when we were in Paris without Dad, Inge lent Mom her apartment there.

I loved the place. The look was bohemian: it had magenta walls, a low platform bed, and an abstract tapestry on the wall. Inge later married the playwright Arthur Miller and one fall weekend when I was about thirteen my parents and I visited them in Connecticut. When we arrived, Inge told us that Arthur was working in the barn. I expected to find him behind a rustic desk working on his next great play. Instead we found him under the engine of a tractor. Later, when I told him I liked the sliding glass doors that looked out at the patio, he said, "Marilyn put them in." I wanted to bow down before the sliding glass.

Inge, who was bony and chic and sharp, sophisticated in an offhand European way, just delicious, had arranged a dinner party for Saturday night. She sat at the head of the table and Mom sat at the other end. I sat next to Inge and asked my rehearsed question: "Do you prefer taking pictures in color or black and white?" She indulgently answered, "That's a good question. Of course, it all depends on the subject. But I would have to say that black and white was my first love. And remains so."

I noticed that Inge kept shooting icy glances down at Mom, who was being very expansive, dominating the conversation at her end of the table, being terribly witty, talking a bit too loudly, acting like it was *her* dinner party.

We never saw Inge Morath again.

Mom and Dad had known Bill and Rose Styron for years and were fairly close for a while. (Bill had had an affair with Wanda back when they were all young, gifted, and boozed.) When our families went to the beach on Martha's Vineyard Bill wouldn't come down onto the sand but stayed lurking in the dune grass, fully dressed, smoking and observing us. Rose, in contrast, was exuberance itself, radiant and generous, with a smile that lit the room. I was with Rose and Mom on the beach the day that Marilyn Monroe died—they talked about it in excited, knowing tones.

Then one year Mom and Dad went up to the Styrons' house in Roxbury, Connecticut, for New Year's Eve. It was just the four of them and another couple. As the night wore on, Mom insulted Rose. Once again Dad reluctantly told me the story, although he refused to share the details of the diss.

We never saw the Styrons again.

I was embarrassed by Mom's insults. It was a reflection on the family and revealed a nasty streak. It was one more reason I felt wary of her. She was on a short fuse.

In 1992, a couple of years after I moved up to Cambridge to live with my partner Stephen, Mom came to visit. She and Alice, Stephen's mom, hadn't yet met. We were all going to rendezvous at a benefit in Boston. Alice was wise and funny and deeply loving, but not sophisticated, with a touching insecurity. At the benefit she greeted Mom with great warmth, opening her arms. In return all she got was a polite smile.

A friend of ours was also at the benefit, a smart, funny woman who had founded a successful import/export business. The next morning Mom came into our kitchen, sat down, lit a cigarette, took a deep pull, exhaled, and said, "Your *import/export* friend seems like a woman who's accepted her *limitations*."

A couple of years later Mom visited again and we all had dinner with another dear—and whip smart—friend. When we got home, Mom lit a cigarette and said, "I like your friend. She's not terribly *bright*, is she?"

Then there was the night in Amagansett. We'd gone to dinner at the home of a woman I thought was a close friend of Mom's. As we were driving away Mom lit a cigarette and said, "She knows nothing, she's a complete idiot, she's a *shop girl*."

This had been going on all my life—driving or cabbing home from dinners and country weekends, Mom lighting up and launching her dissection.

"She is *the* most stricken woman I've ever met."

"He's *completely* uneducated. And vulgar."

One of her favorites: "She's basically a *hausfrau*."

And most damning of all, "They're nouveau riche."

It was a compulsion, this need to exert her superiority. It was also her basic attitude toward her kids: *don't think for one little minute that you're smarter than me.*

I really believe she couldn't stop herself.

16

Mom and Dad loved the East End of Long Island, both for its sea-splashed landscape and because they had friends there. Back then it was bohemian and artistic, full of writers and artists, not all of them rich. Before my parents sold their apartment on Central Park West and bought a place in Amagansett, they'd rent a house there for a month or two and do a lot of socializing. As usual we kids were left free to roam. There was a lot of beach time—I could bodysurf for hours—and bike riding.

The highlight for me was Tina's visits. Hours before her arrival I'd get excited, imagining her on the decrepit Long Island Railroad chugging out from Manhattan. I'd ask to be driven to the station early even though the train was rarely on time. She'd climb down onto the platform, we'd lock eyes, smile, and the rest of the world would fall away.

Tina would settle in at our house and I'd ask, "What do you want to do today?"

"Let's go for a huge bike ride."

So off we went, usually heading toward scruffy Springs, away from the old-money precincts of East Hampton, riding down empty country lanes, weaving and bobbing and talking and laughing between corn and potato fields that gave way to seaside scrub forest and modest brown clapboard houses. We loved Louse Point in Springs, a craggy bay with endless small inlets and a colony of houses on stilts. We'd swim and search for shells and rocks, all dunes and sun and saltwater and sea grass.

We were biking home late one afternoon, our towels over our shoulders, when Tina saw something up ahead, and pointed.

"Look! A deserted house!"

As we got closer, I saw a modest white two-story house set far back from the road. It looked rundown and lonely.

Tina barreled off the road and up the crushed-shell driveway. I was nervous. We were visible from the road and what if the place *wasn't* deserted? "Tina, be careful! What if there's a crazy man hiding in there?"

"You're such an optimist."

"No seriously."

"We'll bike like hell," she said with a big, excited smile.

Tina rode behind the house, out of sight of the road, and I followed. We got off our bikes. It was quiet, just the soft buzz of insects, the still of a summer afternoon.

"Isn't it beautiful?" Tina said.

There *was* something romantic about the peeling paint, the cracked windows and lopsided steps, the tattered curtains.

"I wonder what happened to the family that lived here? Do you think there was a murder?" Tina asked.

"It's weird, just to leave a house to die a slow death."

"Should we see if we can get inside?"

"No. I think we should leave. It's spooky."

"Maybe it's haunted."

"Exactly," I said.

"That's why we *should* go in."

I sighed, knowing that if I turned down this adventure Tina would be disappointed in me. She took my reluctant hand, "Come on, Sabastini!"

Tina had a bunch of nicknames for me, including Sebby, Sebowski, and Sirbasketball.

I followed Tina up the wobbly back steps. She tried the doorknob and it rattled loosely. "I could probably force it."

"That's breaking and entering."

She turned and gave me a sly smile. Then she cupped her face and pressed it to the glass in the door. I did the same. We saw a kitchen with dingy linoleum, hanging rolls of flypaper dotted with corpses, and a chipped farmhouse sink.

"It's like a time warp from the 1930s," Tina said.

"Like a movie starring Jean Harlow who runs off with a flashy no-count to escape poverty and live in the Plaza Hotel." I was *obsessed* with Jean Harlow.

"I was thinking more *Grapes of Wrath*. A poor, stoic farm family who just up and headed for California."

"*Grapes of Wrath* starring Jean Harlow."

"No, I think it was a murder. They fled after a murder."

A little brown bird suddenly swooped into the kitchen—and both Tina and I gasped.

"That bird could be a manifestation," Tina said.

"Of who?"

"The little girl who was murdered here."

"This is the first I've heard of her."

Tina tried the knob again and sighed in defeat. We sat on the ground and looked up at the house. We liked to sit side-by-side cross-legged, knees touching.

"I wish *we* could live here," Tina said.

"Me too."

"We'd have dinner parties with famous writers and artists and opium eaters."

"We'd always set a place for the dead girl."

We were silent, imagining the ghost-bird-girl.

I thought of my family, back at the rented house. Part of me wanted to rush back and share this adventure with them. But I knew what would happen if I did. Mom would scoff at our imaginings, reducing them to cinder. No flights of bird-girls for her. And I knew, not for the first time, that Tina's world was the one I wanted to live in.

Today that afternoon is still fresh in my memory but the associations it triggers have changed. I now see Tina as the doomed bird-girl.

"Speaking of dinner parties, I'm really hungry," Tina said.

We set off for a shoplifting trip to the IGA. It was easy back then, especially in a poverty-free zone like East Hampton. We stuffed Clark Bars and Milky Ways and Mounds Bars into our pockets and waistbands and walked out casual as day. There's a windmill in the middle of the village, surrounded by a small park dotted with trees. We sat under a tree and gorged ourselves into sugar bliss in the softening evening light. There was something paradisiacal about the East End of Long Island—the potato fields, the scrubby sand forests, the diffuse light, the muted colors and, of course, the sea, the sea, the beautiful sea, which had left us coated with salt and deliciously exhausted.

"Let's never go back," Tina said. "Let's just get on our bikes and ride and ride."

Being the more practical member of our twosome, I bit my tongue. But if Tina had started to pedal, I would have been right beside her.

As for our thievery, I don't know why we didn't just pay for the candy, but shoplifting became something I started to do pretty regularly. I think it was partly because I was a rebellious impulsive entitled brat who thought the rules didn't apply to him. And partly because I liked the adrenaline rush, the we-might-get-caught thrill of it all.

One fall night when we were around twelve, Tina and I were at Jemmy's house in the Garden. There were no grownups around. There was a bottle of sherry and Tina and I were alone with it. We'd never had alcohol before.

"Should we taste it?" I asked.

Tina nodded.

We both took a long sip straight from the bottle. It tasted thick on my tongue, both bitter and sweet. We took another sip. Then a third.

We got really high, in a luscious slow-motion way.

Suddenly I wanted to be out in the city. "Want to walk up to Washington Square?" I asked.

Tina nodded again.

We walked up MacDougal Street through the passing parade of beatniks, hipsters, and bull dykes. I *loved* bull dykes, incarcerated or not. Talk about swagger—they made John Wayne look like Tinkerbell. They'd strut past in man-drag with their ultra-femme girlfriends, who were all cleavage and hairdos.

We sat on one of the park's long curving benches, it was late September and the summer humidity lingered, bringing with it the smell of watery hotdog carts and acrid concrete and marijuana. There were drummers playing beside the fountain and people strolling, savoring the night in the city.

The streetlights had haloes. I was so happy, being buzzed, being with Tina, we'd always be together, grow old together, end up side-by-side eating TV dinners and watching game shows. I felt a mix of cozy and jazzed-up.

"Can I kiss you?" I asked.

"Yes."

I kissed her on the cheek. She smiled her sweet half-smile.

I can still see that smile.

And remembering it brings Tina to life with a surge of nostalgia, sadness and ... happiness for what we had, brief as it turned out to be.

17

One summer when I around nine my family took a road trip to Mexico City, where some friends were living. We loaded up our station wagon and headed across the American South. One night we stayed at an old-fashioned cabin motel. It was hot and through the screen door I could hear a billion insects buzzing in the night air. Then from the cabin next door came the sounds of Mom and Dad having a screaming fight. I couldn't make out their words, but their tone was bitter and rage filled. I'd never heard them fight before and I was shocked, fascinated, confused and scared. As the warring decibels escalated it was Mom's lashing tongue that prevailed. The next morning, they were quiet and distant, but Mom's chin was held high, her jaw set. Dad's shoulders hunched and he seemed dazed. I'd never seen him look quite so beaten down before. She broke him. In some weird way it felt like she was making him an example for all of us: *don't mess with me.*

Mexico City was vibrant and color-splashed. We stayed in an old Spanish colonial hotel built around a courtyard and my brother and I played with firecrackers for hours at a deserted playground. I bought ropes of colored sweetened coconut from street vendors and took walks along old stone roads under trees trained to grow at an angle to provide shade. We also did the whole museum thing and even that was bearable, Mexican art and culture being so soulful and exuberant. There were depictions of death everywhere you turned, and Mom explained Mexicans' reverence for dying and the dead. We visited a street market where every other stall seemed to be selling skeleton marionettes and painted papier-mâché skulls. I was enthralled and asked Mom to buy me a skull.

"Morbid," she scoffed before handing over the pesos.

We spent a couple of weeks in Mexico. Dad flew home for work and Mom and we kids drove back north on our own. One hot day Mom seemed restless and distracted behind the wheel, smoking even more than usual. Finally, she said, "I think it's time for you children to learn the facts of life."

The four of us leaned toward her. She lit yet another cigarette. "The man puts his penis inside the woman's vagina. When he has an orgasm, he shoots his sperm into her womb, where it fertilizes an egg. It's life's most beautiful experience. That's why it's called *making love*."

I couldn't believe Mom was talking about sex. My sibs and I exchanged shocked and bemused looks. She went into a sort of fugue state as she spoke; her voice grew thick. I think she was missing Dad pretty badly.

Later, somewhere in the South, Mom decided we would stop for a picnic lunch. We bought the fixings and Mom searched for a spot. She finally pulled off the road into an area of open hilly farmland and fields. We climbed a small rise. It was a hot, still day and we spread out a blanket.

"I wonder who owns this property?" I asked.

"I'm sure the owner wouldn't mind a nice family stopping to picnic," Mom said.

We set out the food and then suddenly Mom's eyes went wide with fear—panic really.

"Hurry, children, we have to go!"

She frantically gathered up the picnic stuff and corralled us. We fled to the car and sped away. There was no one around to see or hear us and I couldn't understand why Mom was so frightened. I felt such confusion and concern for her.

I think now her reaction was the low-level panic that she lived with all her life flaring up into full bloom, a vein of fear that the worst would happen. After all, pretty close to the worst *had* happened to Mom. She'd watched her mother die a gruesome death for eleven long years. I know now that it left a wound that would never heal.

I believe her outburst was triggered by the southern landscape, the open fields filled with existential terror, so far from home and all that she knew.

Another day we stopped at a dusty funky gas station/general store somewhere in Alabama. It was total *Tobacco Road* gothic with red dirt, chipped and dented pumps and the smell of gasoline. The family who owned the place sat outside in the wet heat. They looked like a portrait from the Great Depression, dirty and sweaty and defeated. There was an older woman, a fat older man in overalls, and a large young woman holding a baby. They spoke in a drawl that bordered on dialect and I hung on every word.

After the tank was filled, we got to pick out ice cream bars and were eating them out front when suddenly the young woman's face darkened and she said urgently, "One's a coming!" The older woman grabbed the baby while the man picked up a short stick and stuck it lengthwise in the young woman's mouth. She bit down.

Mom grabbed us just as the woman fell on the ground and started to convulse. I was shocked and spellbound. Mom had to pull me to the car—I couldn't tear my eyes away from the scene.

As we drove away, Mom said, "She's having a fit."

"What kind of fit, Mom?"

"Epileptic. An epileptic fit. The stick is to keep her from swallowing her own tongue."

"Swallowing her own tongue?"

I watched out the back window until the family disappeared from sight.

That night we stayed at a nice motel and I got five dollars in change from the front desk, went to the phone booth and called Tina. I couldn't wait to tell her about the gas station family and the fit. Her line was busy. I tried several times. I hung up and sat there disappointed, realizing that if I couldn't tell Tina about it, an adventure didn't really count.

18

My aunt Wanda got lucky when she met Don Allen at a party in Rome in 1954. She had left Michael, Nicky, and Tina in the care of Hilda, the OB housekeeper, and fled the drudgery of motherhood to have some fun in the eternally sexy city. Don was working there as a journalist. He was from a rich old Northern California family, handsome as hell, with a head of thick black hair and a distinctive baritone. He was also smart, charming and funny. He later worked for UNESCO and would say, "There's a lot of money in poverty."

Don was a real lothario, married five times with a total of six children. He and Wanda began an affair the night they met. They were married in May 1956, and Don bought their house in Westport, Connecticut, near Compo Beach, soon thereafter. My wonderful cousin David came along that August. The house had originally been a summer cottage and it was charming, with beadboard walls and a sun porch, but it wasn't insulated, and it was always drafty and creaky and cold.

Tina was seven when Wanda married Don. She adored him, and he returned her affection. The years he was around were happy ones for her. He encouraged her, acting as a friend and even a dad. He paid her a dollar to memorize "The Owl and the Pussycat." I can see her standing on the back patio and reciting it with such pride:

"And hand in hand, on the edge of the sand,
    They danced by the light of the moon,
    The moon,
      The moon,
They danced by the light of the moon."

On my weekends in Westport, Tina and I would spend large chunks of time planning a party for Saturday night. We'd go into town and buy party favors and snacks and rolls of colored crepe paper to decorate the small TV room. We would pick a time for the party to start and the day would be filled with anticipation and preparation—decorating, putting up streamers, filling bowls with Chex Mix, setting out the noisemakers and pull-apart poppers. We rarely invited any guests, though, except for Nicky or a friend who lived across the street. Usually it was just me and Tina. When the appointed hour arrived, we'd announce, "The party has started!" and we'd pull a popper, twirl a noisemaker, eat some peanuts and then keep doing whatever we'd been doing before the announcement.

The civil rights movement was galvanizing the country and Tina told me about an article she read in *Readers Digest* about how Black men scrimp and save and go without lunch so that they can buy Cadillacs because the cars gave them a sense of pride. The article made her cry. We were both passionate about civil rights, we listened to leftie folk songs and wanted to be part of the movement. We hit on the idea of forming our own civil rights group and batted around a hundred names before settling on YES: Youth for Equality in Society. It had two members. We both had denim shirts and we stenciled YES on the back and wore them to a folk music concert at Town Hall. We were bursting with pride—but of course no one else knew what YES stood for. Beyond the stenciling, I can't remember any other actions that YES took.

Wanda wasn't much of a housekeeper. Unlike our house, which was a model of order and efficiency with set mealtimes and clean clothes, things were haphazard at Wanda's. The knives and forks often had bits of food stuck to them, even when they came out of the dishwasher, meals were random and slapdash, and there was always an enormous bag of cookies open on the kitchen counter.

My siblings and I were left on our own in a cushy environment, Wanda's kids were on their own in a tatty one. Mom's and Wanda's lifelong competition continued on a low boil. One of Wanda's mantras was "Zef has a maid." That explained everything.

On weekends when I was in Westport, Wanda would often show up in the late afternoon from a friend's house and lean against the door jamb with her cheek resting on her clasped palms, a dreamy smile on her face. I thought she was so glamorous and lovely and free. It wasn't until years later that it dawned on me that she was wine-splashed.

At the time I didn't care. In fact, I loved Wanda's laissez-faire ways, the lack of supervision, just knocking around, taking walks along the beach, hanging out with Tina's girlfriends. She was a popular kid. Looking for fun, one fall day a bunch of us climbed to the top of a closed beach pavilion at Compo, using a drain spout for leverage. It was cool being up there. Then all the girls clambered back down but I was too chickenshit and sat up there petrified.

"Come on!" Tina called.

I looked down. It looked far. The sidewalk was concrete.

"Maybe we should call the fire department?" I suggested.

"You sure you don't want the Coast Guard?" Tina said.

I scampered farther up the roof, away from the edge. By now I was all sweaty, sliding toward freak out.

Then Tina shrugged. "All right, here I come." She shimmed up that drainpipe like a squirrel up a tree. She got to the roof, walked over to me and took my hand.

"Come on, Sirbasketball ... make that Sirbasket*case*."

She was so agile and confident that I relaxed and let her lead me down to safety. I remember feeling protected.

If only Wanda and Don could have made it work. One Sunday afternoon after lunch Don made a fire, put on classical music and was playing on the living room floor with David, who was about four. Tina and I were also in the room, playing chess. It was a cozy scene. Then Wanda came downstairs.

"I'm going over to June's for a drink," she announced. "David, come along with me."

Don said, "Wanda, it's Sunday afternoon and I want to stay here, listen to music and play with my son."

"I want to go over to June's for a drink," Wanda said petulant, adamant.

"Go. But David is staying with me."

"David, come along!"

"Stay right here, David!" Don said, an edge of futility in his voice.

David looked stricken. I didn't understand why Wanda was being so insistent. But she got her way and she and David disappeared.

Looking back at that fight I can see it signaled that the marriage was pretty much over. Wanda wanted a drink more than she wanted a husband.

19

Some weekends Tina would come down to the city to see me. One Saturday when we were about thirteen, we decided to go for a long walk. We told Mom.

"All right, but I forbid you to go to Times Square."

Guess where we hightailed it lickety split?

Times Square was truly sleazy back then, way down on its heels, filthy, with piles of litter at the curbs, filled with porn theaters, stripper bars, sex shops, hookers, grifters, hustlers, and lowlifes of every variety—a cavalcade of cock and pussy, pussy and cock, all lit by a lurid panorama of neon and noir and lorded over by the man on the enormous Camel billboard who blew massive smoke rings out over the scene.

"Don't you love it here?" Tina said as we dragged on our Winstons and walked down Broadway and into the Square.

"Yeah. It's scary," I said.

"Life is scary. Look at her," Tina said as we approached a chunky, dead-eyed, Honey-you're-way-too-old-for-this-business hooker wearing teeny-tiny cutoff jeans, a halter top, and platform mules. (A tough look to pull off if you're over fifteen and your name isn't Daisy Mae.) She was leaning against a building with her hips out. A businessman in a suit eyed her and she licked her lips.

"I wonder what her mother would say if she could see her?" I asked Tina.

"I bet she was abused and ran away from home when she was twelve."

"And she's been hooking ever since."

"I wish she could move to Vermont and raise goats," Tina said.

"Should we give her some money?"

"Let's."

We walked towards the hooker, scaring off the john.

"Oh, hi, I'm Sebastian and this is my cousin Tina. We don't want to bother you or anything, but we like you and want to be your friends."

"Maybe you should move to Vermont and raise goats," Tina added.

I reached into my pocket and pulled out some bills. "Here's five dollars."

Her mouth fell open, and she clocked us up and down. Then she grabbed the $5 bill and spit out, "Get the fuck outta my face."

We beat a quick retreat, holding hands, thrilled at the encounter.

We reached 42nd Street, the throbbing heart of the Square. Then I spotted it across the street: the Holy Grail.

"Tina, look!" I said, pointing to a sign that covered the front of a gaming arcade: Hubert's Freak Museum. The name was surrounded by primitive drawings depicting the wonders to be found within: the Hermaphrodite, the Fat Lady, Flipper Boy, Lizard Man. We looked at each other in amazement: could anything be more strange and wonderful? We crossed 42nd Street and walked into a smoky arcade lined with rows of pinball machines being played by skinny speedy low-lifes and hormonal bridge-and-tunnel boys. We followed the signs to the back and headed down a flight of stairs lined with more hand-painted posters extolling the marvels to come, our excitement growing with every step.

We paid something like a buck and entered a large dingy dusty room with a stage along one wall. The half-dozen "freaks" stood in a line in front of a small audience. A tatty master of ceremonies appeared. "Welcome to Hubert's Freak Museum, the world's foremost institution of human abnormalities and deformities! They say Mother Nature knows best. But she was asleep at the wheel when she created these poor unfortunates. Let's meet them, shall we?"

Each of the performers gave a little spiel. They sort of phoned it in—after all, performances were more or less continuous, and it had must have been pretty tired to go through their how-I-got-this-way routines again and again. The fat lady was jovial (and not that fat—today she'd be just another food court chubby) and Flipper Boy, whose hands grew out of his shoulders, was cheerful and extroverted. He looked right at me and Tina and smiled. The bearded lady, on the other hand, seemed deeply morose.

"Why doesn't she just shave?" Tina whispered.

For an extra fifty cents you could visit the flea circus, which the master of ceremonies pushed pretty hard. Tina and I took the bait and followed him into another room, much smaller and dark. There was a table covered with a wood-framed glass box and inside was a teeny-tiny circus made of metal. The MC got all grand, twirling out his words like he was ringmaster at Barnum & Bailey, but I think it was to deflect attention from the fact that the fleas were invisible to the naked eye. The miniature circus was charming and dusty but for the life of me I couldn't make out any fleas.

Buzzing from our adventure we headed over to our favorite eatery—a Horn & Hardart Automat. These places were Art Deco magic in stainless steel and white tile—huge immaculate cafeterias whose walls were lined with tiny little windows that displayed individual pot pies and macaroni-and-cheese and Jell-O topped with a fat dollop of whipped cream. As a bonus, Automats attracted a lot of strange and solitary diners. We got a fistful of change from the lady in the change booth and headed to the windows. I dropped in the coins for my favorite sandwich—two slices of orange cheese on white bread. The door sprung open and it was mine. Coffee came out of an ornate spout that stuck out of the wall and we filled our thick china cups. Then we found a table, lit Winstons and ignored our food. We had more important things to do than eat.

"I don't think they should be called freaks. They're *not* freaks. They're just different and that's a good thing," Tina said.

"And even if they are so-called freaks, what's so wrong with that? With all the racists and creepy mean people in the world, give me the freaks any day."

"They're beautiful in a way."

"And brave."

"Let's write them a fan letter when we get home," I said.

"That's a great idea!" Tina leaned into me and lowered her voice. "Check out the lady three tables over."

She was old and emaciated, with a heavily-powdered face, a red slash of a mouth, smoking a lipstick-stained cigarette and wearing a dark suit with a large bird brooch and a matching hat with a veil that covered her eyes.

"She looks like a minor character in a twisted noir thriller," I said.

"She lives in a residential hotel," Tina said.

"And has no friends."

"And doesn't want any friends."

"She has a cat she hates."

"She worked as a secretary in a private detective agency for forty years."

"And never missed a day."

"She had sex once."

"When she was forty-five."

"And she loved it. But he never called again. Check *him* out," Tina said, nodding in the direction of a man carrying a meatloaf platter on a tray. He was tiny, maybe 5'2", wearing a fedora and a tweed elbow-patched sport coat even though it was summer. He had a round ruddy face and round metal-framed glasses. He walked over to a table, put down his tray, sat, and began a ritual that included shaking out a napkin and putting it on his lap, then neatly positioning his silverware, the salt and pepper, and his plate and coffee cup just so, and finally looking around innocently before taking out a flask and filling the cup with booze, which he sipped before taking a bite of meatloaf, the picture of urban contentment.

"I think he's a *New Yorker* cartoonist," I said.

"Bingo! Never married."

"Visits a prostitute once a month."

"The same prostitute."

"For twenty years."

"He's her last client."

"They don't talk."

"But they love each other in some weird way."

We lingered forever, refilling our coffee cups again and again, high on it all—how grown up we were!—topping it off with a slice of coconut cream pie. A day in heaven with my best friend.

20

Mom and Dad were always looking for places to park us kids during the summer months. My siblings were sent to dude ranches in Wyoming, wilderness camps in Canada, on hiking trips in Hawaii, and on their own European adventures. We were almost always sent to different places. The same was true for our schools. I think Mom was afraid that any alliances between us siblings would threaten her emotional control. She was the chess master, and we were the pawns.

In August 1964, when I was fourteen, Mom—in an effort to improve my French—booked me to stay with a French family in their chateau for a month. Apparently, they were minor royalty, a vicomte and vicomtesse, and their chateau was surrounded by a vast estate. I flew into Paris and Mom picked me up in a rental car and drove me to the chateau. As we headed up the long drive, we passed farm workers with bales of straw on their backs. It looked like a Brueghel painting and Mom said, "Aren't the peasants picturesque?"

The vicomtesse greeted us on the front steps. She was a large buxom woman, grand and formidable, who bore an uncanny resemblance to Margaret Dumont, the pompous foil of many Marx Brothers movies. She ushered us into the chateau and then into a sumptuously furnished parlor, where we all enjoyed tea brought by a uniformed servant girl. Mom and the vicomtesse chattered away in French while I ate cookies. It was all very *la-de-da* and I thought I was going to be in for a deliciously cushy month. Then, as soon as Mom left, the vicomtesse turned off the charm machine and barked to an older servant, "Show him where he's sleeping," and walked away in curt dismissal.

My room was barely furnished, with a narrow bed and ancient lumpy mattress. I soon learned that most of the chateau was threadbare at best. It turned out that the vicomte and vicomtesse, who had thirteen children, were land poor: the estate didn't bring in enough money to pay for maintaining the chateau, not to mention their brood. Which of course is why they tolerated the indignity of taking in insufferable American kids whose parents were impressed by their titles.

The children of the chateau mostly ignored the paying guests. We boarders all stuck together and never spoke a word of French. One of the sons was an absolute queen, a mini Jean Cocteau who swished around, ethereal and grand, at age twelve. I was fascinated by him and felt a kinship—he was my brave and unabashed brethren. One day I smiled at him and said, "Bonjour." He looked me up and down as if I were a specimen of some rather dull species and then waved me off with haughty *noblesse-not-gonna-oblige*.

After a week at the chateau we all repaired via train to their summer place on the English Channel. Mom had told me we'd be spending part of the month at the seashore, and I'd envisioned something like Saint-Tropez, all sun and bikinis and olive groves spilling up hillsides. The English Channel was just plain dreary— gray sand, gray water, gray skies. The vicomte and vicomtesse had a huge (gray) stone house right in town, on the boardwalk that fronted the sea. The staff lived downstairs in a story that was below the boardwalk level. Most of them were girls and there were always local boys hanging around down there, lascivious laughter and delighted squeals filtering up to us. Downstairs was having a lot more fun than upstairs.

One day a new boarder appeared from England, Virginia Litchfield—Viggie. Tall and pretty with long blonde hair she loved to flick, Viggie was about my age, very upper-upper, insouciant and athletic. We hung out together and loved to walk atop the old stone walls that were everywhere. She was forever talking about her daddy, who was very dapper and had two Bentleys. Viggie seemed rather bored by the whole enterprise in her upper-upper way, but I was taken with her.

On the day she was to return home to "the countryside," I said to her, "It's been so much fun having you here, you're wonderful company. Thank you for the laughs and adventures."

Viggie looked at me for a moment, flicked her blonde hair and walked away without a word. I was hurt and baffled, our friendship negated. Did I do or say something wrong? Of course I blamed myself, as always, not realizing that the truth may have been as simple as the fact that Viggie was a stuck-up British bitch. I missed Tina.

Another summer Mom parked me with a family in the English countryside for a month. Like most families that have to take in boarders, there was some resentment. This was an all-female household, aunts and daughters and a powdery grandmum. They had an enormous house with spreading wings filled with nooks, crannies, and window seats, all very cozy-crinkle and English-y, especially on rainy days. On sunny days I loved wandering around the countryside. There was a gypsy encampment not far away that I found exotic and romantic. The gypsies were dark-haired and elusive and lived in caravans, wooden trailers pulled by horses. We were warned not to get too close to them—so of course I beelined right over. Two gypsy boys appeared, and we played a game of tag, cut short when one of them pushed me down for no reason.

The English family's entire world centered around late-afternoon tea. Anticipation built during the day as baking smells wafted out from the kitchen (which the cook forbade us to enter), and trips were made into town to buy clotted cream and other goodies I'd never heard of. The dining room was vast and the massive table—I mean *seriously* massive—was filled from one end to the other with sweets of every variety, including the dreaded pucker-fest, gooseberry pudding. There were a few savories thrown in for show but practically no one touched them. We would sit there and stuff our faces for an hour as the women chitchatted about English-y things like dogs and The Royals and what to have for tea tomorrow.

Our entire family spent parts of two summers touring the Greek islands on a boat we rented with Mom's friend Penny Potter and her three really nice kids. Greece was *the* place to go during those years—it was all you heard about at dinner parties. The first summer I arrived late in Europe and Mom booked me on a small cruise ship from Trieste to Athens, where I would meet up with everyone. The ship was tiny by today's standards, a lovely little gem, like something out of the 1920s, romantic in a lost-world kind of way, and Trieste's main square looked like a sepia dream as we sailed away.

But onboard I fell through the cracks. My name wasn't on the list of sleeping and dining assignments posted near the front desk. I felt embarrassed, as if I'd done something wrong by not getting my name on the manifest. I got all sweaty and flummoxed. It took me twenty minutes to work up my courage and point out I wasn't on the lists. I was put in a room with a businessman who did not appreciate the company, and in the dining room I was shown to a table where a fashionable Italian couple sat. The woman gave me the hairy eyeball and they chatted in low exclusionary tones through every meal.

There was one young male couple in their early twenties on board, both beautiful, lithe, with sleek swimmer's' bodies. They were openly affectionate with each other, swimming in the small on-deck pool and drying each other's backs while matronly women cooed over them. I envied their love. And dreamed of a boy of my own. In fact, I was becoming obsessed with falling in love. It was what I wanted most of all and the longing for it consumed many an hour.

The boat our two families rented to tour the Aegean had a crew of three: the captain; his wife, who did the cooking; and one mate, a stunning young man whom Penny eyed with undisguised interest. I tried to be a little more discreet.

We visited Crete, Mykonos, Santorini, etc., took donkey rides up hillsides and toured ruins, but it was all too furnace-hot and blindingly sunny for me to enjoy. I was bored by all the history, ancient this and ancient that. I wished I was at Compo Beach kicking around with Tina.

Romantic dreams or not, I was distracted by my flaming teenage hormones which had kicked into *holy-shit-I'm-FUCKIN'-HORNY!* In my heart I may have been yearning for true love, but in my body and mind I was desperate for sex.

One night in Athens before we boarded the boat I ducked out of the hotel, determined to have an erotic adventure. I found a plaza with a lot of cafes and activity, and spotted a man sitting alone at an outdoor table. He looked to be in his thirties, attractive in a mild-mannered, English-actor sort of way. I walked over and hovered near him. He looked at me with mild curiosity. I approached his table, surprising myself. I was *never* this aggressive.

"May I join you?"

He shrugged.

I interpreted this as "Yes" and sat down. By this time, I was semi-hard, and I rubbed my crotch discreetly, hoping he would follow suit. He didn't.

"Are you staying at a hotel?" I asked him.

"I am." He had an English accent.

"Do you want to go there?" I rubbed myself again.

"Out of the question."

I couldn't risk bringing him back to my hotel room. "Do you want to go for a walk?" I asked. My throat was dry, and I felt dizzy with want.

He looked me over as if for the first time.

"You're very young."

"I can't help that."

He smiled a little.

"Do you want to go for a walk?" I repeated.

He considered and then shrugged. "All right." He paid the bill while I looked around for someplace to go. I remembered a small construction site I'd passed on my way over, about three blocks away.

"Let's head up here."

I hurried him along into a quiet neighborhood. I had a full-blown hard-on by now. We reached the construction site. It was encircled by a wooden fence. I found the entrance, which had a shed with a driveway beside it. There was no one around.

"Want to duck in here?" I said.

"No. This is not a good place."

"Come on!" I looked around and the coast was clear. I opened my fly and my cock popped out. "Come on!"

I walked into the site, behind the fence. He half-reluctantly followed. I reached for his crotch. He stepped back. I tried again and he let me grab his cock through his pants. I went in for a kiss. He turned away. I started jerking off. He watched. I liked being watched. He finally took his cock out; it was as average as he was. Still, I was past the point of no return—one look and I shot like a bullet.

"Hey, thank you," I said, laughing nervously.

"Yes, well." He frowned in disapproval.

I walked back to my hotel confused and exhilarated and ashamed—which pretty much sums up my emotional cocktail regarding sex in those days. In some weird way the confusion and shame added to the exhilaration, the thrill. Queer sex was wrong and sick, and I was a rebel and an outsider. It was what I wanted to be.

21

The minor French royalty, the English tea freaks, the Greek Isles, the cruise ship—all seem emblematic of my childhood and my folks' parenting. On the one hand, it was generous and well-meaning. Mom and Dad wanted their kids to have varied experiences and a good time, to become sophisticated and worldly. On the other hand, for me at least, it was too much way too soon. I had no confidence and I often hid in my room, lonely, too shy to venture out. I was given independence before I knew how to handle it.

Everything was paid for as if by a magic wand. I had only a vague idea that people actually did jobs they hated just to survive. I had no idea where wealth came from, why some people had it and others didn't. I had no concept of taking responsibility for myself. After all, I went into the kitchen and gave Ruby my breakfast order every morning and when I came home from school my bed was neatly made and all my clothes put away. We were handed charge cards to Bloomingdales, B. Altman's, and Saks, and there were carte blanche accounts at the deli and the drugstore.

Mom was forever saying, "Nice people don't talk about money." It was "déclassé" and "unbecoming" to be motivated strictly by lucre. One of her favorite put-downs was reserved for certain types of go-getters, who were "hustlers and shits." People who pursued money for its own sake were "grubby" and inferior. Money was something you *had*, not something you earned. As my sister Rebecca says, "I thought money grew on trees. Family trees."

During those summers, my siblings were off having their own privileged (delusional) childhoods. Rebecca, the baby, was an adorable redhead, funny, bright, articulate—and addicted to Saturday shopping sprees. David, two years older than me, was handsome, thoughtful, and articulate, catnip to the girls, a proud young prince who found himself without a kingdom. Diana was the least happy of the four of us. Being the first child, a girl, and suffering from dyslexia—for which Mom had no patience but plenty of disappointment—she was a sitting duck for Mom's competitive head games, which took a real toll on her. Still, she was super foxy, a little wild and spent long stretches of time on Ibiza.

I remember once waking up in a private sleeping cabin on a train that was traveling through Switzerland. I raised the blind and saw mountains, green fields, fat cows, rushing streams, geranium-bedecked chalets—a vision of paradise, and I thought, *All this is here for me.*

My head was so far up in the clouds that I was barely tethered to the planet.

I know that privilege, and its loss, aren't sympathetic. But when you're a kid and you grow up with money, you take your situation for granted. A deep sense of entitlement took hold. We were encouraged to be independent—to go out in the world and find our way. The irony was that at the same time we were learning complete dependence.

22

In July 1964, not too long before Tina showed early symptoms of her illness, the two of us went to the Newport Folk Festival. Taking the bus from the Port Authority up to Rhode Island we felt grown up and free. We didn't know where we would sleep when we got there. Back then we trusted in the fates.

We found our way to the festival grounds and sat on the dusty grass surrounded by thousands of other earnest folkies. We saw Pete Seeger, a vision of simplicity and kindness, sing "This Land is Your Land," Woody Guthrie's paean to an America that belongs to everyone. We saw soulful Joan Baez and rough-hewn Johnny Cash. And then we saw Bob Dylan sing "Mr. Tambourine Man"—and we were blown away.

"I want to have his baby," Tina said.

"You might want to meet him first."

"Don't be so literal, Sebastian."

At the end of the afternoon all the performers came out on stage and locked hands, the audience followed suit, and we sang "We Shall Overcome," the anthem of the civil rights movement. I got goosebumps and Tina's eyes welled up. I squeezed her hand.

As we walked out of the festival grounds in search of some grub, Tina asked me, "Do you think we should go down South and register voters?"

"Tina, I'm fourteen years old, you're fifteen."

"So what?"

"So plenty. First of all, we can't drive, and second of all, it's really dangerous. You have to have training and everything." The thought of going to Mississippi, where kids just a little older than us were being beaten and even murdered, scared the shit out of me.

"So, you're chicken?"

I lit a Winston as I tried to think up a witty retort. None came. "In a word—yes."

We slept curled up under a tree in a nearby park and woke up puffy-eyed, disoriented and excited. There was a feeling of big changes coming and we wanted to be part of it. Most importantly we were together and when we were together everything was all right, more than all right, *plain outasight*. We couldn't wait for the mystery of our futures to unfold. I had no clear idea what I wanted to do or be, maybe a writer or an actor, but decisions like that seemed a lifetime away.

Tina's future, on the other hand, seemed to be unfolding pretty quickly.

My folks had rented a house in Amagansett and the day after the folk festival ended, we headed there on the afternoon ferry from New London to Orient Point. It was an unseasonably bracing windswept, whitecapped day. We were hanging out on the top deck when we noticed a middle-aged, coiffed and made-up woman staring at Tina. She smiled at us and approached.

"You're very beautiful," she said to Tina. And Tina was beautiful, with a perfectly symmetrical face, high cheekbones, full lips, soulful amber eyes, flawless olive skin.

"Thank you," Tina said, looking down, modest.

"I'm Jane Pickens Langley. I think you could be a successful model. I'd very much like to introduce you to Eileen Ford, she's a friend. How would you feel about that?"

Tina and Langley chatted for a while and exchanged phone numbers. When Langley left, Tina smiled at me. The sky, the water, the chugging ferry—the day seemed to sparkle with promise.

When we got to Amagansett and told Mom, she said, "Of course I know who Jane Langley is. She's a singer turned socialite, a fixture in the gossip columns." She lit a cigarette and added, "*Not* the classiest lady in New York."

Why did Mom always have to add those dismissive little asides? She never wanted anyone to have a moment, especially one that overshadowed her.

A few days after their meeting on the boat, Langley called Tina. She told her she was booked for the following week to see Mr. Kenneth, aka Kenneth Battelle, the first superstar hairdresser, credited with creating both Jackie Kennedy's bouffant and Marilyn Monroe's underflip. After he had styled her hair, she would proceed to the photographer's studio for her test shots.

When she got back to Westport, she called me. I was waiting by the phone.

"So how did the shoot go?"

"I think it went really well," Tina said excitedly. "First this make-up artist put on a little make-up and then the photographer took over. He was all business but made me feel very relaxed, he played the Beatles. I felt like Twiggy. England swings!"

"That is *so* cool."

"I'm coming into town tomorrow to see the pictures and meet up with Jane. Do you want to come?"

"Yes!"

The next day I met Tina's train at Grand Central, and we walked across town to the photographers' studio. We arrived to find Langley and the photographer—middle-aged, no-nonsense, with a moustache and half-glasses on a string around his neck—going over the contact sheets, looking through a small, lighted magnifier. They gave us quick nods but didn't look up from their work. We stood nearby, expectant.

"The best of these are *stunning*," Langley finally said in a hushed voice.

"She has something very special. A depth in the eyes. I want to work with her," the photographer said.

"I'm calling Eileen today."

"Ford is going to be excited by these. This girl is pure editorial."

"Yes, I doubt she'll be booking a lot of summer-dress catalogues."

They laughed and then, almost as an afterthought, Langley turned to us, smiled, and said, "Come look."

The pictures were striking and soulful, and I was jealous. Tina's magic wheel was starting to turn, and I was just a tagalong with a shameful secret. I felt the balance of our friendship shift, at least in my own mind.

We left the studio and headed up to Central Park West. As we walked, Tina seemed subdued, lost in thought, troubled. I'd noticed that this was happening lately. It was as if she were being pulled into herself—that "depth" around her eyes that the photographer noted looked more like withdrawal to me.

"Aren't you excited?" I asked.

Tina nodded.

"You don't really seem it."

"I guess I'm not the cheerleader type. Besides, I don't really want to be a model. I want to be a poet."

"Couldn't you be both?"

"Yeah, well, maybe, I guess I could."

We reached Central Park South. "Want to walk through the park and get an ice cream?" I asked.

"Sebastian, models don't eat ice cream."

"Do poets?"

"They take one bite and then ponder it for half an hour."

"That sounds like a yes. I promise I won't tell a soul."

About a week later, Langley got Tina an appointment with Eileen Ford. When it was over Tina called me from a pay phone—and this time she *was* excited.

"I think it went really well."

"Tell me everything."

"We talked for a few minutes. Then Eileen looked at the pictures. Then she asked me to walk across the room."

"And then ...?"

"Then she said, 'You'll work.'"

"Just like that?"

"Yes, and one of the models told me that's *the* best thing she could have said."

"That's wonderful."

"You sound jealous."

"That's ridiculous." Tina let me hang there for a moment. "I mean just because I *am* jealous doesn't mean I *sound* jealous. And just for the record, you're treating me to a trip to Europe."

"I was thinking a safari."

The subtle shift in our friendship was growing more pronounced. My natural insecurity grew. Still, Tina was making me part of her exciting new adventure.

"I'm happy for you," I said.

"It's all happening so fast. I'm a little scared. Mom is being weird."

"Weird how?"

"Drinking even more than usual, picking fights with everyone."

"Just ignore her," I said.

"Sebastian, she's *my mother*. We live in the same house."

"You have a point. Maybe just avoid her then. Want to come over and we can go out for coffee?"

"I have to catch my train back to Westport. Mom's taken to checking my homework. It's almost like she's trying to mess up this whole modeling thing for me."

"We won't let her," I said.

23

Tina went on a couple of look-sees and the feedback was encouraging, but Wanda's sudden interest in her academic career increased and she forbid Tina from skipping school to go into the city. In addition, there was Tina's own ambivalence toward modeling. Eileen Ford, however, remained interested and Tina was invited to the agency's Christmas bash at the Waldorf Astoria. She asked me to escort her.

The day of the party arrived. Wanda and Tina were spending the night at 101 CPW. My sibs were away at their various prep schools and Mom and Dad were off who-knows-where. Wanda had a friend with her, an editor at *Seventeen* magazine. The two of them were working their way through a bottle of red wine as we waited in the living room for Tina to appear.

I'd seen the narrow strapless black-velvet gown she'd borrowed from a Westport friend, but only laid out on her bed. Then she walked into the living room, her shy walk, holding back. But there was no holding back her beauty—she looked ravishing.

"Wow, Tina, you look *amazing*," I said.

"You're a great beauty, darling," Wanda's friend said.

And then it began, something so ugly it makes me queasy and heartbroken to write about it, to think about it, even now, over fifty years later.

Wanda's jaw set, death rays flashed from her eyes, and she lit into Tina, the venom pouring out of her: "*What are you going to do for money?!* There are hundreds of pretty girls, beautiful girls, *thousands of them!* You're not so special! *Tell me what you're going to do for money?* So you're pretty, *so what?* Thousands of girls are pretty. You have no money; you have to make money! You're not *that* pretty! There are a thousand girls as pretty as you."

Tina stood there, absorbing the blows, fighting back tears, and finally she said again and again, quietly, from someplace deep inside her, "You're the devil, you're the devil, you're the devil." Still Wanda wouldn't let up, attacking her, berating her.

I went numb. Was this really my Aunt Wanda, my fun glamorous sophisticated Aunt Wanda? What was going on? What was this about? I felt completely at a loss.

Finally, Tina and I left.

The party was in a ballroom at the Waldorf. We sat on the periphery of the room. All around us models and their escorts primped and laughed and danced. Tina just sat there, not talking, far away, sullen and sad, in some kind of shock. I'd never seen her this withdrawn, and I was scared. I know now that inside her brain terrible things were happening, circuits were shorting, delusions and paranoia were unfurling their batwings.

The party broke up early—all those models needed their beauty sleep. Tina's big night was ruined, stomped on by her mother in a jealous rage. Dad had told me that in her heyday Wanda had had several serious, and seriously rich, suitors. Instead of marrying one of them she'd fallen for sexy Monty Montemora. Three unwanted kids soon followed. Now Wanda was in her mid-40s and her beauty was fading fast. She was burning with regret for the mistakes she'd made when she was beautiful and young. She couldn't stand to see her own daughter beautiful and young. I believe with all my heart that, on that night at least, she hated Tina.

When I think back on it and remember Wanda's scorching voice and Tina standing sad eyed behind the couch, first comes the nausea and then cosmic sadness and a strange kind of panic take hold of me. Poor Tina. Poor doomed Tina.

Why didn't I stand up for her that awful night? Interrupt and scream at Wanda to "Shut up, shut up, *SHUT UP!* Leave Tina alone, *leave her alone!*"

But I didn't speak up. I just stood there in shock, uncomprehending, both about why Wanda was doing this and how terrible the toll was on Tina.

We'd spent so many summer afternoons together, me and Tina, our childhoods intertwined like incestuous vines. I loved her so much, more than I even knew. I was her pal, her chum, her buddy. *Oh, how I wish I could have been her protector.*

79

24

Mom used to have these weird instant mini-breakdowns.

During one of our European summers—I think I was around 12—she, Dad, and I were going to the American Express office in Rome to take care of some business about a train ticket. We got there and the office was closed. Mom started stomping her feet and waving her arms around in desperation. "*What are we going to do now?!*" she screamed, teary eyed, freaking out. Then she lit a cigarette and sort of huddled in the doorway with her back to us, making strange sounds. After about half the cigarette, she turned to us, threw the butt on the sidewalk, ground it out, and said fiercely, "We'll get the ticket tomorrow."

Another time, on a Sunday when I was about sixteen, the whole family—plus Diana's hunky but decidedly working-class boyfriend—were going to have lunch at the Algonquin Hotel, the famous literary hangout. We got dressed and gathered in the living room, waiting for Mom to appear. She came into the room, looked us over, and burst into bitter tears, crying, "I can't believe *this* is my family!" She rushed into her bedroom and slammed the door. Lunch was off. We had disappointed her again.

Years later while taking a white mixing bowl out of the refrigerator in Amagansett she dropped it. It shattered. Her face instantly contorted with tears of rage and frustration and loss, and she cried, "*I've had that bowl for twenty-five years!*" Then she ran into her bedroom and slammed the door. Ten minutes later she came out and was all pulled together.

"Are you all right?" I asked her.

"I'm fine," she said, like she had no idea why I was asking.

Mom's fits mystified and frightened me. The way they came on—like lightning in a blue sky. And their magnitude—as if the whole world was coming apart. They made me feel unsteady and tentative around her. What if I did something that triggered one? They also made me feel sad for Mom. I wanted to help her, to make things better. But what if I made things worse? What if she turned on me the way she turned on so many others? Retreat was the safest strategy.

25

While the trappings of their lives were very different, the two Malinowski sisters had parallel pathologies. What was the source of this poisoned well? While Tina and I had speculated that the toxic spring was our grandmother's illness, it was Tina who really brought the theory home. It happened during a conversation after her second hospitalization, when she was staying with us at 101 CPW. Tina had liked her therapist at the hospital and meds had stabilized her psychosis. She was almost like her old self and I was hopeful she would continue to get better.

It was late afternoon, no one was around, and we were sitting on a couch in the living room. She seemed eager to talk. "Can you get me a new mother?" she asked with a wry smile.

"So, Wanda is ...?" I began.

Tina spoke simply. "She triggers a lot in me, Sebastian, weird stuff, dark stuff. I just don't trust her."

"I know she triggers you. I've seen it. Do you remember that party at the Waldorf?"

"As if I could ever forget it."

"Why do you think she did that?"

"I have some theories."

"Such as?"

Tina looked down as she spoke. "Like we've talked about, I think it all goes back to Mom's childhood. For both our Moms. To *their* mother."

"To Elsie Masson you mean?"

"Yes. To her slow death from multiple sclerosis."

"Elsie has always been a verboten subject with my Mom. She never mentions her, and Dad told me not to bring her up," I said. The truth was I rarely thought about my grandmother. She'd died fourteen years before I was born, ancient history, irrelevant to a mixed-up kid in the violent swoon of adolescence.

"Think of what that must have been like for them. They spent their entire childhood watching their mother die this slow and agonizing death."

I'd never given serious thought to this before, pictured it in my head. The ravages of the disease, the loss of muscle control, the speech and vision problems, and the effect it must have had on Elsie's daughters. It was revelatory. This was my first glimmer of understanding as to why both Mom and Wanda were prone to rages, erratic behavior, and rare, short-lived displays of affection.

"It must have been so traumatic for them," I said.

"And the thing is, they just stuffed it all down," Tina said. "And they're *still* stuffing it down. I've learned in therapy that you can't just stuff bad shit down. It will fester and come out in some weird way. I think it's why Wanda drinks so much."

"And why Zef is so angry."

"I think the trauma formed, and deformed, their characters," Tina said.

"And ours, too, I guess."

We looked at each other, grasping the unspoken truth: that Wanda had played a big role in Tina's madness. And that my own self-destructive behaviors and roiling insecurity were tied to Zef and my terror of her. And then there were the other extended family members who were schizophrenic, or subject to disturbing fits, or abused drugs, or had zero impulse control.

"It's almost like there's a curse on our family," Tina said. "The Malinowski curse."

I reached out and smoothed her hair. "Maybe we can break the curse," I said.

Sadness swept across Tina's face and each of us knew what the other was thinking: that the horse had already left the barn. But she managed a heartfelt hopeful, "Maybe we can."

Although I didn't realize it at the time, our talk was important. Tina's illness didn't exist in a vacuum. Stepping back for the first time, I could see the contours of the context, of the links between all of us in the extended family. It would be many years of therapy and many hard knocks before I fully understood how my grandmother's illness generated monster waves that swamped, to one extent or another, her children and her grandchildren. But that afternoon in our living room I took the first step towards awareness and understanding and maybe even becoming an adult.

And it was Tina who led the way.

26

Although I'd exhibited some of the classic early signs and symptoms of homosexuality—obsessively redecorating my bedroom, worshipping Black girl-groups—I for sure figured out I was gay when I was about thirteen. The muscle-building ads on the back of my *Archie* comic books (another sign—*real* boys read Marvel comics) clued me in when I popped a stiffy looking at them. I also realized pretty early on that being homosexual made me different, an outcast carrying a dark secret that would complicate my life. Balancing that was my embrace of outsiders and the seductive knowledge that I was one. Shame vs. pride duked it out in my psyche. But those ads were so exciting—those muscles, those skimpy bathing suits hinting at the wonders within.

Our apartment was on the third floor and my bedroom looked out onto Central Park West, at that time one of the most popular cruising areas in the country. Night after night hundreds of men would prowl up and down the park side of the street, furtive and bold, lust and longing. I would look out my window and know I wasn't alone.

One bright sunny day I looked out and saw two scraggly homeless-looking men—one Black, one white—sprawled out on a bench, making out. They had their pants down around their ankles and were playing with each other's enormous hard cocks. This went on for a long time, at least an hour, with people walking by—middle-aged men, families, little old ladies, junkies and skanks, all glancing over, not batting an eye, continuing on their way. The Upper West Side—rundown, exhausted, filled with queers and drug addicts—was like that back then.

One Saturday I went to see a Doris Day/Rock Hudson movie at Radio City Music Hall with a friend from the UNIS. I went into the men's room to pee. The man at the urinal next to me—tall, thin, wearing tight slacks and a windbreaker—stood back. He was hard. My flesh shivered in excitement. We waited until the men's room cleared out, and then he went down on me. It was so exciting that I went back later in the movie and found another obliging gentleman.

I started to let neighborhood men pick me up. One guy was very sweet, a waiter from Venezuela, he sent me home with packs of cigarettes he got at work. Then one day I ran into him in front of my building. What if someone in my family saw us? He smiled and said, "Hello."

"Get the fuck away from me," I spit out, feeling mean and creepy.

His sweet face fell.

The lexicon of the day echoed in my head—gays were sick and disgusting, barely human, sinners against God, effeminate little fairies. I started to wear a black leather jacket, trying to butch it up a little. Who did I think I was kidding? I looked like a *Scorpio Rising* reject.

One night I saw a television news segment on homosexuality. In it, they interviewed Dr. Irving Bieber, a psychiatrist who claimed he could cure it. I looked up his office number and a few days later snuck out to a phone booth over on West End Avenue, out of range of my family. I was sweaty and my heart was pounding as I dialed. A woman answered.

"May I speak to Dr. Bieber, please?"

"May I ask who's calling?"

I resisted the urge to hang up and choked out, "Richard ... Richard Jefferies."

"And this is in reference to?"

"I would like to see the doctor."

"Hold on a moment."

Once again, I fought down the urge to hang up. I was flushed with shame, sure all the pedestrians walking by knew that I was a pathetic fag making a desperate plea for help.

"This is Irving Bieber."

I blurted out, "Can I come and see you? I don't want to be a homosexual."

"How old are you?"

"Fifteen."

There was a pause and I felt myself start to sweat. Then Bieber asked, "Would you describe your parents as well-to-do?"

"Well ... yes."

"Claire will book you an appointment."

Bieber's office was dark and hushed and filled with the thick lingering shame of his patients. Claire, middle-aged and poker-faced, sat behind a desk.

"The doctor will be with you shortly," she said without a smile.

I sat, jittery and clammy, vulnerable, a raw nerve. A thin effeminate man with an umbrella came out of the inner office and made a follow-up appointment. Then I was shown in. Bieber looked about fifty, bespectacled, imposing and grave.

Again he went straight to the bottom line, "I can help you, but the first thing you must do is talk to your parents and get them to agree to pay for my treatment plan."

"Is it expensive?"

"Seventy-five dollars an hour."

It wasn't the money that freaked me out, it was having to tell my folks. I gulped air and said, "No. I can't."

He shrugged, as if it was my loss.

I left.

His vibe was so creepy. I found out later that Bieber was one of the great villains of the gay rights movement. He had written a landmark 1962 study that claimed to prove that homosexuality was a curable disorder, and he had led the fight against the American Psychiatric Association's 1973 removal of homosexuality from its list of psychiatric disorders. He wrote: "A homosexual is a person whose heterosexual function is crippled, like the legs of a polio victim."

I didn't know it at the time, but I'd walked right into the belly of the beast. Luckily, I walked out again.

27

The day after my misbegotten mission I waited until the apartment was empty and called Tina. This was before her first psychotic break.

"I need to talk to you about something," I said.

"Are you all right?"

"Yeah, yeah, I guess so. Maybe not, I don't know."

"Tell me."

I felt like there was a lot at stake for me. I took a deep breath and blurted out, "I'm a homosexual." Just saying the words made me feel a little lighter. The secret was out.

There was a pause and Tina said casually, "I kinda suspected as much."

"You did?"

"I'm not deaf, dumb and blind, Sebastian. It's a cool thing to be, if you ask my opinion."

I felt lighter still. I'd never heard homosexuality described as *cool*. Only Tina. "You think so? Really?"

"Definitely. Look at the brilliant writers and artists and musicians who've been homosexual. Anyone can be a heterosexual. Being a homosexual makes you special. I think it's totally wonderful and groovy."

My eyes welled up and I sighed. "So, you still want to be my friend?"

Tina laughed. "If you thought you could get rid of me with this little homosexual ploy, think again."

"You're such a good pal, cousin," I said.

"Homo power!"

We laughed and laughed, a balm for my soul.

Now that I was out to Tina and had her blessing, coming out to other people, like my parents and sibs and friends, would be so much easier. And if they didn't like it, too damn bad. My cousin Tina was totally down with it.

28

The summers we didn't spend in Europe or the Hamptons, I was sent off to camp. In the summer of 1965, when I was fifteen, I decided I wanted to stay in town. One of Mom's great maxims was, "*No one* stays in New York in the summer." This only made me want to do it more. The country bored me. All those trees. I told my folks and as usual they relented. So, I had my first summer in the city.

Tina visited and I spent some time with her in Westport, but most of the time no one else was around. Mom and Dad had rented a house in Springs and my sibs were off at various camps and adventures. I had the apartment to myself for long stretches, which was dreamy. I loved waking up to a day filled with ... *nothing*. No school, no family, no trips, no cathedrals, no archery. Nothing. I'd started smoking pot and now I didn't need to do it sitting next to the open window in my bedroom. I could toke up on the vast living room couch, I could go to the deli and get a Sara Lee cheesecake and eat the whole thing, I could stay up until 2:00 and sleep until 11:00. I realized that I had no problem amusing myself, and that I loved my freedom more than anything in the world.

There were reasons no one stayed in New York in the summer. The whole decaying city seemed to wilt. The air was so bad that you gathered fat black specks of soot on your skin and clothes. The heat was a swampy nightmare. The uncollected trash stank. I went to the movies a lot, sliding into the delicious air conditioning with my Junior Mints.

I loved summer weekends, when Midtown felt especially deserted. I would wander around looking in shop windows, checking out the architecture. One furtive, leering man or another always seemed to be following me, adding an erotic charge.

One evening I was wandering around Midtown East—where office buildings bleed into residential neighborhoods—when a well-dressed middle-aged man approached me.

"Hello there," he said.

He wasn't my type—too refined—but whatever, I enjoyed the attention. "Hi."

"How would like to make forty dollars?"

My ears perked right up. "I'd love it."

"Follow me."

"Follow you where?" I asked, a little wary.

"I know a place where we can ..." he lowered his voice, "... have some fun."

"What kind of place?" My excitement was growing; it felt so secret and erotic.

"You'll see. Come on, I mean do I look like Jack the Ripper?"

He had a point. I followed him east and then into a passageway that led to the back of a low-rise residential building. Halfway down the passageway there was an alcove. He nodded for me to step into it.

He knelt before me, opened my pants, and pushed them down around my ankles. Then he chowed down. And he took his time doing it. I wasn't that into it, but my dick stayed harder than Aztec arithmetic—I was at that age where your dick has a mind of its own. Being outdoors, danger, real or imagined, lurked at the edges and upped the thrill.

After I blew my wad, he blew his, with my dick still in his mouth, moaning so loud I worried that someone would hear him. We made ourselves presentable and he handed me forty bucks, four times my weekly allowance and a nice chunk of change back then.

"I want to see you again," he said. I nodded, trying to contain my excitement at the two twenties dancing in my pants pocket. "Where can I meet you?"

I didn't want to meet him again, forty bucks or not. He was too ... *soft*, his hands, his manner. I knew already that I liked more of an edge.

"Sometimes I go to the Museum of the City of New York," I said. I never went to the Museum of the City of New York; it was a dull and dusty mausoleum.

"Will you meet me there next Saturday at five?"

"Sure." I had no intention of meeting him there. Why did I send this benign gentleman on a wild cock chase? It seems kind of twisted to me today, but at the time I somehow thought I was being polite.

We parted and I practically kicked up my heels. I had turned my first trick!

I knew about turning tricks because I devoured every book and magazine that I could get my hands that mentioned homosexuality. My bible was John Rechy's 1963 masterpiece *City of Night*, an autobiographical novel about his days as a hustler in various big cities across the country. Set in YMCAs, crumbling piers, cruisey parks and all-male hotels, the novel pulsed with yearning and sorrow and loneliness and sex-sex-sex. I found it deeply romantic and erotic. I wanted to be part of Rechy's world. And now I was. It was thrilling. I was desired. I had power. And who can't use a little extra cash?

Like all of New York, Grand Central Station was ratty around the edges in those days. The men's room was off the main waiting room, down a flight of stairs. A couple of years earlier I had gone down there innocently to pee while waiting for a train to Westport. There were two long rows of tall marble urinals opposite each other and when I stepped up to one, the man next to me stepped back to show off his hard-on. I quickly noticed a lot of hard-ons and men jerking off. Again, the hint of danger implicit in public sex added to the charge. I had only a few minutes to look, but on future jaunts to Westport I left the house earlier—after all, I didn't want to miss my train.

While I never hooked up with anyone, I did have fun looking and playing with myself. And being a teen, I garnered some attention, although I was hardly the only kid there. I'd see other teenage boys at the urinals, looking around in wide-eyed wonder, pulsing with heat.

It all seems kind of strange today, when a connection is just a swipe away, but before the Internet a lot of gay boys were initiated into sex the same way—in men's rooms and locker rooms. It makes perfect sense considering the opportunities these places provided, but I think it also contributed to a disconnect between sex and affection and even love. It was all crotch focused. The rest of the person didn't really come into it play.

I soon realized that some men were only excited by anonymous sex—if you started talking, wanting to connect on an emotional or intellectual level, it shattered the fantasy and could end the encounter. I was guilty of this myself. If I went home with a man and he immediately gushed about his new thrift-shop throw pillow, it was a turn-off. Once when I was a teen a local man picked me up on West 72nd Street. He was masculine and unshaven and, I thought, working class. We went to his apartment, which was book-filled, and then his cat appeared, and he said, "Meet Oedi-puss." I said I was allergic and split.

Many gay men quickly outgrew this focus, but many didn't. And I think it caused serious emotional confusion for a lot of men of my generation and made it difficult for them to form relationships. Sex and affection were distant planets. Some men, of course, were fine with this. After all, it was liberating, they were getting laid, it was a fuck-you to the uptight Republican culture, they liked being single and free, and it was a lot of fun. But for other men, who longed for love or at least some sort of emotional bond, it could be tough. I fell somewhere in between. While I've always felt a connection heightened the excitement, I certainly wasn't above falling to my knees in a dark back room.

29

About a week after I turned my first trick, I was on one of my weekend walkabouts and decided to drop into Grand Central again. By then I'd figured out that the benches close to the men's room entrance were pretty cruisey too—suburban husbands hiding behind newspapers, lounging lascivious hustlers, older femmes with dye-pot hair styled to conceal their bald spots. On this Saturday there was a very sexy redhead youngman who looked to be in his mid-twenties sitting on a bench with his legs spread. He had pouty lips and knowing eyes and wore tight black slacks and a white tank top that showed off his naturally toned body. A nascent belly and a slightly battered air of having been around the block a few times only made him hotter. He had a copy of the *Racing Form* on the seat beside him and he kept scanning the room, clocking the men coming up from the men's room. I sat down near him. He looked over at me, poker-faced, wary.

Two cops came through the station's main entrance, which was in the middle of the waiting room. The youngman immediately picked up the *Racing Form* and perused it. The cops looked around and kept walking into the station's main hall. The youngman put down the *Racing Form*. We eyed each other again, but he was still wary. I smiled at him. He considered it and then smiled back—he had such a sexy smile, slightly lopsided, with half-lidded eyes.

"A guy's gotta be careful around here," he said. He had a working-class accent, Brooklyn or the Bronx. "It's not the uniforms you gotta worry about, it's the plainclothes."

"Really?"

He scooted over a little closer and I could smell the slight tang of his sweat. He looked me over. "How the fuck old are you?"

"Fifteen."

"The chicken hawks are going to love you."

"Chicken hawks?"

"Guys who like 'em young." I loved learning this lingo.

I sure wanted to kiss this ginger. My leg was bouncing in agitation.

"Relax, man," he said.

"I'm sorry, I ... um ..."

"You're new, aren't you?" I nodded. "Curtis," he offered.

"I'm Sebastian."

"*Sebastian?*"

"It's not my fault."

He laughed. "You look like a rich kid."

"Kind of, I guess."

"This is a *job* for me," he said with an edge of pride and defiance.

"I guess you can set your own hours." He didn't smile. I took out my Winstons and lit one, trying to keep my hands from shaking. "Would you like a cigarette?"

He shook his head. "You sure you wanna be doing this?" I nodded. "Okay then. You want me to tell you a thing or two?"

No, I want you to kiss me. "Sure."

"Downstairs is the happy hunting ground. But pick the right urinal. You don't want the nickel and dimers, old guys who want to pay you five bucks to suck your cock. Look for fancy suits, gold watches, you know, the rich guys like to show off. They're going to want to see what you got before they shell out. You hung decent?"

I was taken aback by this question and didn't want to oversell my assets. "I guess."

"So, once they show interest, put it away and start to walk upstairs, but turn around and nod at them. If they follow, you got 'em."

"But where do we go?"

"A lot of your tricks will be staying in hotels, but most won't bring chicken back to some fancy-ass hotel. There's risks involved."

SEBASTIAN STUART

"So then what?"

"Follow me."

I could hardly believe this was happening. I flashed on *City of Night*. I was stepping into a secretive underworld, one ruled by men and sex, sex and men.

We went out onto 42nd Street and headed east a block to Lexington Avenue. "This place is safe, they pay off the cops. So just bring 'em here."

We crossed Lexington to an old four-story brick building with a small red neon sign reading HOTEL out front. The office was at street level, the size of a phone booth. A chubby bald man inside was engrossed in the *Daily News*.

"Hey, Merv." The man looked up from his paper. "This is Seb." Merv gave me the once-over, nodded, and went back to his reading.

"You're good now," Curtis said. He licked his upper lip and I swooned.

Curtis and I headed back to Grand Central. I was proud to be seen with him. I was part of a brotherhood.

"How much do you charge?" I asked.

"Twenty's the going rate for a BJ. If they want you to fuck them, double that. If they want to fuck *you*, triple it. But, you know, everything is negotiable. And if you think they might be plainclothes, ask them if they're a cop. They have to tell you."

Curtis looked at me, and I knew he knew I was crushing heavy on him. He flung a casual arm around my shoulder. "Anything else you want to know?" I got a strong whiff of his sweet sweat and popped a semi-boner. We reached the entrance to the station. I screwed my courage to the sticking place and asked, "Do you want to fool around?"

Curtis smiled a wicked smile of satisfaction, and then he softened, "Oh baby, I'm not queer."

This sure threw me. "You're not?"

"Fuck no. I got a girlfriend. Wanna see her picture?" He took out his wallet and flipped it open. On one side there was a picture of a pretty girl in a tiny bikini. "I told you this is a *job* for me."

I was so confused. "You're not gay?"

"Don't take it so hard. I'm what you call straight trade."

The odds that Curtis was really straight were low. He was playing a role, and the picture of his "girlfriend" was a smart touch. For some gay men, a straight guy is a huge turn-on. That was Curtis's demographic. And that pic of the chick had its intended result: it made me want him more.

Back in the waiting room, a man walked by us and eyed Curtis, stopped, lit a cigarette, looked back.

"Duty calls. See ya around."

I never did see Curtis around. But I was grateful for his sentimental education. In fact, I put it to use that same evening. After enjoying dinner at a curbside hotdog stand, I went back down to the men's room. A slender man in his 40s, wearing a well-tailored pinstriped suit, was pretty aggressive in showing his interest and following me upstairs.

"I must have you," he said in what sounded like a German accent. "I'm staying at the Regency, room 1038. We'll enter separately."

This guy was nervy. The Regency was one of New York's fanciest hotels, but I'd been to fancy hotels. "I know a closer place," I said.

"Lead the way."

We walked over to Lexington, and he paid Merv $20 for the room. Upstairs, the place was ragtag and rickety. Our room had one of those old-time metal-framed beds and a grimy window. It smelled like decades of cigarette smoke, whiskey, and sex. There was a sink in the room, but the bathrooms were down the hall. I loved it—it was so film noir. I was sure that in the room across the hall a gin-soaked femme fatale was working her wiles. And I was about to work mine.

"Strip and then stand on the bed and masturbate," he said.

I obliged. He took out his cock and jerked off as he watched, repeating like a mantra, "Sexy boy, sexy boy, sexy boy." When it was over, he reached into his wallet, pulled out a wad of bills, peeled off five twenties and tossed them on the bed. "What do you think about that?" he asked.

Holy shit! "Thank you!" A hundred bucks was a lot of money for ten minutes of "work."

"No, thank *you*. You're a sweet boy."

He left. I lay on the lumpy mattress in a semi-euphoric state, drinking in the seedy splendor of the room. I couldn't believe how much power I had. At home I was at the mercy of emasculating Mom. Now I was hurtling away from my family, their significance receding. I got under the scratchy sheets and thin blanket and fell asleep. When I woke up about an hour later, it was dark out in the dark city, the sex city. I dressed slowly, wanting to prolong this moment of grace.

About a week later I went back to Grand Central and sat in the waiting room near the men's room entrance. A tall blond man in his early 30s, wearing a suit, sat down a little distance from me, and glanced over.

"Nice night," he said in a low, tense voice, not looking at me.

"It is nice. Not too hot," I said, copying his tone, not looking at him. Could he be a plainclothes cop?

"You want to make some money?"

"Maybe."

"What's the catch?"

"Are you a cop?"

"No."

"You sure?"

"I work in real estate."

"Okay."

"You know a place?"

"Yes."

"Is it safe?"

"Yes, it's a hotel, they know me."

"Let's go."

I stood up and spotted his wedding ring. Hot.

We walked over to the hotel on Lexington. I walked past the entrance and nodded at him. He walked up to Merv and paid for the room. I followed him upstairs. In the safety of the room I got a good look at him—he was really built, really nice looking. I couldn't believe he was going to pay *me* for sex.

"I'm going to take a quick shower," he said. He stripped down. His body was like a college jock with a few years on him. He smelled like Old Spice. He wrapped a towel around his waist and left. I got naked and waited. He returned and took off the towel. His cock was *massive*. He wanted to 69. Fine with me, except I could only get about a third of that thing into my mouth. I did my best, as did he, and we both shot.

Then he scooted around and kissed me. It was so unexpected. He was the first man I'd ever kissed; most johns had no interest in affection. His hot tongue slid into my mouth and roamed around. I returned the ardor. We started making out. For a long time. Like straight kids at a drive-in. It was just so dreamy and exciting, writhing around, touching his body, his cheeks, his hard-again cock. Suddenly it became weirdly emotional for me. I felt something I never had before—a surge of feeling toward him that transcended the sex. I was *falling in love* with him. He *must* be feeling what I'm feeling. I felt it in his kisses. We both came again and pressed our sticky sweaty bodies together, finally parting with sweet reluctance.

I lay there, spent in every way, and we touched each other, gently, tenderly, greedily. I was imagining what would come next: we would lie there and talk about what had just happened and when we would meet again. Instead he hopped off the bed, pulled his wallet out of his pants and handed me a twenty. I didn't even want it. He quickly got dressed. I raced to keep up with him. The whole mood shifted. Weren't we going to talk?

Down on the street, he clapped a hand on my shoulder, "That was nice. Thanks."

"Aren't we going to ...?"

"No, we're not. I have a wife and two kids waiting for me at home. You take care." He turned and strode away.

I stood in front of the hotel and a great rush of loneliness surged over me. Our passion had felt real to me, and yet he had negated it, brushed it off with a clap on the shoulder. We hadn't even exchanged names. He was off to his family. I would never have a family. Gay men didn't have families. I didn't *want* a family. Did I? I was gleaning some early lessons about being queer. It could be very lonely.

We didn't know where we belonged. Society had rendered its verdict: we were sick. Pity was the best we could hope for. For the majority of queers, especially those outside big cities and simpatico professions, coming out wasn't an option, unless you were prepared to lose your job, your friends, and your family. And so you stuffed it down and denied this core part of your being. Gay men constructed elaborate cover-ups, emotional and practical. Effeminate men lived in danger of verbal and physical assaults. I knew I was fortunate to be growing up in an accepting, artistic milieu with liberal folks. Yet later, when I was in college in San Francisco, Mom sent me a letter in which she wrote, "We saw all the fairies and dykes parading in Central Park. The poor things."

I turned more tricks and had sex a few times in the Ramble, a woodsy cruising area in Central Park. I quickly learned that while these encounters were fleeting, they were intense. An intimate human connection was often made, and that gave them meaning. They told us we weren't alone. And that, despite all the shame that society piled on us, we were human beings and we deserved respect. And maybe most important, we learned that, even for us, love was a possibility.

After Labor Day, when my family returned and school started, my tricking was curtailed, but I managed to slip in a few adventures. I know now that I was slumming. I would be going back to Central Park West, while hustlers like Curtis had nothing to fall back on. They were street kids, barely holding on, with few prospects.

But I loved having a secret life, coming home with a pocketful of bills and then having dinner with my oblivious family. I didn't even tell Tina about my adventures until a couple of years later. I wasn't afraid or ashamed to tell her, I just wanted this hidden world to be mine alone, illicit, dangerous, and so fucking erotic.

Today I understand I was seeking validation and attention, and maybe not too wisely. But that kid back then loved the charge, the sense of power, the exotic locations, the humid city and its dark promise.

I loved my lonely summer in the city, not having to answer to anyone, each new day mine to fritter away, drifting through the heat and haze, not a thought, not a care, not a clue.

30

No doubt about it, I was Mom's favorite. I don't know why she picked me over my brother—my sisters' gender had, of course, disqualified them at birth—but she did. She was affectionate with me now and then and I was spared the worst of her contempt. She constantly goaded my siblings until almost every exchange was a test of wills, a jousting match—and Mom always won. The smoldering vein of frustration and rage that runs through my family can be traced to the thousands of battles, large and small, lost every day.

With me, though, Mom kept the criticism and baiting on a low boil. "Use some elbow grease, for Christ's sake!" "What is *wrong* with you?" "You never do *the work*, Sebastian." When I did something right, her attitude was, "Of course you did, you're my child." When I did something wrong her look of dismissal or anger did the job. And between her criticism and her anger there was disappointment.

Still, what I endured was mild compared to my siblings. My sisters were overweight, and Mom never missed a chance to disparage them. I think if Diana had told Mom she had a week to live, Mom's response would have been, "You still have to lose weight."

Of course I was glad to be the favorite—I had a halo of protection. But it also led to some resentment and I sometimes felt serious, at times overwhelming guilt about my favored treatment, especially since there was always someone around to say reproachfully, "Oh, *come on*, Seb, you *know* you're Zef's favorite." These words were designed to throw me on the defensive. They worked, often sending me into a spiral of depression. These feelings were compounded by my guilt about being a letdown to Mom and Dad—expelled and underachieving—my guilt about being queer, and my guilt about Tina's illness. All in all, I was a bundle of roiling guilt and self-loathing. Sometimes it waylaid me for days. And being the favorite meant Mom invested her affection and expectations in me, and that was some pretty heavy baggage. I couldn't carry it, that's for sure.

One scene brings the dynamic home. Every Christmas Mom made an elaborate broccoli-pudding type dish, some old Tyrolean recipe. It was built around a conical mold and involved a food processor, broccoli and breadcrumbs and whatnot and was baked and served with hollandaise sauce. Making it took hours. That broccoli pudding defined Christmas at our house.

One Christmas when I was in my mid-20s I was hanging out in the living room in Amagansett with my siblings and a couple of other family members, a fire was going, it was a cozy scene. I was sitting on the arm of one of the couches, a perch that gave me a view into the kitchen. I could see Mom, wearing her blue apron and laboring over that broccoli pudding, put upon, blowing her hair off her forehead.

Someone said, "*What* are we going to do about Zef?" and *zap!* the sluice gates opened and the invective poured out—she was trashed up and down the block. And there she was, poor Mom, making her broccoli pudding.

I wanted to defend her, to say, "Look at what she's doing for us!" But I didn't say anything. I was straddling two worlds, two allegiances, and I wanted to stay in favor with both. I was a wuss.

Favorite or not, Mom could gut me with a word or two. When I was around thirty-five, a screenplay I wrote with my friend Robert Rubinsky was optioned by the actress and director Lee Grant. Lee has had a long and fascinating career—she's won two Oscars and directed features and documentaries, including the 1985 documentary *What Sex Am I?*, an astonishing look at transvestites and transsexuals that was thirty years ahead of its time. By any measure Lee had accomplished far more than anyone in my family. She was also a delight to work with—full of ideas, fun and warm—and when we met at her sprawling West End Avenue apartment, she always fed us.

When I told Mom I was working with Lee, she shrugged and never asked me about the project's progress. A few months later, she, Dad, and I were driving in from Amagansett, adrift in a miasma of desultory chitchat and disappointment.

Finally, Mom asked, in a disparaging tone, "How's that *Grant* woman?" I was proud to be working with Lee, but Mom turned it into less than nothing. I felt diminished. But I didn't stand up to her.

When Mom had cataract surgery, I went to see her at the hospital. Dad was there and she was in bed, one of her eyes bandaged. Mom threw up her arms and cried, "Come hold me!" Her gesture shocked and frightened me. I recoiled but quickly caught myself, went to the bed and gave her a strained hug. Her need was so great at that moment, so primal, and it was directed at *me*. Where did it come from? She'd never behaved like that before. At her most vulnerable she cried out for *me*. It scared the hell out of me.

31

When Tina and I were in the ninth grade, she started talking a lot about the Farrows, a show-biz family who had moved into an old estate in Westport. One of the kids, Stephanie, was in Tina's class at Staples High, and they'd become friends. The mom was a former movie star named Maureen O'Sullivan, most famous for playing Jane in a series of Tarzan movies. The dad was a movie director, John Farrow, who had recently died, which had led to the family's move east from Hollywood.

One sunny Saturday Tina took me to meet Steffi. The estate was large, with a stream that had been dammed up to form a small lake, but the grand house was barely furnished. The Farrow kids—Johnny, Prudence, Stephanie, and Tisa (Mia was already off on her starship)—were not only great-looking, fair and freckled, but were also warm and welcoming, funny, wry and knowing. They passed around a joint and a bottle of wine. The Farrows weren't the first show-biz family I'd known, but they had a sparkly glamour that hooked me. And I loved that there were no adults in sight.

The family soon moved into the city, to a sprawling apartment on Central Park West, just two blocks up from me. I saw quite a bit of them. Their building was a rental, home to quite a few show folk, a bit rundown, with a part-time doorman and no seating in the lobby.

Maureen O'Sullivan was warm and charming in a 1930s movie-star way, vivacious, with a breathy voice and terrific legs. She adored her children. I think she was struggling a little financially. She was usually off in California looking for work, so the kids were on their own.

Steffi was about as pretty as a girl could be, and funny, and I developed a wicked crush on her. She went to a fancy Catholic girls school on the Upper East Side, taking the 79th Street crosstown bus. One afternoon I sat on the huge stone bench in front of the Museum of Natural History and waited for her to get off the bus. I was going to pretend I just happened to be sitting there—what a coincidence! Bus after bus arrived, the doors opened, but no Steffi.

Johnny Farrow liked Tina and they became a loose couple for several years—holding hands, making out. I became great pals with Prudence. She was smart, a little nutty (always a good fit with me), and had an idiosyncratic take on the world, surprising me with offbeat observations and insights. I adored her. We loved to ride the city buses for hours on end, looking out the windows and commenting on the people and buildings. She, too, was striking—tall and thin with enormous saucer eyes, short curly hair, high cheekbones in a roundish face. We used to go out drinking with our fake I.D.s and guys were always asking me, "Is *she* really with *you*?" Luckily, I've never had much of a male ego and I felt proud to be seen with her.

Prudy and I had a blast knocking around town and dancing in bars—"Love Potion #9" was our favorite song—but she had a serious side and could be intense at times, boring into you with her wide eyes as if everything was of great import. A couple of years later, when I was living in San Francisco, the Beatles wrote "Dear Prudence" about her. She'd been at an ashram in India with them and didn't come out of her tent for days at a time. I could just picture it and I hoped she was okay.

Drugs were everywhere in my social circle, especially pot and LSD. I took my first acid trip when I was fifteen, with Phoebe, a friend from UNIS. Phoebe's parents were rare book dealers, and she was super bright and precocious, still had her baby fat, and was insecure in the most adorable way. She dressed like a budding beatnik in black tights and turtlenecks and Capezios, and developed a Streisand-like persona, kooky and loveable, both hyperarticulate and at a loss for words. She loved sophisticated older men who recited poetry and had wives. She was an only child, and her parents didn't seem to take much interest in her. I sensed a fragility, which made me feel protective of her.

Phoebe lived in a rambling apartment on West End Avenue. She had her own wing, down a long hallway, so it was easy to hang out at her place and never see her parents. One night I was over there, getting high on reefer.

"I have some LSD," Phoebe said.

"Where did you get it?"

"From a friend."

"Have you taken it before?"

"No, have you?

"No."

"Should we take it?"

"Let's," I said. So many of my friends had tripped that I felt some peer pressure to keep up with them.

We placed the tiny squares of acid-laced paper on our tongues and they quickly dissolved. As we waited for the acid to hit, we decided to walk to Lincoln Center, which was graceful and new, all clean lines, a breath of fresh air in the grimy struggling city. The acid came on little by little and by the time we got to Lincoln Center we were peaking, and I realized *Whooooa-holy-fuck-fuck-this-drug-is-SERIOUS!* Fifteen-year-olds probably shouldn't eat acid.

Phoebe seemed anxious and sweat broke out on her brow.

"Are you okay?" I asked.

She nodded and shook her head at the same time. Not the answer I was hoping for. We walked into the plaza and approached the circular fountain at its center. Suddenly it spurted up in a fearsome *whoosh!* of red-tinted water—*or was it blood?* Phoebe screamed in terror, turned and ran out of the plaza into the teeming city. I froze in place. People were looking at me. Why had my girlfriend run away screaming? Things were not going well.

I took off after Phoebe in full freak-out mode. I caught up with her on Central Park West. Her eyes were size of Frisbees and filled with panic.

"Let's try and groove on the trees," I said inanely.

Phoebe ignored me and ran over to a well-dressed guy in his thirties and said, "Help me!"

The guy walked over to me, grabbed me by my lapels, lifting me up, and asked Phoebe, "Is this guy bothering you?"

My mind was doing backflips and my stomach was lodged in my throat.

Phoebe pulled herself together enough to say, "No, he isn't."

The guy let me go. Relief flooded over me. But now what? Phoebe was shaking.

"Listen, Phoebe, let's walk up to my house, my folks are away, we can calm down."

We somehow arrived at 101 CPW, crossed the plush lobby and got in the elevator. Unfortunately, Desmond was the operator on duty. He was a weird little Irish guy who was missing the top digit on his left index finger. His wire-rimmed glasses magnified the size of his darting beady eyes and made them—to me at that moment at least—look like they were popping out of his head. Desmond was *very* loquacious. And you were literally a captive audience, with the elevator's metal accordion gate standing between you and freedom. He'd get you to your floor, turn, and start flapping his jaw.

Sure enough, Desmond closed the gate and took me and Phoebe up to the third floor, turned and started yakking. The fact that he was looking at two kids with their eyes flying around in their heads and their mouths gaping open didn't seem to register. Phoebe wigged out, crying, "We're trapped! *We're trapped!*"

Desmond reluctantly let us out and we went into my apartment, where we immediately ran into Ruby, who wore this cool purple rinse in her hair. Phoebe took one look at her and cried, "She has *purple hair!*" Ruby was not amused.

I finally got Phoebe to the den and suggested we sit and try to calm down. Fat chance. Within minutes I was escorting her back over to her place. The rest of the trip was less eventful. I spent several hours staring at a textured lampshade, sure it was a miniature diorama of ancient Athens. Phoebe sat on the edge of her bed smoking cigarettes and talking about the universe and death and the married men she'd fucked.

I'm happy to report that Phoebe (not her real name) is alive and well, busy in retirement doing all sorts of interesting things.

32

In 1962 Mom got a job as an editor at *Life* magazine. She was both a show horse and a workhorse and she quickly started to move up the food chain. On most Monday nights she'd fly out to Chicago, where the magazine was printed, to put it to bed. She'd arrive home on Tuesday just as we were leaving for school, looking flushed and triumphant. All her extra hours and hard work paid off and in 1965 she was named its Entertainment Editor.

Thus, began Mom's glory days.

In that pre-digital era, *Life* was the pop-culture pinnacle, the most popular magazine in the country, and Mom was the big kahuna—every publicist, star and producer's holy grail. She could pick up the phone and get great seats to any show on Broadway a half hour before curtain, arrange private screenings of the buzziest flick in plush midtown screening rooms, book a last-minute lunch at the Four Seasons. Mom would sweep in wearing her power like a badge, often with her favorite child in tow. It was heady and fun for me to step into that world. Everything we did felt supercharged, and I loved meeting all the stars. I was proud of Mom and felt as if our family's status had zoomed up a whole lot of notches.

Mom reveled in it all. As her confidence grew, she started to dress sexier and hipper, Pucci pants and a gold-link belt, cracking one night when she was wearing a studded black leather belt, "I'm into S&M." I don't think her kids would argue with that.

Mom was always coming home and making pronouncements: "Dick Avedon says Better Midler is *the next* immortal," or, after supervising a photo shoot with Barbra, "Streisand is beautiful from some angles and plain from others—and she knows *exactly* which is which."

When Bette was in the first flush of her stardom, she came up to our apartment to pay a courtesy call. She sat on the couch, a publicist beside her, looking vulnerable and a bit dazed, was soft-spoken, nothing like her raucous stage persona. About a week later Mom and I went to Madison Square Garden to see the Rolling Stones. We were walking down an endless deserted corridor when a tiny creature appeared heading our way, tottering on her heels. It was Bette, and again she looked lost, telling Mom she didn't have a ticket but wanted to see the show. Mom hooked arms with her, saying, "Come on." She marched up to the box office, pulled rank—and Bette was in.

The Stones were phenomenal that night. (Mick = God.) The next week we went to see Elvis at the Garden, sat in the same great seats, and the contrast floored me. The King, bloated and sweaty, phoned it in, encased in a silvery jumpsuit that looked like it could stand up on its own volition. The audience was full of three generations of Elvis-freak women—grandma, mom and teen sitting side by side, hairdos high.

Mom took me to the taping of *Liza with a "Z,"* Liza Minnelli's iconic TV special, directed by Bob Fosse. It was one of those pumped-up crackling New York nights, like the whole town had its finger in a socket. There was a tall striking older woman vamping up and down the aisles wearing a silver lamé gown and matching turban—skinny as lightning and twice as electric (and, I realize now, speeding her fucking skull off). I was dazzled.

"Who is *that*, Mom?"

"That's Kay Thompson. She wrote *Eloise.* She's a *dreadful* woman."

I wondered how Mom knew Kay Thompson was a dreadful woman. I liked *Eloise.* But Mom spit out her words with such force, fierce and final, that I was cowed into silence.

Liza was amazing that night, at the peak of her talents. *Life* had recently run an article on her and the writer of the piece had become chums with Liza. After the show he took us backstage. Liza appeared in her dressing room doorway and looked at Mom blankly. The writer leaned down and whispered to her, "*That's Zef Stuart from Life.*" Liza threw up her arms, cried, "*Zef!*" and ran to Mom.

Dad's career, meanwhile, had stalled, and he was living in Mom's Technicolor shadow. He was working hard to make a film of James Baldwin's short story "This Morning, This Evening, So Soon," a sad subtle look at the breakup of a marriage. Dad had written the adaptation himself and had signed up the legendary cinematographer James Wong Howe to shoot the film and the brilliant composer and performer Peter Schickele to write the score.

James Baldwin came over for dinner a couple of times. There was always great expectation and excitement beforehand. He was a gentleman, soft-spoken and at the same time exotic and fabulous, with a voice like honey and those hooded eyes that made him look like the world's wisest lizard. On his first visit, as we sat around in the living room, I batted my green eyes, hoping he'd pay a little attention to me, but while he was polite to all of us kids, he really wanted to talk to the other grownups about big issues, especially race, and the latest books and literary gossip.

Dad held readings of the script and invited potential investors but was never able to get the movie made. The air seemed to ooze out of him, and he began to have bouts of melancholy. It was only later that I grasped what a profound disappointment that must have been.

Dad did produce and direct a short film called *That's Me*, based on a skit developed at Second City, the Chicago improvisational theater troupe that's been a training ground for many great comic talents. Dad had seen Alan Arkin perform the skit and was inspired to turn it into a movie. It was Arkin's first flick, and it was nominated for the Oscar for Best Short Film. Colleagues urged Dad to move to Los Angeles and parlay his nomination into directing gigs, but he was a resolute New Yorker and declined. Like a lot of east coasters at the time, Mom was scathing about LA, calling it a cultural wasteland that turned out commercial dreck. And when Mom was scathing, it was best just to take cover.

That's Me is about an unemployed Puerto Rican man who loves to sit on a bench in Central Park with his guitar and play folk songs. His earnest social worker arrives and tries to talk him into getting a job. He turns all the social worker's arguments around on him, saying he's happier with no responsibilities, even it means he has very little money. It's a charming film, warm and funny and humanistic, like Dad.

But I'm afraid the message of "jobs aren't really necessary" and "'tis nobler to a minstrel be" may have made too strong an impression on me.

33

I was a bad boy.

Starting when I was around thirteen, I used to go around with a screwdriver and steal metal signs off the sides of buildings and pry those cool medallions off the front of Volkswagen bugs. I amassed a huge collection of plaques, many of them brass. I can see the appeal of the VW medallions, but what the hell I saw in a plaque announcing a doctor's office I'll never understand. One day Dad discovered some of the booty in my closet and became angry (or at least as angry as he got). He told me they were worth hundreds of dollars and that I had to go back to all the doctors' and lawyers' offices and apartment buildings and return them. I didn't and he never mentioned them again.

A few years later my badness found a willing partner in my friend Jan. We traveled in the same New York semi-rich-kid circles and there was always some new cafe or diner that would become everyone's hangout for a few months. We'd all go and smoke cigarettes and gossip and flirt. Jan was a nice funny up-for-anything girl with frizzy black hair, sharp cheekbones and a distinctive not-quite-pretty face. I think she knew I was gay but still crushed on me, and I dug her too, in my gay way. She had a trendy sister, Gigi, who loved to dance to the Supremes in front of the full-length mirror in her bedroom while she smoked a joint. Like so many parents in our circle, Jan and Gigi's made only cameo appearances.

Gigi floated on the fringes of the Warhol crowd and one night she said to us, "Come on, let's go down to the Factory."

We walked down from East 57th Street, where Jan lived, to a nondescript midrise loft building on East 47th, and followed Gigi upstairs.

The Factory was one huge room, its walls covered in tin foil. Gigi and Jan

WHAT WASN'T I THINKING?

disappeared and I stood alone, taking in the scene. There were ratty sofas filled with lounging acolytes who managed to look both languid and tense at the same time. A couple of men were checking me out, but I felt out of place and awkward. I didn't really understand the scene and felt sort of square. There was soul music blaring and a few dancers in the middle of the room, including the doomed superstar Edie Sedgwick, striking with short silver-blonde hair, saucer eyes, and amazing legs. She was wearing a long white t-shirt, black tights and black heels, and kept looking around nervously. Even back then I could tell how insecure she was.

Then I noticed Andy standing a few feet behind me.

"Hi," he said, with a little wave. Then he giggled.

I was shocked that Warhol was interested in me, but flattered.

Andy came closer. A short swarthy man, wearing a black leather jacket and a black leather cap covered in pins and medals, came over. (Gigi told me later he was the celebrity hair stylist Ara Gallant.)

"Who *are* you?" Ara asked, getting up in my face.

"My name is Sebastian, I'm here with Gigi. It's a pleasure to meet you," I said, holding out my hand for him to shake, falling back on the manners Mom had drilled into us.

Ara ignored all that and said, "I want to suck your cock."

Andy smiled in encouragement.

Geez, was Andy going to watch while Ara sucked my cock? And where would we do it exactly, since the Factory was so open? I was puffed up by their attention but nervous, trying to get my bearings. Sex was the farthest thing from my mind. "Maybe not tonight," I said.

I went and found Jan. "It's kinda boring here, isn't it?" she said.

"It is, kinda. No one is really talking. It's almost *too* cool."

"Listen, there's a party up on Park."

We headed uptown. The party was in one those enormous Park Avenue apartments that seem to go on forever. It was filled with rich kids, but we quickly learned that the parents, though out of sight, were in residence. Cardinal rule: if the parents are home, the party will be a dud.

As at most of these parties, there was a spare bedroom where everyone tossed their coats and purses onto the bed. Jan and I went in and I impulsively opened a purse and saw three twenties inside. I looked at Jan. She looked at me. I pocketed the cash. Then we looked at all the other purses on the bed. Grifter minds think alike: *Free money! Fun money!* I felt a killer rush race up and down my body. This scene was a lot more exciting than the Factory.

"I'll be lookout," Jan said, going out into the hall and scanning both directions.

I rifled through more purses and quickly netted about $300 in cash. A serious score.

Then we split, giddy with excitement, and headed straight for La Brasserie, a glamorous underground restaurant in the Seagram Building that featured a central staircase perfect for grand entrances. We both had fake I.D.'s we'd bought for five dollars at a Times Square arcade. We used them to order Tom Collinses, a totally girly (and delicious) drink. After a couple of rounds we moved on to foie gras and lobster.

I wish I could say my thievery was a one-time stunt, but back then my moral compass flew right past True North and landed on Cheap Thrills. I was a rebel in a Brooks Brothers shirt, and I was doing shit that was wrong. Speaking of Brooks Brothers, in those days you could just charge things by telling them you had an account and giving them a bogus name and address. No proof required. It became my fav store.

Now and then I still feel guilty about my thievery, and almost fall into a shame spiral. Then I think of John Waters, the patron saint of bad boys and bad girls. I hope he'd give me a benediction.

34

As I mentioned earlier, my bad boy behavior extended to UNIS. I had a lousy attitude, my grades were in the basement, and I smoked. In the middle of the eighth grade, just before Christmas break, they kicked me out. I never understood the specific reasons, if there were any, but after I was elected class president, I think the honchos felt I had to go.

Mom and Dad didn't seem particularly upset by my expulsion. There were no reprimands or explanations demanded. In fact, we never talked about it. They just took me over to Collegiate, an all-boys school that claims to be the oldest in the country, we had a talk with the headmaster, and I was admitted in January.

Collegiate and I were *not* a good fit. First of all, there were no girls and girls were fun and unpredictable. Rich boys were a huge bore. Then there were the mandatory jacket and tie, chapel and Latin and sports. Worst of all was the sound the chairs made when they scraped against the cafeteria floor. I kept my head down and trudged from class to class, hating each one more than the last.

Dad noted my antipathy to the school and how it was bleeding into my general moody isolation. He started to ask me into his home office to talk. These talks were excruciating. I never knew what to talk *about*. I certainly wasn't ready to open up to him about being gay.

I would sit there squirming, frequently asking, "Can I go now?"

Dad would answer, "Not yet. We still have a lot to talk about."

I now believe that those awkward, halting conversations strengthened the unspoken bond between us. Dad was reaching out and trying to help me. There were a few laughs now and then, some sarcasm, some irony, random thoughts and opinions on people, politics, summer plans, school—no animosity, just stumbling attempts at connecting by two people who loved each other.

After a year and a half at Collegiate, I told Mom and Dad I didn't want to go back and they said, "Okay." Apparently Collegiate had let them know the antipathy was mutual.

We were sitting in the living room after dinner, discussing my next move.

"What about boarding school?" Dad asked.

"I want to go to public school here in the city." I thought this would be a nice change of pace and fit in with my outsider image of myself.

Mom and Dad both lit cigarettes.

"Sebastian, that's *ridiculous*," Mom said. "The public schools in this city are *appalling*."

"You won't get a good education," Dad said.

Who cared about getting a good education? "I want to go to public school," I repeated.

"Walker, talk some sense into him."

"I think you should think it through, Sebastian," Dad said.

"I have." I hadn't.

I could actually feel their resistance fading. The air in the room got softer and they exchanged a resigned, sheepish look. As usual, they never insisted on anything.

Mom sighed and ground out her cigarette. "Alright then. But don't say you weren't warned."

I didn't have the grades to get into the good public schools—Stuyvesant or Music and Art—but I did find a school called Charles Evans Hughes on West 18th Street in Chelsea. The vibe was relatively mellow and I enrolled as a sophomore in September 1964.

I loved Hughes. It was like stepping into another world. The school was built for 2,500 students but had 4,100. It was about 95 percent Black, with the rest Puerto Rican and maybe a hundred white kids. Half of one floor housed a school for disabled students.

I learned pretty quickly what it feels like to be in the minority. Kids looked at me sideways and skeptically. I was nervous for a week or two, then forgot about it.

In fact, I totally dug it. The Black girls had cool names like Jaybird and LeRae and Veda. I became friends with Veda. She was smart and charming with a wry sense of humor. I had her over for dinner and she brought me around Harlem. Many of her friends and family lived in the projects and I was amazed to see living rooms with linoleum or concrete floors. When I walked in, I was definitely Honky from Another Planet. Mouths opened and eyes widened.

The white kids at Hughes were mostly working-class, with a smattering of middle-class kids of all races. The leader of the middle-class pack was a warm, bright, earthy, funny white girl named Judy Finn, who held court at a nearby coffee shop.

Judy and I hooked up online a few years back and had a long talk on the phone. She remembered my first days at Hughes: "I saw you around school, but you seemed very shy and I wasn't sure what to make of you. Then one day you were on a staircase behind a blind girl. She dropped her books and said, 'Somebody pick up my motherfuckin' books.' You picked them up and handed them to her and she continued up the stairs without thanking you. Then she dropped her books again and said, 'Somebody pick up my motherfuckin' books.' You picked them up and handed them to her again, and again no 'Thanks.' When she dropped them a third time, you said, 'Pick up your own motherfuckin' books.' That's when I knew you were okay."

Judy brought me into her circle. I used to hang out at her apartment on 126th Street and Riverside Drive. Her mother was a small Jewish woman, grim and determined, a Communist who trudged to her job every day. Her father was a handsome twinkly Irishman who never seemed to have a job, adored Judy, and loved having her friends around.

Judy's mom was a member of the W.E.B. DuBois Club, a communist social group. Out of curiosity I went to a few meetings with Judy. They were filled with downtrodden-looking people in dark wool coats carrying sandwiches in neatly folded brown paper bags. I decided that communists had no sense of humor, were martyrs to their poverty, and worst of all were totally unglamorous.

Conor, another friend from Hughes, lived around the corner from Judy. He was pure Irish, his aunt ran the numbers, and his ancient gaga grandfather lived in a large crib and yelled out mumbo-jumbo. Whenever we needed money we'd go into his aunt's bedroom, take a book off the shelf, and remove one of the endless twenties that were stashed in the pages.

We used the money to buy pot. You could go into a bodega in those days and buy nickel and dime bags. We were all major potheads. I spent hundreds of happy hours on rooftops getting stoned with my new friends. We'd just pick a random building—once you got out of the fancy precincts a lot of buildings had no front door-lock—and head up to the roof. The view was always cool, and we'd smoke and laugh and talk—of course I have no memory what about.

My favorite teachers at Hughes were Miss North and Miss Clark, elderly spinsters who looked like they'd stepped right out of the 1930s. They wore mid-calf navy-blue serge dresses with short sleeves and lace collars, and they kept their gray hair pinned up. They were holdovers from a different city, a different school system, and yet they cared. They taught hard, fair but firm. Miss North was thin and bristled with energy. She was my guidance counselor, which meant that I visited her office now and then.

Miss Clark was ample and slow moving. Her office was across the hall from Miss North's and one day she walked in carrying a newspaper. Ever polite, I stood up and she rewarded me with a warm smile, before saying, "Miss North, did you see this article on education in the *Sun* today?" She handed Miss North her copy of the *Brooklyn Sun*, a newspaper that is now long gone.

Miss North was also my math teacher. My math scores were so abysmal that I—along with a few dozen other kids—was in danger of failing. She scheduled an exam to give us all one last chance. I actually studied for it and passed by just a hair. She rewarded me with a big smile. Miss North was a brave dear unsentimental woman with a quiet moxie that I've never forgotten. I loved her then and I still do.

Hughes had discipline problems and there were hall monitors, little middle-aged ladies who walked up and down the halls and were supposed to keep things under control and protect us.

The school had three huge metal staircases, one in the middle of the building and one at each end. You reached them through padded swinging doors, each with a small diamond-shaped window. One day I walked out onto a stairwell and was accosted by two boys.

"Give us your money," one kid demanded.

"I don't have any," I said.

He punched me so hard I flew across the stairwell, hit the wall and crumpled to the floor. Then he came over and kicked me in the head and stomach. "Maybe I do have a few dollars," I said, handing them over.

The boys fled down the stairs and as soon as they were gone the door swung open and a hall monitor appeared.

"I saw the whole thing," she said, "Now go get cleaned up." And that was that.

A wildly sexy and macho Black kid, handsome and muscular, really a porno dream, would appear at Hughes now and then. He would strut around with a swooning queen on each arm. There was a small contingent of Black queens at school, boys who pomaded their hair, wore tight shiny clothes and vamped it up with high-pitched voices, swishing and swaying down the hallways. If you were femme, it was hard to be closeted in the Black community. It was too honest. I heard queens get harassed a few times, but it was pretty mild, even jokey.

I rarely went to the cafeteria at Hughes, it was so depressing, with inedible food and dingy décor. But one day I was there and the macho boy walked through, a queen on each arm. He stopped at my table and started flirting with me. I was so excited and flattered by his interest that I got all tongue-tied. Then one of the queens pulled him away, hissing, "You don't need a *white bitch*."

I wished we could have gotten to know each other better, preferably in a dark empty classroom. But I never saw him without his swoon squad and I sure as shit didn't to want to ignite their ire.

Hughes may not have been an academic powerhouse, but I was definitely getting an education.

My very favorite thing to do during my two years at Hughes was to visit the ancient Walgreens on 8th Avenue and 19th Street. It was right out of an Edward Hopper painting—dark wood trim, dusty shelves, slanted light, a quiet, lonely vibe, and a small luncheonette with a few tables, a Formica counter and round chrome stools with red vinyl seats. I'd sit at the counter, order a grilled cheese and coffee, and linger, smoking Winstons.

Every day without fail a group of four drab middle-aged women employees from the huge Con Ed (now Google) building on 8th Avenue would come in for lunch. They ordered egg salad or BLT sandwiches and coffee and sat there expressionless, talking in droning monotones about office minutiae or the weather. One day one of them was out sick and it was like you'd flipped a switch. The three remaining women were chatty and animated, leaning towards each other, dishy and alive, their voices singing. *Every word* they spoke was to disparage their missing colleague. They trashed her from here to next Tuesday.

I was shocked and even had an urge to interrupt them and defend the poor absent creature. I was so confused—why did they have lunch together every day if they felt that way about her? I felt a terrible aching pity for the woman, at home nursing her cold, wondering how her friends were getting on without her.

A lot of gay men lived in Chelsea. It was just north of Queer Central, the West Village, and the rents were lower. Once in a while I'd let a man pick me up. The sex was usually pretty desultory because I was so nervous and had no idea who I was or what I wanted. Hustling had been transactional and both parties knew their role. I felt much more insecure with a random pickup. So, I'd mostly just lie there and let them do me.

Sometimes the sex was okay but there were no emotional sparks, which was what I longed for. I was obsessed with true love and I couldn't wait for the day when I would meet the boy I was destined for. We'd kiss, the sky would split open, and our two would become an ecstatic one. Or something along those lines.

Just about everything in my confused head and heart was inchoate, unformed, based on shards of hope and yearning.

35

One night Tina and I were at the Farrows alone, in the library. I don't remember where the Farrow kids were. Tina handed me a can of soda and watched with a wily smile as I drank it.

Pretty soon I started to feel queasy and my vision got wavy. "Tina, did you put *acid* in that soda?" She nodded and smiled.

As most druggies know, acid trips take some psychic preparation, and I was in *no way* ready. "Why the fuck did you do that? I'm freaking out!"

She didn't answer. She just got up and left the room. I sucked air and willed myself to come down from the high. It didn't work. I went looking for Tina, calling her name. I checked the bedrooms but there was no sign of her or anyone else. I began to panic.

I heard the front door open and a lilting, "Hello?" I went into the front hall and there was Maureen O'Sullivan, looking a little tipsy. She gave me warm smile. She was wearing a short metallic gold dress that really *popped!* on acid.

"Sebastian, how lovely to see you. Where is everyone?"

"I don't know."

"Well, I'm sure they'll turn up."

I had to find Tina.

"It's nice to see you, Mrs. Farrow. But I have to get going."

"Oh, don't rush off! Why don't you stay a minute?" She took my hand and led me into the library. I was so fucking high, I was struggling to keep my bearings. Maureen went over to the console and put on a record. Sinatra sang "Fly Me to the Moon."

I was already *on* the moon and wanted to get back to terra firma.

"Why don't we dance," Maureen said, twirling around. Was she trying to seduce me?

"I ... I ... I ... would love to, but I really have to get home."

I fled the apartment. Tina wasn't at my house either. I walked around the neighborhood looking for her, sweaty and jumpy and frightened. Finally, the acid started to wane and I went home and curled up on my bed, wet with bitter acid sweat, my thoughts racing and ricocheting.

What was happening to Tina?

Why had she done this to me?

A few days later she called me and said, "I'm sorry I gave you that acid without telling you."

"Why did you do it?"

"I don't know. But I'm sorry."

"I accept your apology."

The call was short and left me with more questions than answers. Tina's bouts of silence and withdrawal were becoming more frequent. When she came down from Westport to visit me for the weekend, she would often lie on the bed in David's room (he was away at boarding school), sometimes for hours at a time. When I tried to engage her, she said nothing, just stared up at the ceiling expressionless. I didn't understand what was happening. At first, I was sympathetic, but I grew increasingly annoyed. I wanted her to snap out of it. I wanted us to go back to having fun together.

One Sunday a few months after the acid incident we were alone at 101. It was a still afternoon and we were hanging out in the kitchen. Ruby kept an open stepladder in one corner. Tina was sitting on the top rung, quiet and distant. Then she said, in a strange matter-of-fact voice, "I'm going crazy, Sebastian."

I was gripped with terrible foreboding and didn't answer for a moment. "What do you mean?" I finally asked, hoping my voice sounded calmer than I felt.

"I hear voices. Voices in my head."

The quiet kitchen, the afternoon light, I felt a fear rat scurry up my spine.

"Voices?" I asked. "What do they say?"

"They say my name. Over and over. They tell me people are looking at me. That people are after me. That they want to kill me," she said in a monotone.

I had no idea how to respond. I know now that Tina was half into madness and half out, still sane enough to realize that something horrifying was happening to her.

I can still see her on that stepladder, elbows on her knees, with a forlorn and faraway look on her face. I can still hear her words—*I'm going crazy, Sebastian.*"

The acid mickey now made more sense. Tina was jealous of my friends and family and especially of my sanity. She wanted me to join her in the Land of the Mad. We'd always been so close and now she'd been shot down and I was still airborne. I realize now that she was enraged at her fate. Of course she was. Who wouldn't be?

As I relive that moment in the kitchen now, the pathos of Tina's destiny is clear and overwhelming. In some essential way her future was over—and she knew it.

Tina's behavior grew more erratic, okay one day, shut down the next. Hope and promise and fun were replaced by confusion, anger, loss. And shock. And guilt, so much guilt: *why had Tina gotten sick and not me?*

Because she hadn't had a full-blown psychotic break yet, no one in the family besides me paid much attention to her alarming and deepening withdrawal. When I told Mom and Dad, they shrugged it off. Later, after her psychotic break, they tried to help Tina, but at first they made it clear they considered it some sort of phase. While Wanda was concerned, she simply wasn't emotionally there for Tina. She too minimized what was happening.

In the months and years that followed, as the disease's grip on Tina tightened, she became almost incapable of engaging. The insane live in a small self-obsessed world. Just writing this brings back those early months and makes me nauseated and afraid. *Poor Tina, poor sweet baby.*

Schizophrenia is a take-no-prisoners disease. Back then there were few effective treatments. The best outcome was to gain some control of the symptoms through medication and therapy, and hopefully stop any full-blown psychotic breaks. Today, thanks in part to better meds, many schizophrenics—worn down by the agonies of the disease—"age out" and stop having acute episodes. Many go on to build safe, small lives for themselves, damaged but functioning.

As Tina slipped further into madness, my hopes for our future together began to fade. My best friend, my soul mate, my knock-about buddy and pal, my sounding board, my buffer and counterweight to Mom, was being sucked away. How would I manage without her?

The day after our talk in the kitchen, I found Tina lying on my bed like a corpse, looking straight up at the ceiling, arms at her sides. In some weird way I was glad she had moved from David's room to mine. Maybe it brought her some small comfort.

"Are you okay?" I asked. Stupid question. She didn't answer. I suddenly felt a wave of love for her. My throat tightened. "Do you want me to lie next to you and hold you?"

She paused and said, "No."

I was hurt, not understanding that she was on a solo journey.

I wish I had lay down beside her anyway.

36

I was at Charles Evans Hughes for two years, and while I loved it, my restless soul was up for a change. Mom kept mentioning a boarding school in Connecticut, not far from Tina, that a couple of family friends sent their kids to. Apparently, it was loose and artistic and had a lenient admission policy. One day in late June we drove up to take a look.

The school was in Ridgefield in the heart of bosky, rich Fairfield County. We drove along winding roads until we came to a wooden sign hanging on a tree: "The Shapley School." We headed down a long tree-lined drive, parked and looked around. The campus was originally an inn and the grounds were crisscrossed by old stone walls; there was a small lake and a collection of drafty, rambling buildings. Everything was chipped and peeling and musty, rundown and wistful. A motel wing had been added to the inn at some point and that's where the classrooms were. Adding to the campus's odd charm, the girls' dorm—which perched atop a little hill—was a cool 1950s split-level ranch house. I was smitten.

As soon as we got out of the car a tiny birdlike woman flew out of the main building and started chattering away in an English accent, "Hello hello *hell-o*, welcome *welcome*! We're frightfully busy! And you must be Sebastian!"

I wondered if she was hopped up on diet pills, but I found out later she was flying high on Christian Science. She led me to an interview with the school's founder, Carl Shapley, while she gave Mom and Dad a tour of the campus. Because school had ended for the summer, there were no kids around.

Shapley had a large sparse office overlooking the lake. He was around 40, very intense, with a smooth sharp face, all points and angles, Beatle bangs and mad sparkly eyes.

"Such a pleasure to have you visit, Sebastian. I believe most schools teach students what they *can't* do and be," he said, his cadence rising, "We turn that *topsy-turvy!* I believe a child should mold his own curriculum, impromptu, improvised. Let your imagination roam freely over the geography of your soul!" He got all red-faced and a vein in his forehead throbbed.

"Wonderful," I said, thinking, *I have no idea what's he's talking about but, boy, this place sounds like fun.*

I signed up and started in the fall.

It turned out that the Shapley School was only a few years old and that Carl and most of the teachers and staff—we called them his groupies—were Christian Scientists. They all had those mad sparkly eyes, like they were in on some delirious secret that gave them magical powers. The faculty included an ancient silent-film star named Faye Marbe, who would put on full makeup and a mink coat and parade around campus looking like a figure on the prow of an old schooner.

My schoolmates were mostly refugees from other schools—flunkouts, dropouts, and kicked-outs. For most of us Shapley was our last chance to get a diploma. There were fewer than a dozen kids in the senior class. My roommate was Danny Leber, a chubby, insecure, funny and imaginative kid from Scarsdale. It was his second year, and he loved the place. Like a lot of the other students, he had found acceptance there.

The welcoming assembly consisted of Carl Shapley giving a high-fidelity version of the sermon he had preached to me in June. "What a glorious year it's going to be! You children, students of the human heart, will be leading the charge." It sounded like he wanted to put the inmates in charge of the asylum. I was down with that.

After UNIS, Collegiate, and Hughes, I had definitely landed in another educational galaxy altogether.

My first class was philosophy. I walked over to the motel-classroom to find Mrs. Fangel, an Italian aristocrat who had married a Yankee lush, sitting at the head of a long table. She was a buxom woman with olive skin and a hooked nose—she looked regal and emanated tidal waves of profundity.

"Children," she said, looking at each of us in turn, pulling us into her bottomless pool of wisdom. "*Socrates!*" The word hung in the air. Finally she spoke again and I heard *cogito* and *dialectic* and *determinism*—the kind of words that give me a headache. It was like she was speaking some language she'd invented called Abstractish. But I adored her just for being her, so frigging deep.

The current events teacher was "Mr. Swanson from Wisconsin" (as we called him behind his back). He ignited a class war on campus. After letting us know he didn't have much money, he barely contained his resentment towards the spoiled brats in his charge. He had a long white beard and a folksy manner, wore suspenders and called his pudgy wife "Mother." The two of them were aliens from Planet Midwest.

We smoked *a lot* of pot at Shapley. Often we would duck into the woods during lunch, or even before breakfast, and get blitzed. I'm sure it was no fun to teach a bunch of incoherent glassy-eyed kids, plus the Swansons lived in the boys' dorm and literally got wind of what was going down.

One bright January morning Swanson walked into my French class and said, "There are some gentlemen here who would like to see you, Sebastian."

"Who? What?" I said, shocked, looking at Swanson's smug face.

"You'll find out soon enough. Now follow me."

I walked outside to find two cop cars parked in front of the dorm. I felt a frisson of fear. A policeman approached me. "Are you Sebastian Stuart?"

"I am."

"You're under arrest for possession of marijuana." My breath stopped. He read me my rights as he handcuffed me. *Holy shit, this is really happening.* I was led to a police car and driven to the town jail, where I called Dad, who bailed me out and hired a lawyer. Turns out the cops had a found a small bag of pot in my desk drawer.

As my court date approached Mom and Dad got their local friends to write letters to the judge in my support. Mom drove up from the city to take me to court in depressing downtown Danbury. Understandably she was in a foul mood, all clenched and antsy, and I was feeling guilty for putting her and Dad through this and for being such a fuck-up in general.

The courtroom was pretty empty and when my case was called, I went up with my lawyer and stood in front of the judge. I watched as he read the letters on thick embossed stationary from tony Connecticut addresses. Then he looked at me and said, "I'm putting you on probation. If you stay out of trouble for the next year, the charge will be erased from your record."

That was it. I was free to go. Privilege had saved me. If I'd been a poor Black kid I might still be in jail. Seriously. I knew I'd dodged a bullet and I felt guilty but grateful.

37

A few months after my court date, I got that call from Mom about Tina's psychotic break in Central Park and her admission to Gracie Square hospital. Visiting her had left me hollowed out. I went into denial about both the seriousness of her disease and my grief over losing my best friend. I leavened the denial with irrational optimism. Tina was getting good care. She'd get better.

Tina couldn't turn to her father for help. Monty Montemora had long ago gambled away his restaurants and everything else. As for his fathering skills, after he and Wanda divorced, he never contacted his kids. Monty was a classic type— handsome rake, big talker, selfish shit.

When I was about thirteen Monty managed to get another restaurant going, a burger joint on far East 34th Street, which was sort of a no-man's land back then. Tina and I visited one day. The restaurant was pretty empty, but Monty was all smiles and ordered us burgers. He didn't ask Tina any questions, not one. There was nothing between them, just nothing. After we ate our burgers he gave Tina five dollars and we left. It seemed deeply weird to me, that a parent could care so little about his own kid. Tina was quiet for the rest of the afternoon, her brow knitted, unsettled and confused.

Monty gambled away that restaurant, too.

Tina never saw him again.

Fast forward fifteen years to 1982. Monty was living in a residential hotel on West 34th Street. He started calling Nicky, who was a NYC public school teacher. He'd spin out his latest comeback scheme and then ask to borrow fifty bucks, which Nicky always gave him.

One day I got a call from Nicky.

"The police called me. My father died of lung cancer."

"I'm so sorry. Where?"

"In his hotel room. I have to go clear out his things."

"Do you want some help?"

The hotel was awful, dark and oppressive, down-and-out on West 34th Street. We walked down a hallway that smelled like urine and mold and a billion cigarettes. Nicky had brought along some black garbage bags for her father's belongings.

"Have you been here before?" I asked.

"No. He would never let me come, we always met at a coffee shop."

We found his room. Police tape covered the door, warning us not to enter. We tried the door anyway. It was locked. There was a fire escape at the end of the hall and we climbed out onto it, opened a window, and clambered into his room. Not a pretty sight.

There was a single bed and a dresser with the drawers open, clothes spilling out, sheets and towels strewn around. There was blood everywhere, in splatters and in big, dried clumps, like he had spit his lungs up. The room smelled like decay and death and shit. I gagged. I wondered how long his body had been there before someone found him.

Nicky looked around, fighting down tears.

"Can you handle this?" I asked.

She nodded and opened the closet. A few cheap suits. There was no desk, just a pile of medical paperwork on the dresser top. I found a stack of stationery in the top dresser drawer.

"Look at this, Nicky."

The top of each page had been rubber-stamped "Vincent Montemora, Restaurant Consultant." The ink was splotchy, the stamp crooked.

"At least he was still trying," Nicky said.

The seedy sordid hotel and Monty's death brought home to me how far our family had fallen. I remember feeling creeped out but also morbidly fascinated by the gruesome room. Tina's father had died there. And now she was sick. It was such a long way from Wanda's salad days as a top model with a dashing husband.

"Have you told Tina?" I asked Nicky. Tina, then 33, was living upstate in Woodstock and we were in sporadic contact.

"I called her."

"What did she say?"

"'Oh.'"

Looking back on Monty's life helps me to understand why Tina got sick and I didn't. Schizophrenia is centered in the prefrontal cortex, a part of the brain that's weakened by stress, especially during adolescence. Well, Tina had plenty of stress, including an undermining alcoholic mother and an AWOL father. There was no one to counter this neglect and abuse. Don Allan was around for a few years and he was so good for Tina, but watching the collapse of his and Wanda's marriage may have added to her instability. Mom and Dad tried to help, putting her in Gracie Square and, I found out years later, sending her to a series of expensive psychiatrists. I will always love them for their efforts. But, like me, they didn't understand how fierce and intractable the disease was. They were fighting a fire-breathing monster with a cap gun. And they couldn't afford to keep up the fight.

It only took Nicky and me a couple of minutes to case the room. We were both fighting nausea.

"I don't want anything," Nicky said, and we left the way we'd come in.

I can't help remembering that awful day, that awful room. I wish I could forget it. I think of the dried blood as Tina's blood.

38

When it came time to apply to colleges, I picked the three cities that sounded the most romantic to me and were—just as important—farthest from my family: New Orleans, Los Angeles, and San Francisco. I applied to Tulane, Occidental, and San Francisco State. While I knew I was fleeing my family, I also needed to get away from the confusion, guilt and sadness Tina's disease was causing me.

My grades were mediocre at best and the first two schools nixed me quickly. Then one sunny spring morning I was in bed reading when I heard the dorm phone ring.

"Hello, darling," Mom said. "You've received a letter from San Francisco State College. Shall I open it?" I could tell she already had. "... You've been accepted. I suppose congratulations are in order. Though I don't think the school's reputation is much of anything." Mom had to get her little dig in, but for once I didn't care.

I went outside and sat on the front steps in the sunshine, euphoric. I was heading to California, land of sunshine and freedom! The realities of college—going to class and reading and learning and all that—never entered my head. I had no concrete image of my future, just a sense that it would be filled with adventure and mystery and, of course, that I would meet the boy of my dreams, the sky would slide back and we two would become one.

And San Francisco! The city had a reputation as the freewheeling forefront of the exploding counterculture, which was anti-war, anti-materialism, pro free-love and peace and macramé. And San Francisco was *gay*. *Life* magazine had published a big story on how it was the homosexual mecca of America. I read it so often I practically had it memorized.

But first I had to get through the remaining months at Shapley. After the drug bust several kids were withdrawn and the school sort of deflated. Then the faculty's paychecks bounced, Mr. Shapley was replaced as headmaster, and his coterie of Christian Scientist groupies followed him away. It was announced that the school would be closing permanently, and a gloomy nostalgia hung over the campus. There was a desultory graduation ceremony—I think six of us got diplomas. My high school career limped over the finish line.

39

As the plane landed in San Francisco, I could barely stay in my seat—here I was seventeen, on my own, arriving in the promised land. I was breaking free of Mom and all the old East Coast strictures, free to become my true self (whoever that was).

I got off the plane and looked up to the blue California horizon—the first thing I saw was a bleak denuded mountain covered with huge letters reading: *Welcome to South San Francisco, the Industrial City.* Wait, they have *industry* in San Francisco? That was kind of a downer.

For my first night Mom had booked me into the Gaylord Hotel on Jones Street near Union Square. Someone at *Life* had told her it was a "perfectly decent" hotel. It turned out to be wonderfully atmospheric in a 1940s traveling-salesman way, the lobby home to fringed lampshades and standing ashtrays. As to where I'd stay on night two, I was on my own. I was adamant with Mom and Dad that I didn't want to live in the dorm. They shrugged and suggested the college housing office.

A classmate from Shapley was from San Francisco and she'd given me her address up on Russian Hill. After checking into the Gaylord, I walked up to Russian Hill in the twilight and found her house. I was sure she'd invite me in for dinner, maybe show me around town a little. Instead I found a note she'd addressed to me stuck in the mailbox. In it, she told me she was leaving for college. She also listed a bunch of fun stuff to do in the city. I stood there, flooded with loneliness.

Yet as I walked around the neighborhood I was dazed and dazzled, amazed to discover secret staircases, palm trees, hidden dells, and cypresses shaped like giant bonsai. The architecture was a mishmash of quirky California-modern, old elegance, Art Deco, Victorian, craftsman bungalows. I came to a street that dead-ended in a flight of steps. The city spread out below me, twinkling and enchanting, glamorous and noir. It was all just so beautiful, completely unlike any other place I'd ever been. I knew the East Coast and Europe, but San Francisco was a strange hybrid, an urban dreamscape, unmoored from all my touchstones, the other side of the looking glass, wonderland.

As I stood looking out over the city, a well-dressed man approached.

"It's a lovely view, isn't it?" he said. He was in his 40s, with a kind face.

"It sure is."

"I recognize your expression—this is your first visit to the City."

"I just got here today. I'm going to SF State."

"That's Telegraph Hill over there with Coit Tower on top, and below us are Chinatown and North Beach."

It looked vibrant and beckoning, a small urban valley pulsing with lights and humanity.

The man looked at me for a long moment. "Would you like to get something to eat? Or a cup of coffee?"

I felt some connection to him, but not enough. He was just so ... respectable. I wanted someone kinetic and edgy, maybe even dangerous.

Beware of answered prayers.

"No, thank you. I'm sorry, but I really want to just walk around and see things."

He looked disappointed but said, "I understand. Welcome to the City." He walked a few steps away and then turned back and said wistfully, "You'll like San Francisco."

I wondered why he was sad. Looking back, I think he knew something it took me years to learn—that San Francisco, for all its charm and magic, is tinged with sorrow. It's *too* beautiful—and on the other side of all that beauty lays the abyss. I think that's why people throw themselves off the Golden Gate Bridge. If you can't find happiness here, where can you?

The next day I found a furnished weekly rental in a funky residential hotel a few blocks from the Gaylord, at the edge of the Tenderloin, the city's sleazy underbelly, a 'hood filled with hookers, hustlers, junkies, grifters and porn shops. The room had a large bay window and I thought it would be fun to smoke a joint and sit at the window watching the world go by.

I found my way up to Haight Street, a teeming bazaar of head shops and cafes, hippies sitting on the sidewalks, their dogs on rope leashes, there were guitar players and kids resplendent in velvet bellbottoms and fringe and headbands and frilly Victorian blouses. It was cool and colorful, like nothing back in the boring old East.

I bought some weed from a street kid. When I got back to my room, I rolled up a joint, sat at the window, lit up and got ready for a dream within a dream. Nothing happened. I'd been burned.

I found a wonderful restaurant run by a Chinese family that served both Chinese and American food. It had a long counter filled with solitary diners and cozy booths framed by filigree woodwork. A four-course dinner cost eighty cents and included a bowl of watery soup, a small chunk of iceberg lettuce, a slice of meatloaf with mashed potatoes and soggy green beans, and a dish of Jell-O with a little dollop of whipped cream on top. I loved to linger there and people watch. It reminded me of being with Tina and I missed her something awful, imagining how much she would love this restaurant, this city. I made mental notes of all the things I wanted to tell her, but mostly I just wanted her with me, inhaling this strange and wondrous adventure.

I'd arrived about a week before classes started and I hadn't visited the campus yet. School seemed like an abstraction. I just wanted to explore.

After my week at the hotel, I moved to another, cheaper one even farther into the Tenderloin, where I took a room for another week. I met a Mexican-American boy from Arizona there. He was nice looking and very sweet, and I wanted a friend. I asked him if he wanted to take a walk and we headed over to Union Square.

"How long have you been here?" I asked him.

"Two months."

"Do you like it?"

"I miss my family."

"Do they know about you?"

"No." He looked dejected. "I wish I wasn't ... *gay*."

"But you are. We both are."

"I know that. That's why I came here. But I don't like it. I want to go home and marry a girl and settle down. I want to have children." His voice had a bitter edge. Back then gay men having children was beyond imagining.

"But don't you want to be true to yourself, to who you are?"

"We're not normal people, we're freaks."

It was disappointing to hear him parrot society's disdain for queers. "We're normal for *us*," I said. "And what's so wrong with being a freak? An outsider? I like being gay."

"I'm happy for you then," he said begrudgingly.

We headed back to the hotel.

"Do you want to come up to my room?" I asked.

"Okay."

We made out a little on the bed but neither one of us was that into it. We quit halfway through. He sat on the edge of the bed, morose.

"Do you think you will go back home and marry a girl?"

"I don't know, man, I just don't know," he said, confused and sad.

When he left, I felt hollow. I pitied him. He was battling himself. But I couldn't let it infect me. The last thing I wanted to do was marry a girl and have babies. I wanted to be a wild child.

At some point I must have taken the endless Muni trip out to San Francisco State and registered for classes, but I have no memory of it.

40

After two weeks I was ready to get out of the Tenderloin and I began searching newspaper ads for a real apartment. I found a listing for a furnished studio on Noe Street just off Market Street, in the heart of the Castro district, which back then was sleepy, working-class, largely Irish and Scandinavian. The gay invasion began shortly thereafter. I made an appointment to meet the owner.

Standing in front of the three-story building was a thin Chinese man of indeterminate age. He was smoking a non-filter cigarette and enjoying it immensely.

"Hello, I'm Sebastian."

"Nice to meet you," he said.

He led me into the building, up the stairs to the top floor and into the apartment. There was a foyer with a built-in dresser and closet, a black-and-white tiled bath, a perfect 1940s eat-in kitchen, and a large living room with a nubby maroon horsehair sofa and chair and windows that looked out to the roof of the low-rise building next door. The apartment had a wonderful smell—slightly musty, woodsy, with a hint of fog. But there was no sign of a bed.

"Is there a bed?" I asked.

The man laughed. Clearly, he'd been waiting for his cue. He walked over to a blank wall and pushed in one side of it. Like magic the wall spun 180 degrees and a metal-framed Murphy bed appeared. He pulled down the foot of the bed; it unfolded and—*presto!*—the room was complete.

I was swooning. I'd always loved the idea of living in one room, having a small simple life. It just seemed so romantic. This apartment was perfect. The rent was $100 a month.

"I'll take it."

He nodded. I wrote him a check (Dad was sending me a monthly living allowance), and he handed me the keys. I went back to the Tenderloin and picked up my suitcase and took a cab back to Noe. When I was settled, I took out my camera and photographed the apartment, the bed, the building, and the neighborhood. I had the pictures developed and sent them to Tina. Suddenly, in my own San Francisco apartment, the future was a beckoning canvas, and anything seemed possible—even Tina getting better.

She called me a few days later.

"Hi, Sebastian." Her voice sounded slightly sluggish, but I could tell she was making an effort to sound like her old self. It was touching.

"Tina. How are you?"

"I'm better. I'm staying on Central Park West for a little while. Your parents are so good to me. I got your pictures. The apartment is wonderful. It's like an old movie about an alcoholic from Kansas who runs away from his wife and children to drink himself to death in the big city."

"I'm not there *quite* yet. But it's so cool. I wish you could see it." There was an awkward pause; she was in no condition to come out to SF. "I mean I wish I could see you."

"You're having a real life, Sebastian."

"I wouldn't go that far."

"Have you started college?"

"Yes."

"What's it like?"

"Well, you can smoke in class, so that's a plus. It's kinda boring really."

"There are a lot of distractions in that city. You stay out of trouble."

"That doesn't sound like much fun."

"Please ..." Her concern for me was so genuine, my throat tightened.

"For you, okay. Say hi to Ruby for me."

"Sure thing, Sirbasketball," she said with jaunty bravado that couldn't disguise her melancholy.

I hung up feeling guilty. I hadn't asked Tina about her therapist, her medications, her delusions and hallucinations. Thanks to my hardening denial of just how sick she was, I'd been Pollyannaish, wanting things to be "up."

But maybe that's what Tina wanted from me. I hope so.

41

Dad was working for ABC News on a documentary and he spent a few days in San Francisco en route to somewhere. He was staying at the posh St. Francis Hotel, where I met him and enjoyed a sumptuous breakfast. He seemed preoccupied, even troubled, but I chalked it up to work stress.

"I'm eager to see your apartment," he said after breakfast.

We rode the Muni together and went upstairs. I'd cleaned the place and bought flowers.

"This is nice," Dad said. "You should get a girlfriend." I froze and blushed and he quickly added, "Or a roommate." He was handing me an invitation to come out, but I wasn't ready.

"How's Tina doing?"

"She's doing all right. It's somewhat disruptive having her at the apartment. She never cleans up after herself. I don't think your mother or Ruby want her there much longer."

"Where will she go?"

"Into a hospital. It will have to be a state hospital."

"Please look out for her, Dad."

"I'll try my best."

We went downstairs, out onto Noe Street. It was time to say goodbye.

"Have you given any thought to what you'll want to major in?" Dad asked.

"Not really."

"You don't have any idea how you want to make a living?"

I'd been writing feverish poetry and so I offered, "I want to be a poet."

Dad winced. "That's fine, but what about earning money?"

I shrugged. "Is earning money so important?"

Dad looked pained. "Yes, it is. That's something we need to discuss." He lit a cigarette and took a long pull. "I don't know if you realize how much everything costs these days. Shoes, schools, trips, it all adds up so quickly. My income isn't enough to cover it. Even with your mother's added."

"How are you paying for everything?"

He sighed before answering, "I dip into my capital." He looked around beseechingly, as if for a savior to come and end this discussion. "I don't have much money left, Sebastian. You can't count on my supporting you."

"That's okay," I said casually. It would be a gross understatement to say I didn't grasp the implications of what he was telling me.

Today I understand what a tough talk this was for him. I don't know if I didn't believe it, didn't understand it, or just denied it—probably all three—but his heartfelt warning fell on deaf ears. It didn't seem real, especially since he was sending me a check every month and staying at the St. Francis.

I was off in my solipsistic, narcissistic dream world, where there were no jobs defacing the landscape.

We shook hands—what an odd and formal goodbye that seems to me now—and he headed back downtown. I was relieved to see him go.

42

San Francisco State was isolated at the very southwestern edge of the city, bordered on one side by Park Merced, a vast apartment complex, and on the other by the Stonestown shopping center. The campus itself was filled with low-slung buildings and basically looked like a really huge suburban high school.

I registered for classes like Writing and Sailing. I'd studied maps of the campus and fixated on a small man-made lake, imagining long hours spent lolling on its bucolic shores. It turned out to be barren and weed-choked, ringed by wide roads.

State had a lot to offer, including a well-respected writing department. Its Poetry Center—founded in 1954 with money donated by W.H. Auden—was famous and there were some hotshot poets on the faculty.

None of that interested me.

The streets did.

I quickly realized that I could open one of my apartment windows and climb out onto the flat roof of the building next door, which fronted on Market Street. At night I liked to climb onto the roof, walk over to the far edge, and sit with my legs dangling over.

One night I was sitting there looking out at the quietude when I had something of an epiphany: I wanted more—more sensation, more excitement, more thrills. Here I was living in this amazing city and I was ... lonely. And a little bored. I said to myself, in a voice I can still hear, "I'm going to go find some adventure."

I started hanging out with street kids around Union Square, a ragtag bunch of druggies, runaways, and hustlers. Men approached me for sex, and I started to turn tricks again. I was a terrible hooker—passive, inhibited, self-absorbed, deluded in thinking that there was something more than sex going on, that the men gave a shit about me beyond my body. I didn't need the money, but I needed the validation, the attention, the kicks. Being desired gave me a feeling of worth and power.

The Union Square kids talked about a famous hustler who worked the Oak Room bar at the St. Francis Hotel. The Oak Room was all-male back then and was legendary as a discreet place for high-class hustlers to score rich johns. You had to wear a jacket and tie to get in. I was *not* a high-class hustler—I was street trade and didn't even own a jacket and tie. Anyway, this hustler, who was Hispanic, was reputed to have the biggest dick anyone had ever seen, eleven inches for real. He was also apparently short, homely and in his early forties. His M.O. was to wear a blazer and tie and *very thin* gray flannel slacks and to stand at the bar, his massive snake outlined under the light fabric. The closeted businessmen from Omaha and Wichita would ogle it and he would let them brush up against it. Once. After that the meter started running. Word on the street was that he started at a hundred bucks. After hearing the guys talking about him a few times, I was curious to see what he—and his endowment—looked like.

I was hanging out in the Square one night when one of my comrades said, "There he is."

He was indeed short and homely, with a scrunchy, troll-under-the-bridge face. He looked around, crossed Powell Street, and walked up to me.

"I'll pay you fifteen dollars to come home with me," he said. Fifteen bucks was the going rate for a BJ either way.

"You will?"

"Yes. But there's one condition."

"What's that?"

"I get to fuck you."

I let that sink in. Even though I'd been around the block a few times, I'd never been fucked. I told him. He shrugged. I looked at his equipment through the slacks. "Do you think I could handle that?"

"One way to find out." He looked at me with that narrow-eyed, single-minded stare I was coming to recognize in total tops, the stare that seems to whisper: *I want to fuck you into a coma.*

I looked at his piece again and felt desire sweep away my doubts. "Okay."

His apartment was like a fancy hotel suite, thickly carpeted with heavy drapes in beige and violet, and soft lighting, all soothy and smoothy. Perfect for making Omaha feel right at homo. And, yes, Virginia, it *was* eleven inches—that thing was so big it had its own zip code. And no, he didn't go slow and easy. In fact, it felt like I was being torn in two. Which I guess I kinda was. Afterward I took a shower and watched with detachment as bloody water curled down my legs. Even the bathroom was like a hotel, with miniature bottles of shampoo and conditioner and body wash.

Back in Union Square, there were lots of eager ears among my hustler comrades, which I happily appeased.

Do I wish my first time had been more Romeo and Romeo? Nah, not really.

I became friends with some tranny (transvestite, not transsexual) hookers who worked the area. Today the word "tranny" can be an un-PC term, but these kids wore it proudly. They were a brave and exotic and twisted tribe, turning tricks with men who didn't know they had dicks, often in alleys and doorways in the Tenderloin. The risks were twofold—first that the cops would bust them, and second that the john would discover they had a dick and would rough them up or refuse to pay.

Josie, a skinny pretty hard-ass queen, wanted to be my soul mate. She was from Redondo Beach and she was a speed freak, shooting crank and going on four-day runs. I always passed when I was offered the needle, but I dug getting stoned on pot and watching the antics. Speed freaks talk *veryveryfast* and their adventures in the skin trade made for fun listening. We'd hang out in funky flats South of Market where nobody ever slept and the parade never stopped—there were fevered confabs in the corners, macho guys into queens, lots of screaming and laughing, outfit roulette with heels and mini-dresses and cock-tucking, dinner was Ring-Dings and miniature Table Talk pies that came in little white boxes with a cellophane window that let you see the pie inside.

There was an after-hours club called Doyle's, around Market and Church. It opened at 2 a.m. after the bars closed and was so much fun—the crowd was gay boys of all colors and sizes. The music was great and the vibe was love.

All around us in the city gays were starting to speak up, demanding an end to police raids of bars. SF was the epicenter of the nascent gay liberation movement and you could feel it percolating. One of the drivers of the change was the Tavern Guild, an alliance of gay-bar owners that created a grapevine where information and news could be disseminated. I avidly read *Vector*, the monthly gay magazine put out by SIR (Society for Individual Rights). I went to a couple of meetings of a gay group at college and to gay poetry readings and discussions. There was always fervent talk about the importance of coming out.

We were tiptoeing into the political arena and you could feel the groundswell at Doyle's. I loved feeling that I was a part of it. Boogieing at three in the morning with a rainbow of fellow gay boys felt like a defiant celebration of our outsider queerness.

Doyle himself lived upstairs. At around 5 a.m. the club would close and a band of us would head up to his place, where we'd lie on the floor smoking joints and listening to our anthem: the Chambers Brothers "*Time has Come Today*":

Time has come today

Young hearts can go their way

Can't put it off another day

I don't care what others say

They don't matter anyway

Listening to that song today I'm transported back to Doyle's—the twirling lights, the dancing, reefer smoke, the laughter and love, and all the lost boys I was proud to call my friends. We'd emerge into the San Francisco dawn, which smelled like damp and eucalyptus and the tattered promise of California.

43

One of my favorite things to do in the afternoon was to visit the Strand Theater on Market, a down-at-the-heels movie palace that was a throwback to the Depression era. It played double features, with cartoons and newsreels in between and the patrons basically moved in for the day, settling into their seats with food, drink, cigarettes, and sometimes the newspaper spread around them. The crowd was marginal, *Day of the Locust* SF-style–plus-sized women in housedresses, powder-faced old ladies with perfect circles of rouge, skinny old men who had missed the boat and were glad they had, some threadbare families. The last few rows of the balcony were cruisey and the men's room was always hopping, but I ignored all that. I was there for the atmosphere, the movies, and most of all for the giveaway game between shows.

Your ticket stub was numbered and the lights would come up and the master of ceremonies would come onstage full of bluster, holding a metal bucket. He'd start throwing silver dollars into the bucket really hard, the thrilling clank of money ringing out through the theater, counting each one until he reached the prize amount, usually around twenty dollars. Then he'd spin a huge colorful wheel that *slooooowly* slowed before landing on the winning number. There'd be a scream and some woman in a muumuu and slippers would rush up to the stage as the rest of us watched in envy, the clanging doubloons echoing in our ears.

One day after leaving the Strand I ran to catch the Powell Street cable car and hopped on board. An odd-looking gay guy–he was wearing thick black glasses because of a walleye that made him look deep, like Jean-Paul Sartre–said to me, all pissy, "You walk too fast. You'd be sexy but you walk too fast. Walking fast is *not* sexy."

I was taken aback but intrigued, so the next Saturday I went up to Haight Street and practiced my new walk—it was long and slow with some side-to-side hip action. I hadn't gone a block when a handsome light-skinned Black man, who looked about forty, approached me and said, "You have a sexy walk."

"I'm trying."

He laughed. He had a gorgeous smile. There was some definite heat. "My name is Eddie."

"Sebastian."

"Cool name. Wanna head into the park and smoke a joint on Hippie Hill?"

"Definitely."

Hippie Hill, a short walk from the entrance to Golden Gate Park, was an iconic landmark of the '60s. It was jammed with drumming circles, Hare Krishnas, stoned hippie chicks dancing topless with their eyes closed, guitar players, trippers and dopers. If you looked more closely you'd also see bleary homeless teen addicts under the trees, skinny and sallow, their forlorn mutts asleep beside them, and lecherous old men lurking on the periphery ogling the half-naked chicks.

We sat on the hill, Eddie took out a joint and we smoked. He was one charming guy, with a ready smile and a devilish twinkle in his eye. I moved a little closer to him.

"I'm from New York City. What about you?" I asked.

"I'm from right here. My dad is a judge. And right now, he is surely judging me. You see, I have a wife and two kids."

"And you've left them?"

"Yup. You know, I realized I was getting older and it was now or never. That's the long version. The short version is I want to go straight to hell." He smiled again, "Want to come with me?"

I shrugged.

And off we went.

44

Eddie had friends all over the city and we visited them one after the other in his big blue Pontiac. We usually all ended up in bed. Eddie shot both heroin and speed and was forever imploring me to join him. For several weeks I resisted. Then one day, in some unknown apartment, he said, "I have something new."

"What's that?"

He took out a little piece of folded glassine paper and opened it to show me a white powder. "This is pure medical-grade methamphetamine."

I'd hung out with enough speed freaks to know about the clenched jaw, the paranoia, the rank sweat, and the *mile-a-minute* all-night yak fests. "Maybe not for me."

"Oh, come on, sweet boy." He put a hand on the back of my neck and kissed me. We made out and I melted. "Eddie wouldn't steer you wrong, we'll have us some fun."

"I've seen junkies," I said halfheartedly.

"We're not junkies, baby, we're just cats digging life, liberty, and the pursuit of a high." He kissed me again.

I felt a tug-of-war inside my psyche. On one side was doubt, on the other was dare. *Hey-hey-hey, get high, baby, get high* whispered the devil on my shoulder. He was such a seductive little fucker.

"... Okay ..."

Eddie's eyes sparked. He tapped some of the powder into a spoon and then filled a hypodermic with water, which he squirted into the spoon. He mixed the powder and water until the powder dissolved. Then he put a tiny piece of cotton in the water and drew the mixture back up into the needle through the cotton. He worked slowly and methodically, with hushed edge-of-seat reverence.

"Roll up your sleeve." He wrapped a belt around my bicep and tightened it, making the veins on the inside of my elbow stick out. "Virgin veins," he said. I was holding my breath. Then he pressed the needle tip against the vein and blew, sliding it in with an almost imperceptible prick. He depressed the hypodermic and shot the mix into me, then he slowly pulled out the needle.

I jumped up and starting dancing, my whole body pulsing with ecstatic energy. I felt like Superman. Well, Superboy.

"One pill makes you larger, and one pill makes you small," Eddie sang, laughing.

I didn't sleep for three days as we went from apartment to apartment, shot up, drove over to Oakland, got naked, shot up, smoked Kools, *talkedandtalkedandtalked,* break the night, fracture the night, fracture the day, what day is it, who cares, we're out there in some strange place beyond exhaustion, wired and wild, our own private jagged dreamy Idaho, fly-fly-*flying* high ... until finally we collapsed into a ruined pile of sweaty flesh on some bed somewhere.

That was my initiation.

Eddie had a cardboard box filled with porno magazines that he'd cart around and spread out on whatever bed we happened to be in. He heard about a hotel on the edge of the Tenderloin where the rooms were easy to break into. Just find an empty room, jimmy the door, and have a private shooting gallery. We went there one sunny afternoon. It turned out to be the same hotel where I'd spent my first week in San Francisco. Using a credit card Eddie jimmied open the door to a room identical to the one I'd spent that week in, with its bay window looking out at the ragged streets.

We got naked and he spread the porno all over the bed. I started to cook up the crank, one of the first times I'd done it.

I tapped the powder into a spoon. *Tap ... tap ... tap ...*

"That's probably enough," Eddie said, a little wary.

... tap ...

I did the hypodermic/spoon/water/cotton ritual. Then I pulled half the mixture up into a needle. I handed it to Eddie and then filled a second needle. We both tied off and shot up at the same time.

!!HOLY MOTHER OF FUCK!!

My body turned bright pulsing red and my head felt like it was going to blow off my neck and fly out the bay window.

Eddie just said a simple stunned, "... *Whoa.*"

We were standing there frozen and freaking with our mouths open and our eyes bulging and our hearts hammering, when the door to the room burst open and the hotel manager and a security goon barreled in. Their eyes went from naked Eddie to naked me to the porn to the needles. Their shock quickly evolved into anger. I ducked behind the open bathroom door while Eddie jumped into his pants and turned the charm machine on overdrive.

"I'm sorry, we're on our way out of here, so sorry, we don't want any trouble, I'm so sorry, please, we'll be out of here in two minutes."

Eddie tossed me my clothes and I dived into them. I guess the manager didn't want to deal with the hassle of calling the police and pressing charges. "You got five minutes to clear out," he said, "and if I see you around here again, I'm calling the cops first."

Once again, I'd dodged a bullet. I was becoming proud of my exploits. They felt authentic, edgy, rebellious. Talk about deluded.

I remember shooting up acid one day—I was peaking even before all the blood and drug had flowed into my veins. I looked down, tripping out of my gourd, and there was a hypodermic filled with billowing clouds of blood stuck in my arm. That was *seriously* intense. Another time I shot up downers in a hotel in North Beach and woke up 24 hours later with my contacts glued to my eyeballs.

Everybody lived in cheap hotel rooms. There was one adorable short sexy girl, a hooker, from somewhere in South America. She was very funny in a cha-cha-Charo way and I loved hanging out in her hotel room. She would pull down her pants and jab a needle into her ass cheek, it was called "skin popping." One night I was hanging out in her room with another kid and there was a knock on the door. It was a paunchy middle-aged john. The bed was in an alcove and she led him in there and they fucked two feet away from us, he grunting like a wild boar the whole time.

There was the skinny boy hustler from the provinces who came to town and turned into a raging queen in front of my eyes, his T-shirt and jeans morphing into dangly bracelets and cork mules. He was whip-smart, too. When he was speeding, he would talk a blue streak, a runaway train, all word play, saying things like "Granted—to quote Lee at Appomattox."

People were always giving themselves perms at four in the morning—what better time? There were some real bitter queens, ugly and mean, who would cackle and put spells on their rivals by jabbing needles into tiny effigies, and throw open the bathroom door when you were taking a shit, and eat huge tubs of ice cream right out of the container and never share. Lonely boys were everywhere, along with men cut adrift from their marriages and lives who'd come to San Francisco and now were at a loss, chasing hustlers and runaways. There were so many strange characters—Dickens by way of Burroughs by way of Genet—and I found it all enthralling. Crazy time was spinning around me.

45

I had pretty much stopped going to college and was just hanging out. A couple of men took me out and paid attention to me, but I was looking for big love—the boy who would ride with me into a thousand sunsets.

One night at Doyle's it happened.

Dale's reputation preceded him. The gay boys at Doyle's used to pine over him—he was dark and moody and drove a motorcycle.

When I met him, he didn't disappoint. Dale was from Columbus, Ohio, where his family ran an Italian restaurant. He was about nineteen, handsome in an off-kilter way, with black hair and eyes, a mouth pulled down at the corners, a large nose and a sensitive soulful mien that he covered up with macho bravado, engineer boots, a motorcycle cap. He didn't have a job but spoke vaguely about going to medical school "someday." We all had endless "somedays" back then.

Like a lot of us, Dale was a lost kid—a queer who had to leave home to find freedom and love, and escape ridicule and shunning, even from his own family. We were a reckless ragtag tribe, searching for ... *something*. Allen Ginsburg's holy ecstasy? A home? We didn't know what it was, but we were sure it was out there. For me, Dale was that something. Lost or not he wore it well, he spit out his words—smart stuff, ironic, beyond his years.

I took one look and fell hard—this was the manchild I'd been waiting for. Riding Dale's motorcycle through Golden Gate Park and out to the ocean at dawn was as close to heaven as I'd ever come.

I *think* Dale liked me. We hung out, and he came to my apartment for long make-out sessions that didn't include much sex. He talked about books, movies, medicine, and politics. He was a lot wiser than I was, and much more cynical. And he was so *soulful*, his dark eyes like bruises. You could see the hurt. Sometimes he'd allude to being kicked out of his house by his dad, but generally he was pretty close-mouthed about his pain.

One dreamy dawn, after an all-nighter at Doyle's, Dale offered to drive me home. I assumed he would come up to my pad and we would crash together. When we reached Noe Street, I got off the bike. He didn't.

"Aren't you coming up?" I asked.

"Nah."

I felt hot tears coming. "Why not?"

He looked at me and smiled sadly. "I have to keep moving."

I felt a wave of desperation. "But you need to sleep," I pleaded.

"I'll be okay."

"Please come up, Dale. *Please.*"

"Oh, Sebastian ..."

"I thought we were ... I don't know, *boyfriends.*"

He exhaled, looked down. "... I'm not there yet."

I felt like I was drowning, and choked out, "Do you like me?"

"Sure, I like you ... but I like my freedom more." He reached up and cupped my cheek. "We'll see each other soon, baby boy."

Gutted, I stood on the pavement and watched his motorcycle disappear.

Dale never officially dumped me because there was nothing to dump—the whole relationship was pretty much in my starry eyes. He took up with a much prettier blond number, who gloated to me about *his* motorcycle rides.

I fell apart, went into a waking coma, walked the streets numb, stopped eating. I gave up my apartment on Noe and moved into the funky Paramount Hotel on Market near Church. My room was in the front and had a large bay window. The hotel's red neon sign flooded the room in a ruby glow, lurid and noir.

I went out of my head in that room. My great dream of finding true love, of my whole future really, was shattered. Nina Simone singing "To Love Somebody" would come on the radio and I would lie on the bed breathless and dizzy with heartache.

One night I looked out the window and saw Dale down on Market Street! I rushed outside and ran up to him from behind, grabbed his shoulder—a stranger spun around and demanded to know what I wanted. Another night Dale actually *did* show up. He was coming off a drug run and just wanted a place to crash. While he slept, I went out for pancakes at the diner next door. I can still remember eating those pancakes in a contented haze, knowing that Dale was asleep in my room and that when I went back, he would be there, in my bed, mine for a brief interlude.

I was in serious trouble and on some level I knew it. With Tina sick and my heart broken, I was adrift in the great sea. Frightened, I wanted to go home.

I called my folks for a plane ticket. I didn't give them any reason and they didn't ask for one. As I was packing, I decided to leave a lot of my clothing behind, nice stuff from Brooks Brothers and J. Press. I just didn't want it. The hotel was run by an Indian family and as I got in my cab to the airport the wife ran out of the hotel to tell me about the clothes in my room. I shrugged and said I was leaving them—her face lit up and she turned and flew back inside.

Then the cab took me to the airport and my first year in San Francisco ended.

46

I arrived back in New York in late spring, 1968. The next day I went over to ratty, neglected, but still riotously blooming Central Park and sat on a bench in the sun, numb and drained, but feeling safe and cozy back home with Ruby, clean sheets and dinner every night.

I'd made a big decision. I was going to let my family know I was gay. Tina was the only person back East who knew, and I felt a sharp need to come out to everyone. I decided that Ruby would be the least judgmental and help pave the way.

One afternoon a couple days after I got back, I walked into the kitchen. Ruby was mashing potatoes. She gave me a big smile.

"There's something I want to tell you," I said nervously.

"What's that?"

"I'm gay. I like boys and not girls."

Her mouth twisted down in disgust and she said, "Get out of my face."

My whole body flushed with shame and hurt. I felt like I'd been stabbed in the throat—and the knife stayed in. We didn't speak for the next week. Then one afternoon I walked into the kitchen for some juice. Ruby was baking a cake.

"Sebastian," she said.

"Yeah?" I said, keeping my guard up.

"What you said to me, if it's true, that's who you are. It's all right."

Her words helped but the hurt stayed fresh. I realized that I'd been living in a bubble in San Francisco. That in most places and to most people I was still an object of derision or pity or worse.

With so much happening in my life those past few months, I'd stopped calling Tina. I didn't want to unload my trauma on her—she had plenty of her own. So I didn't really know what kind of shape she was in, I just had secondhand reports from Mom and Dad. But now that I was back East, I wanted to see her.

It was a little over a year since her first psychotic break in Central Park. Dad couldn't afford to keep her in Gracie Square for longer than a few weeks, so she'd moved, briefly, into 101 CPW. That soon became untenable—Tina would make messes in the kitchen and bathroom and appear at dinner parties mumbling to herself. She was involuntarily committed to a state mental hospital in Central Islip, Long Island, where she'd now been for about ten months.

Mom and Dad had rented a house out in Springs for the season and one morning I set out from there to hitchhike to visit Tina. I stuck out my thumb and before long a man in a convertible sports car pulled over. Middle-aged and nicely dressed, clear-eyed, he radiated sobriety and decency.

"Where are you going?"

"To Central Islip."

He nodded. I got in and off we went.

"What's in Central Islip?" he asked.

"I have a cousin who's in a mental hospital there. She's crazy."

He frowned. "Crazy is a very broad diagnosis. I'm a psychotherapist."

"She has schizophrenia."

His face grew grave. "That's a terrible disease. It's intractable. How old is she?"

"She's nineteen, a year older than me."

He nodded. "Schizophrenia often manifests in late adolescence. The only treatments available are anti-psychotic drugs, which only treat the symptoms and are only sporadically effective and often have nasty side effects. What's your cousin's name?"

"Christina—Tina."

"I assume Tina had a psychotic break."

There was something about this stranger saying Tina's name that got to me. He spoke with such empathy, I felt a connection to him, I trusted him, it was almost intimate.

"Yes."

"Are you and she close?"

"Very close. We always have been. I love her."

"Tina has been dealt a terrible fate. But it's not easy on the people who love her, either."

"Are you saying she'll never get better?" I asked, afraid to hear the answer.

"She may not. But there are remissions. And some schizophrenic's age out, or at least the worst episodes abate." That sounded hopeful and I grabbed onto it. "But that doesn't usually happen until they reach their mid-thirties. She, and you, have a rough road ahead."

So much for my hopes. "What should I do?"

"If you can, get involved in her treatment. Make sure she isn't being overmedicated. And that she has a therapist she responds to. Try and get family support for her. Schizophrenics often antagonize those closest to them and end up very lonely. They act out because they're angry. Their lives have been snatched away. But remember, she can't help it."

"Do you think she will age out?"

"That's impossible to say, but she could certainly stabilize with the right medications and good therapy. Listen, this is where I turn off."

As he drove away I felt some mix of relief and foreboding. The stranger in the sports car had given me what I needed to hear—a reality check. It was almost like he was sent to me, to educate me about what to expect, and to suggest what I could do to help.

The hospital was depressing even in the early summer sunshine—huge, sprawling, the lawns patchy, the windows grimy. I found the main entrance, walked up to the desk and said, "Hi, I'm here to visit one of the inmates."

A nurse standing nearby snapped at me, "They're not *inmates*, they're *patients*."

I felt like I'd been slapped. Hard. But I deserved it. "You're right, of course, I'm sorry."

"And you're too late, visiting hours are over."

Another slap. Why hadn't I called and checked on visiting hours? On my first assignment, I'd failed Tina. I was pathetic. That kind man would be disappointed in me. My shoulders hunched in shame. I went outside and looked up at the tall building. Tina was in one of those rooms, probably lying on her bed staring at the ceiling, while I was out here in the sunlight. I felt a familiar wave of guilt.

Suddenly none of it made any sense. Mental illness, Tina's whole situation, her future, my future. It was too much for me. Fuck Tina and her stupid fucking schizophrenia. I reached for my denial armor and suited up. But it didn't quite fit. The truth had penetrated. And that pissed me off. I didn't want to have to take care of Tina. That was a shitload of responsibility and I hated responsibility.

A few days later I took the Long Island Railroad to Islip and got a cab to Tina's hospital.

I was directed up to a dayroom. It was truly the ninth circle of hell—cigarette smoke as dense as fog, unwashed patients wearing hospital gowns or Goodwill rejects, either slumped in druggy comas or pacing around in fitful agitation, often talking to themselves, the smell of ashtrays, Lysol, and serious body odor cut with a tang of urine and soggy cafeteria food.

I saw Tina before she saw me. She was watching one of the wall-mounted televisions. She looked stiff and miserable, her hair sticky and matted. She was sitting erect with her hands in her lap, her mouth slightly open. She looked a decade older. The whole roiling mix of my emotions dissolved into pity and concern.

"Tina?" I said hopefully.

She looked up at me like it was the most natural thing in the world for me to show up. "Sebastian," she said in an affectless voice.

I hugged her, grabbed a chair and sat beside her. I could smell her sweat. Still it felt good to be close to her, and I leaned my knee against hers.

"How are you feeling?"

"Okay."

"You look good," I lied.

There was a pause, and she engaged a bit more, leaning toward me, opening her heavily lidded eyes. "How's San Francisco?"

"It's wonderful, but I did get into some trouble."

"You did?"

"Yes. With drugs."

"Be careful, Sebastian."

"I'll try."

"That's what you said last time."

"I think I may have learned my lesson." In truth, I wasn't at all sure I'd learned anything. "But I'm here to see you. I met a really nice man the other day and he said people with schizophrenia can get better."

"He did?" Tina's eyes sparked with hope for just a flickering moment.

"Yes. He said *you* could get better. And not live in a hospital. Do you like your therapist?"

"He's okay."

"Do you know what drugs you're on?"

"Thorazine ... and trazadone and ... I forget the others." Her mouth twisted down.

"Please, Tina, remember you can get better."

"Yeah, sure I can," she said. Then she lit a Marlboro and looked at the TV.

"You can age out of this, I promise you can."

She turned to me and gave me an ironic, bitter smile. Then she seemed to retreat back into herself.

"Can I bring you anything?"

"Yeah. A new brain."

"I think they're on sale at Bloomie's."

I actually got a little chortle out of her. I found a row of vending machines and bought her candy and chips and soda. As I crossed the dayroom, her fellow patients covetously eyed the bounty.

"Next week I'll bring champagne and brownies."

"No walnuts. I'm allergic."

"I know *that*." I leaned down and kissed her on the forehead.

"And Sebastian?"

"Yes."

"Thanks for coming."

"Wild horses, baby, wild horses couldn't keep me away."

In the months that followed, Tina stabilized and was released from the hospital into a halfway house in Queens. One late August evening, shortly before I returned to San Francisco, I answered the phone at 101. There was a pause—I could hear traffic noises—and then Tina, her voice barely audible, said, *"Please ... help... me ..."* She hung up before I could say anything.

I imagined Tina at a street corner phone booth on some noisy Queens boulevard—motherless, fatherless, afraid and falling—putting in the coins and dialing. The image was too much for me. I was afraid Tina's illness would consume me. Half of me wanted to push it, and her, away. Half of me wanted to be the best friend I could be, and to save her.

47

I'd scared myself during my year of living cluelessly, so when I went back to San Francisco State in the fall of 1968 I moved into the dorms—two bleak slabs at the far end of the campus near the woebegone lake. The rooms, with their concrete-block walls and built-in furniture, looked more like prison cells. SF State's original mission had been to train teachers and the kids in the dorms were a pretty diverse bunch.

I went to the student counseling center and told them I was anxious. They quickly wrote me a script for Valium. I started popping them like peanuts, but they only made me more anxious and jittery. I looked in the PDR (*Physicians Drug Reference*, aka the junkie's bible) and learned that some people have a paradoxical reaction and Valium ups their anxiety. I stopped taking them and substituted more marijuana.

A student strike started at State that fall. The strikers were demanding the establishment of an Ethnic Studies Department, arguing that Black, Hispanic, and Asian history, lives, and truths weren't represented in the existing curriculum. The strike lasted until the following March and was one of the largest and longest in American history, with many professors joining the picket line. At its peak the uprising got lots of media attention all over the country. It was emblematic of the era.

The strikers' demands were eventually met. Today I understand how important that strike was, but at the time I didn't really know or care, I was just into the excitement of the huge demonstrations, the signs, the chants, the solidarity. There were hordes of riot police, some on horseback, and kids were being arrested by the score. I felt like I was part of the whole '60s protest thing.

But I was still attracted to the dark side and would head downtown and hook up with some of my old comrades, shoot up, go on speed runs. It was strange to stay up all night, out in the city with tranny hookers, and then come back to the fog-shrouded dorms just as the wholesome future-teachers were heading to breakfast. I kind of loved the jangly buzz.

One day in the dorm cafeteria a nice-looking fella with twinkling eyes sat next to me. His name was Charlie. He drove a cool little white Jaguar XKE and we quickly became inseparable pals. We visited dive bars, heard Janis sing at a Holiday Inn in Corta Madera, went to free Grateful Dead concerts in Golden Gate Park, smoked a lot of pot in our dorm rooms, and listened endlessly to *Music from Big Pink*. At 2 a.m., after a long night of pot and music, we'd drive to Denny's for pie, coffee, and laughs.

Charlie and I went down to Puerto Vallarta over Christmas. It was a buzzy place to be. Elizabeth Taylor and Richard Burton had put it on the map when, after Burton filmed *The Night of the Iguana*, they'd bought a house in town. Charlie and I arrived by bus to find a sleepy, romantic village with gorgeous beaches and fabulous Spanish-colonial architecture. We found a room in an old hotel built around a central courtyard, very atmospheric and Tennessee Williams-y. The hotel, and the town, attracted a lot of hip druggies, glamorous young things on the cusp of burning out, and single older women who had moved to Mexico because it was cheap and they could enjoy a ritzy lifestyle and get laid by Mexican boys. We dropped acid and went swimming in a river. A little way downriver, women were washing their clothes against the rocks.

On Christmas day Charlie used the pay phone in the hotel lobby to call his mom. I didn't bother. My folks didn't know I was in Mexico.

I did call Tina at the group home in Queens where she was living.

"Merry Xmas, Tina."

"Hey, cousin."

"I'm in Mexico."

"Olé."

"You sound solid."

"I'm feeling better. I'm seeing this shrink who specializes in ... meds, getting me on the right meds."

"Sounds like he's doing a good job."

"I have a crush on him. That helps. I want to be a good little patient."

"Whatever it takes. Give him my number in San Francisco. Tell him he can call me anytime, if there's an emergency, or if he just wants to talk about how you're doing."

There was a pause and then she said simply, "Thanks, Seb."

"Hey, that's what cousins are for."

"Hasta la vista, baby," Tina said.

"You're my funny Valentine."

"It's Christmas, you idiot."

I hung up and stood in the shabby hotel lobby with its trickling fountain and flowering vines, feeling like I'd just gotten the mother of all Christmas presents.

48

I lived in San Francisco for seven years and I moved about eleven times. I was restless and when I got bored, I moved. I liked the whole concept of moving, of picking up and finding someplace new, usually a room in an existing household. Each new set-up intrigued me. It was like walking into a movie halfway through, you had to play catch-up.

The dorm, with its terrible cafeteria food and earnest, upbeat students, started to give me the heebie-jeebies. I went to the college housing office and found a room for rent in a bland neighborhood just east of the campus. The street was lined with tiny identical attached houses, the "ticky-tacky little boxes" Pete Seeger sang about. My new landlords were an elderly couple, Oklahoma transplants. The woman—who insisted I call her "Mammy"—was bowlegged and walked with a side-to-side gait, like a cowboy. Pappy was older and unwell. With his round bald head and benign smile, he was a dead ringer for Mr. Magoo. I think he had dementia.

Mammy took to me. She had tons of energy and was the talkative type. She did everything for Pappy, who sat and watched TV all day. She belonged to a big Baptist church on Market Street and was always after me to come to services, telling me about the wonderful youth group that met afterward. To make her happy, one Sunday I went. The youths might as well have been another species, all dressed up in polyester suits and dresses, sipping punch and talking about sports and homework.

One afternoon I was sitting in my room. It was one of those sort-of-foggy/sort-of-not San Francisco days when it's a little too humid, the world is still, and life feels meaningless. I had some heroin, which I rarely used, and a needle. I decided to shoot up. I did, and then got all itchy in my skin. A minute later Mammy clip-clopped up the stairs, appeared in my doorway and said, "I'd give my right arm to have you as my son." I felt a mix of pride and guilt and then a moment of strange longing in which I imagined I was indeed Mammy's son, living a tidy little life in this room at the top of the stairs.

My shoplifting compulsion was thriving, and I would go to the Emporium in the nearby Stonestown mall and walk out with three or four pieces of clothing at a pop. It was easy. There was never anyone around, customers or employees. Pretty soon my closet had no room left. I never thought about the morality of what I was doing, although I had a rule about only stealing from large chains, never the little guy. So idealistic.

As for picking that forlorn neighborhood: What wasn't I thinking? It was as far from bohemian-hippie-happening San Francisco as you could get. Nearby, at the corner of two ugly, traffic-clogged boulevards, there was a branch of a long-gone open-air fast-food chain called Doggie Diner, known for its iconic sign—a huge dachshund head wearing a chef's hat. I would go there and sit for long stretches, especially at night, nursing a cup of watery coffee, watching the passing parade (which was entirely vehicular), and waiting for something to happen. Nothing ever did. And yet I imbued it all with some weird inchoate glamour. What can I say—I was young and free and under the spell of California.

I had a friend from the dorm named Linda, a chubby fun lively sturdy California girl. She used to come see me at Mammy's and Mammy tried to play matchmaker, telling me what a nice wholesome girl she was. Then Linda discovered diet pills and got skinny and suddenly she was all pretty and sexy. She couldn't handle her new self, all the men wanting her. She disappeared from school. About a year later I ran into her near a freeway off-ramp south of Market, skinny and barefoot and jittery, her feet dirty, in a short skirt, with an older Black man with Ike Turner hair. She said, "I'm in trouble," and kept walking.

"Can I help? ..." I called.

The man turned and hissed, "Get lost, motherfucker!"

They disappeared down the street. Linda had fallen through the cracks. It was easy to do. I'd done it myself the year before. Attention is seductive. Add drugs and sex and the potential brew can easily turn toxic. I decided I didn't want to live on the dark side (though I remained open to the occasional visit). I've tried to track Linda down over the years, with no luck. I hope she was able to pull herself back from the edge, I hope she's had a happy life. She was such a sweet kid.

After a while I grew tired of the banality of Mammy's 'hood. I went back to the housing office and found a room in a house on 47th Avenue in the Outer Richmond, just two blocks from Ocean Beach. It was its own world out there. You could go six blocks east and be in the sunshine, but our little corner of the city would remain foggy all day. There were always surfers around and funky little sandwich shops, the smell of the sea, and best of all Playland, an old amusement park on its last legs.

The house I moved into was owned by a chubby gay man named Seymour, a defeated former teacher who had lost his job after some inappropriate touching of a student. The touching was nothing more than hair-stroking—at least that was Seymour's story. He wore cardigans and shuffled and looked like he was about to burst into tears. When I first went to see the room he wasn't home but I met his other tenant, Jerry, a wasp-thin butch-y queen who had been kicked out of the Navy for being queer. Jerry asked me what the room was listed for at the college housing office and I said, "Eighty dollars a month."

"Tell Seymour it was listed for $60." That kind of subterfuge pretty much summed up the vibe in that sad household.

Like hundreds of other houses in the Richmond and Sunset neighborhoods, it was an attached row house with a parlor, a dining room, kitchen, and two back bedrooms on one floor, with the garage below. I rented the larger back bedroom. At night I could hear the crash of the surf, the barking seals, and the cackling of "Laffing Sal," the scary mechanical lady who sat in a glass booth over at Playland.

Playland was a relic of distant days, mostly deserted, all its bright carnival colors faded in the salt air, the bored barkers had wrinkly smokers' faces and the merry-go-round music sounded lonely and malevolent. The place was like a film noir that had been haphazardly colorized. I loved to ride the bumper cars even though there was rarely anyone to bump, and then to stroll over for a bite to eat at one of the small row of restaurants north of the park.

Since Seymour rented out both back bedrooms, he slept in the parlor, in his clothes, on a daybed. He had a Siamese cat who ignored him all day. At around 10 p.m. Seymour would lie down on his daybed with the cat perched on his chest and chain smoke *an entire pack of cigarettes* while he and the cat stared at each other. He never smoked except during this nightly ritual.

Jerry, who smoked fiendishly and drank beer all day but had one of those wired skinny metabolisms, befriended me and told me all his Navy stories. One night he went drinking at a local straight bar and he was harassed. He stormed out of the bar and fell on the sidewalk, breaking both his wrists. Even with two casts on he managed to drink his beer and smoke his cigs. Another night he slunk into my room and "had" me. The next day he said, "I had no idea how fabulous you were." It felt undeserved—all I'd done was lie there while he did his thing. Well, maybe I squirmed around a bit. I guess you'd call it a mercy blow.

I noticed a lot of comings and goings in a house down the block. Everyone looked young and hippie-ish, there was laughter and the smell of pot. It was a refreshing contrast to the gloom and doom at Seymour's. I started talking to one of the boys who lived there, and he told me there was a room for rent. A week later I moved into the large room in back of the garage that looked out to the yard.

The house was rented by a young woman named Kathy, who sublet rooms. Kathy, who had blonde hair and prominent teeth, a ready smile and a wise heart, was a quintessential San Franciscan. She'd moved to the city from Michigan, a wonderful, liberal, idiosyncratic woman. I was crazy about her. She took me to services at the legendary Glide Memorial Church, where I grooved to the Rev. Cecil Williams' raucous sermons and the all-inclusive love vibe that rocked the house. Although I considered myself out, I still had some shame and trepidation and didn't really talk about being queer with straight people like Kathy. But she had me pegged and driving to church one Sunday she got me to admit that I was gay. It felt scary and great, like a big weight was lifted.

Kathy's house was an odd hodgepodge. There was a dank little space in the front of the basement—part of the floor was dirt and you couldn't stand up all the way. It was basically a crawl space, but a moody young guy rented it and he would drop acid and stay in there for the whole trip. *Yikes!* Another corner of the garage was cordoned off by a sheet, behind which lived a thin redheaded Jewish woman named Rachel who was a fugitive member of the Weatherman Underground, the secretive ultra-left organization that advocated the violent overthrow of the government. I never found out who she was hiding from, but she was always slinking around and didn't like to come out until after dark.

Kathy's house was a semi-commune. I grew my hair to shoulder length and wore bellbottoms and baked bread, including a whole-wheat challah that sent Rachel into raptures. People from all backgrounds came and went. We shared a disdain for the status quo, a desire to drop out and forge a more idealistic future. Today that sounds naïve and futile but back then it brought meaning to our lives and created a tenuous unity among us.

The fragility of that bond soon played out in front of me. At one point a girl from a rich old California family moved in with her boyfriend. The other women in the house were middle- or working-class and they would have women's consciousness-raising group meetings in the living room. I eavesdropped on them from the kitchen. They loved to gang up on the rich girl. One time she burst into tears and one of the other women scoffed, "There's nothing worse than a woman who *cries*. I'm not falling for *that* trick." The rich girl moved out pretty quickly.

A lesbian couple, both named Judy, moved in. One was dark and Jewish, from New York, and the other was a blonde Midwesterner. The Judys were older and had just missed the gay-liberation train. They were beaten down and morose, especially New York Judy, who drank and had been in theater years before. One gloomy afternoon she told me she didn't really want to be a lesbian. But the Judys were bright and kind and funny and we became friends. I liked them a lot, loved them really. They were touching, trying to make a life together. I was taking some acting classes at State and theater-Judy decided she wanted to direct a production of Saroyan's one act *Hello Out There*. It's about a man in jail and a girl who befriends him through a window, with miscast me as the prisoner and the way-too-old-for-the-role other Judy as the girl. We rehearsed for weeks, but theater-Judy had no theater lined up. She would talk about it all the time, but never did anything, too busy drinking and being glum.

A cat lived in the house and one night it had kittens in the bathroom. The only people home were me and the Judys and we would periodically check on the cat's progress. One of the kittens was stillborn and theater-Judy flushed it down the toilet while the mom was still giving birth to more kittens. Other Judy wondered if it was the right thing to do, but theater-Judy got defensive and insisted it was. She was wrong. The mom cat starting mewling and howling, looking for her baby. It was awful. It was almost as if theater-Judy was trying to teach us a lesson, to show us that life was bitter and tough, so wise up, sucker.

An exuberant girl named Jocelyn moved in with her too-serious hippie boyfriend. He went to a masonry job every day and came home mournful and covered in plaster dust. At first, she made him dinners with brown rice and sprouts but he was kind of a downer and she got bored. Jocelyn had a great figure with pert breasts she loved to show off and a cute pixie face, but she wore thick glasses. Then she got contacts and suddenly she was this really hot hippie chick. She started bringing men—suited, respectable, no-doubt married men—home during the day when her hangdog boyfriend was at work. Jocelyn's orgasms were legendary. They went on for a good fifteen minutes, with a slow build and a crescendo so loud you felt like she could be heard across the whole Richmond district. It really did sound like she was giving birth or dying. She was completely uninhibited and would appear triumphantly from her bedroom afterward, flushed and naked. The men slunk out, tying their ties, and she was always saying things like, "It's good to know a lawyer." One day she said to me, "I know I'm a deep person because whenever I read a saying by someone like Benjamin Franklin, I can relate to it."

A gay boy named Timothy moved in. Like me he was, well ... not butch. We both immediately recognized a kindred spirit and became fast chums. Timothy was from nearby Daly City, creative and artistic and pots of fun, we'd draw for hours or put on music and dance around the living room. Other kids he knew from Daly City moved in, and when Kathy moved out, we took over the house.

Timothy had a dark brooding sexy boyfriend named Michael who never spoke. *Ever.* His profound silence led me to believe he held great depths. One day we found a hidden sandy embankment next to Sutro Heights Park and made out for *hours*, until our mouths hurt. I sort of fell in love with him, but I could never get him to talk. Eventually I got bored.

When I was writing this book, I tried to track Michael down. I discovered someone with his name who was born in 1949 and died of AIDS in 1993 in San Francisco. I remembered our long ago afternoon of love in the sands of Sutro Heights as if it had happened yesterday, his musky smell, his probing tongue, his hand on my cheek, and I felt sad about his death. I'm glad I can carry his memory.

49

I lived on 47th Avenue for about a year and a half. Then I decided I wanted to live closer to the action and so I moved into a room on Frederick Street in the Haight, in a large flat rented to a thin sparkly gorgeous Black man who was always rubbing oils on his skin, and his white girlfriend, a raven-haired bombshell. I'd watch as they spent whole afternoons smoking dope and getting dolled up to go downtown to the movies. They'd vamp up and down the flat's long central hallway, which ended in a full-length mirror. One day I came home to find them having sex on my bed, with oils and whips spread around. They wanted me to join in. Flattered but flummoxed, I politely declined.

My room was large and airy, with a beautiful view of the Cole Valley and the Sutro woodland beyond. I painted it yellow and was happy there. I got a job at a coffee shop on Haight off Stanyan. It had a long horseshoe-shaped counter with stools and was owned by a middle-aged Irish guy named Irish, who also owned a sparsely stocked florist shop in the next block. Irish was a gruff burly guy, a former hustler who was always bragging about the size of his dick. He had an obese wife with nubby little brown teeth, her small features lost in a blur of flesh and chins.

I was the coffee shop's kitchen kid. I cut the French fries, which were made with fresh potatoes, and did the prep work and the cleanup. It was my first job, and I took a lot of pride in doing it well. Irish told me I could always have a job with him. Dream big. I actually loved the work. Leaving the kitchen sparkling gave me a feeling of accomplishment.

I also loved all the characters who came in and sat around nursing a cup of coffee. Even though it was on Haight Street and the Sixties were exploding right outside the door, it attracted very few hippies. Instead the crowd was kind of a throwback to old San Francisco—skinny loners who smoked unfiltered cigarettes, pairs of senior women with silver-rinsed hair, distracted men with hairy ears and rumpled newspapers. The place never got very busy.

One day I was coming out of my bank on Haight Street when a man approached me. He seemed nice enough. He was soft spoken and he told me a long story about how he couldn't get his money out of the bank without a hundred dollars in cash, collateral of some kind, which he would instantly repay. I listened sympathetically and told him that I'd love to help him out, but my checkbook was in my apartment up on Frederick. If he wanted to walk up there with me, I would grab the checkbook and we could come back to the bank and get the money. I brought him up to the apartment, offered him something to drink and gave him a glass of water. We walked back down to Haight, I got the money, walked out, and handed him the bills. He told me he'd be right back and disappeared around the corner.

I was such a naïve kid, seemingly sophisticated and knowing but actually clueless, without an ounce of good judgment or common sense. Still, I loved my days in the yellow room on Frederick Street.

50

For a couple of years, I didn't go back East. I talked to my folks now and then, short catch-up calls. Except for Tina I felt little connection to my family, and I was truly-madly-deeply in love with California. Tina had been in and out of mental hospitals and halfway houses, her disease see-sawing. I tried to call her every couple of weeks or so but the truth is that the calls left me so tangled up in blue—*is she better, is she worse, guilt, why her and not me, more guilt*—that I dreaded them.

Then in the fall of 1970, Mom called me. "Sebastian, your father and I visited Tina up at Hudson River Psychiatric Hospital. What a depressing place! But Tina's doing *much* better. She seems stabilized and she was lucid, even friendly."

I knew Tina had been in Hudson River Psych and in our erratic phone calls over the few past months she'd sounded increasingly coherent and stable but hearing it from Mom carried extra weight. "You're kidding, that's wonderful news."

"Her doctors feel she's ready to leave the hospital and perhaps go into a group home and then, if she continues to improve, find a place of her own."

I had a sudden brainstorm and felt my adrenaline spike. "Mom, instead of a group home, do you think she could come out here and live with me?"

There was a pause. "I'm not sure that's the best idea."

"Oh, come on, Mom, California would be great for her. I'll find us an apartment."

I could tell Mom was intrigued. For one thing it would give her some distance from Tina. "Let me speak to your father about it." I knew from the tone in her voice that it was a done deal.

I hung up and had a moment of doubt: was I really up to taking care of Tina? What if she had another psychotic break? These doubts were outweighed by my love for her and my desire to take care of her. And I had selfish reasons: Tina was smart, funny and fun. She inspired me.

I called the pay phone that served Tina's ward. They tracked her down.

"Hello?"

"Tina, hi, it's me."

"Hi, Sebastian."

"That's Sirbasketball to you."

"Dribble-dribble."

She sounded so strong and sane. My throat got tight with anticipation. "Mom called and told me you were much better."

"I only got better because I couldn't face the meatloaf here."

"Hey, whatever it takes. Mom said that you're going to be leaving the hospital soon."

"I think so," she said, a note of uncertainty and fear in her voice.

"Listen, I had an idea. Instead of moving into a group home, why don't you come out to San Francisco and live with me."

There was a pause, and I could feel Tina's tender hope through the line. "Are you serious?"

"I'm totally serious. We can get an apartment together. We'll cook and make friends and take walks."

There was another pause, and I knew that we were both having the same thought: *Could this really happen?*

"I would *love* to come out," Tina said, fighting to control the emotion in her voice.

"I'll call Mom and Dad and get things rolling."

"Oh, thank you, Sebastian. Thank you, thank you."

"Hey, that's how *I* feel."

Looking back, I can see how naïve I was about Tina's disease and how unprepared I was to take responsibility for her. But at the time her imminent move to SF was another high note in my California symphony.

51

I found us a furnished apartment just off Duboce Park. It was on the ground floor and a bit dark, but cozy. The big day arrived, and I went out to the airport to pick Tina up. When she walked out of the gate there was a moment where I saw her before she saw me, and she looked so much better, almost her old self, her face fuller, lighter. Then she saw me and we both smiled—a new adventure was beginning.

Over the next months we turned that dark apartment into a home. We cooked and bought fresh flowers and Mallomars, we took epic walks and went to museums and poetry readings and talked and talked, having a lot of laughs and making friends. Just about every boy who met Tina was smitten. My college friends (yup, I was still in college) would come over and just stare at her, puppy eyed. She was on low-dose meds and often stayed up late into the night writing poetry.

Sometimes I'd look at what she had been writing. Much of it was incomprehensible to me. But I chalked that up to my literal-minded antipathy to poetry in general. Tina seemed happy, and we were happy together.

I had a couple of motorcycles during this period, one of my absurd attempts to prove to myself that I was butch. I loved the image of riding a bike and once you got going it was a blast, but I could barely coordinate the clutch and accelerator and the bike would almost fly out from under me. I never owned a helmet. Once Tina and I were roaring down Route 1, south of the city, when we hit a metal plate in the road and went flying through the air. Luckily, I was able to straighten the bike and nail a landing.

Most terrifying was the time we came back from a jaunt to Berkeley and I tore across the Bay Bridge, weaving from lane to lane, passing everything in sight. Tina was the perfect motorcycle passenger–she sat with her arms around my waist and moved with me like my shadow. When we got to other side, a CHP motorcycle cop pulled me over and told me switching lanes on the bridge was illegal. He kept staring at Tina and let us off without a ticket.

I signed Tina up for a reading at SF State's Poetry Center. It was at night and Tina was nervous heading out there. The room was full, and some well-known poets were there, including a handsome guy who was connected to the Center. Tina started to read, and the room fell silent. I don't remember what her poems were about, but they were vivid/arresting/rhythmic, and she read them with growing confidence. When she finished the room was buzzing and Tina was surrounded by admirers, including the hunky poet, who told me the work was "striking" and that he wanted to hear more. I could tell he was taken with my beautiful, gifted cousin.

We went home on such a high. I think it was one of the happiest nights of Tina's life. She had talent, her poetry was good, it wasn't incomprehensible crazy-girl poetry, garbled and dissonant, it had order and meter and a cascade of sounds and meaning and allusions.

I wish I could relive that night and see Tina that happy. Years later, when we both lived in New York and she had been through several more psychotic breaks and had entered the world of the permanently damaged, she gathered up all her poems in an unruly handwritten bundle, took them to a copy shop, walked over to Grove Press and dropped them off. She never heard back from the press and was so disappointed. But that night on campus, as we poured out into the damp San Francisco air, the future looked full.

Only one of Tina's poems survives. She wrote it when she was a little girl and Nicky has never forgotten it:

I dreamed I went on a ferryboat
A ferryboat that would float and float
One day I really went on one
It was bright and shiny as the sun.

52

I continued my shoplifting hobby, now with Tina along. It made us feel like outlaws and we *did* need clothes and were living on a modest monthly check from Dad. Of course, my sense of entitlement played a role. Why should I have to pay for that sweater?

One day we were at Macy's downtown and I got busted. The store was in the mood to be tough and they called the police, who arrived and loaded me into a squad car for a trip to the city jail on Bryant Street.

I arrived in the late afternoon and they showed me to a huge holding cell that was lined with two rows of bunk beds, with concrete tables in the middle. The place stank of cigarettes and industrial cleaners. There was only one empty berth left, the bottom bunk of the bed farthest from the hallway, way down at the very end of the cell, far, far away. As I walked down to it the other prisoners eyed me like I was a fresh-baked pie. Which made me very anxious. People devour pies.

I quickly returned to the front of the cell and sat at one of the tables. Lying nearby, on one of the front bottom bunks, was a gnarly old white guy who looked homeless—and happy to be warm and on a real bed. He'd squirreled away a couple of hotdogs and was munching on one. The other stuck out of his shirt pocket.

After a few minutes a thickly built Black man came up to me.

"How you doin'?"

"I've been better."

He opened his palm to reveal a metal spoon. "Take it."

"I don't want it."

"You *better* want it. You *gonna* need it."

My anxiety spiked.

"You sharpen that fucking thing, rub it against the concrete. I'll use it to protect you when the lights go out. Otherwise they all goin' bust you right open." He nodded in the direction of a clutch of about a half dozen men who were watching us. They looked tough and mean. And hungry.

I felt myself start to sweat.

"Yeah, I'll protect you, but you gotta be my woman tonight."

"I'm sorry, but I really don't want the spoon and I don't want to be your woman tonight."

My anxiety was racing towards *freak out.*

"You gonna be my woman tonight."

The thought of being his woman scared me shitless. But so did the thought of being gang raped.

I looked him in the eye and choked out, "Look, I was caught shoplifting, okay, no big deal. I'm just here overnight. I just want to get through it. Please! I really, *really* don't want to be your woman tonight. Okay? Okay?"

He listened, took it all in, and paused. Then his eyelids fluttered, and his pupils rolled up like a slot machine and he tossed it all out—the criminal mind in action. "You gonna be my woman tonight. Or *else.*"

"No, I'm *not* going to," I managed, my hands shaking.

He shrugged and looked at me like I was crazy. Then he got up and walked away. That was the end of that.

Fat chance.

For the rest of the afternoon I stayed in the front of the cell near the corridor. Guards and trustees passed by regularly and that made me feel somewhat safe. There was an identical cell across the way and this unbelievably sexy boy in a sleeveless tee shirt was strutting around, grabbing his cock and looking at me—it was total Jean Genet, *really* hot. I yearned to be in that cell. I'd be *his* woman any night. I imagined how he would protect me (between kisses).

As the evening wore on there was growing anticipation among my cellmates —and escalating dread in me. The men circled and eyed me, practically drooling. The lights were finally turned out and I took the long walk down to my bunk.

As soon as I lay down, the pack of men walked towards me, silhouetted by the light from the corridor. They circled my bed and started to grab at me. With some kind of manic strength, like moms get when their kids are pinned under cars, I pushed through them and ran to the front of the cell where I grabbed the bars and started to scream. The men ran after me, threw a blanket over my head to muffle my screams, and pulled me off the bars.

I went into a total frenzy, kicking-punching-screaming-flailing—and suddenly they backed off. I tore off the blanket and saw why. An older guard had appeared outside the cell.

"You gotta let me out of here! They tried to rape me! They started to beat me! I can't stay here, they'll kill me! You gotta let me out of here!"

The guard looked me up and down and muttered, "You look crazy to me."

Better crazy than gang raped. I was moved to a private cell. It had no blanket or mattress, just a metal bed sticking out of the wall and a seatless metal toilet. But to me it looked like the Ritz.

Frustrated that they didn't get my young ass, the inmates turned on the old man with the hotdogs and for hours his screams echoed through the jail. I felt terrible and guilty, thinking I was partly responsible.

The next morning, I was led into the courtroom, where I saw an anxious Tina in the gallery. The judge looked over my charges and said, "Maybe you need another night in jail."

I pleaded, "Please, your honor, they tried to rape me last night." She looked at me for a moment and then let me go.

To celebrate, Tina and I went out to lunch at a Foster's Cafeteria. We were both shaken up, but we tried to hide it. Maybe being an outlaw wasn't all it was cracked up to be. We picked at our macaroni and cheese. Then Tina quoted one of our favorite Dylan lyrics, "To live outside the law you must be honest."

"What does that mean?"

"I think maybe it means we should cool it with the shoplifting."

"Yeah, that's probably what it means," I agreed.

53

Tina knew my friend Danny Leber from the Shapley School. We'd all hung out a few times back East and they liked each other. Danny wanted to move to San Francisco, so the three of us made plans to get a place together. Before Danny arrived, I started looking and ended up renting a house in St. Francis Wood, one of San Francisco's priciest and most conservative neighborhoods, more like a posh suburb. It seemed like a good idea because it was near SF State.

It was a big house owned by a nice Swiss man who stared at Tina. We told him we were married. Dad sent us about $500 a month, but the rent was high and once we'd paid it, we didn't have much money left over for furniture, or even food. We slept on mattresses on the floor but sprung for desks for each of us. The living room had a fireplace and a bank of large arched windows. We bought white sheets and dyed them the most hideous purplish color in the bathtub and hung them on rods—*bingo!* hideous purplish curtains. And no furniture.

Danny arrived, and we settled into a ridiculous domestic arrangement. I don't remember any cooking, in fact I'm not sure we had a stove, but we had fun, at least for the first couple of months. One night we went to see the Cockettes, the legendary acid-drag troupe, at the Palace Theater in North Beach. This was in their early days and they were zingy/ecstatic/madcap—the costumes, sets and make-up were psychedelic folk art, all glitter and swirls, whirls and twirls. At the end of the show they invited the audience onstage and the three of us went up and danced, whooping and hollering. We streamed out into the North Beach night elated.

Danny became a Cockettes groupie, so I got to know a lot of them. The legendary Hibiscus was the queen bee. He had this amazing and original drag, flowing outfits, glitter-encrusted eyebrows and beard, all topped with huge headdresses that were sort of Aztec-meets-acid-meets-gender-fuck-meets-Liz-Taylor-in-*Boom!* There were always things like dawn gatherings in the outer reaches of Golden Gate Park, where everyone would show up in full regalia, having been up all night putting it together, wired from whatever drugs they were on and the excitement of the new day. One pretty blond queen from LA began to imitate Hibiscus's look, especially the amazing headdresses, and they had an ongoing feud we called the Clash of the Acid Queens.

Hibiscus was from New York, from a show-biz family, and he was wicked sexy, with a lithe body and endless energy—a star who reveled in his stardom. He took me up to his attic atelier one night. It was filled with his artwork and costumes and headdresses, a mattress on the floor, a dormer window open to the moon.

Hibiscus moved back East at some point and became a hooker. The last time I saw him was in the late 1970s. He was putting on a show at the Second Avenue Theater in the East Village. I went to a rehearsal. I forget what it was about, but it wasn't drag. He was trying to go legit, but he was kind of burned out, jittery and scattered. The show was bankrolled by his #1 john, a paunchy indulgent fellow. Hibiscus died of AIDS in 1982, one of the first of my friends to fall. My old pal and former Cockette, Adrian Milton, tells the story of first meeting Hibiscus back in San Francisco. Hibiscus had taken a meditative vow of silence and just smiled. The last time Adrian saw him was at St. Vincent's Hospital in Greenwich Village. It was near the end and he'd lost the ability to speak, but he managed another sweet smile.

There was a rural gay movement going on, a sort of a back-to-the-land-we-never-lived-on-in-the-first-place thing, bread baking and toenail painting. Danny and I drove my old Chevy up to a large gathering somewhere in southern Oregon, where a gay commune owned the entire side of a mountain, with a gorgeous swimming quarry. Carloads of queer hippies and queens and musclemen and street kids and whatnots descended on this tiny town. Some of the rural gays were a bit older, bookish and demure and sort of self-righteous. They lectured us about trampling on the native plants and the proper etiquette for shitting outdoors, but we just wanted to take drugs and have fun.

There were outdoor shows and lots of music. At an Isadora-Duncan-inspired fairie dance circle I met this *incredibly* hunky shirtless guy who had just gotten out of the Marines. We found an empty teepee and he wanted me to go down on him. Twist my arm. He lay back and presented the goods. Impressive. For the first twenty minutes I thought I'd found the Holy Grail, then it got really boring and my jaw started to hurt. I didn't want to be rude, so I kept it up for another ten minutes. Then I made an excuse about meeting friends.

At night everyone converged inside an immense barn and made music. I was up in the rafters and got into this call-and-response hooting thing with someone on the other side of the barn. We couldn't see each other but we kept it up for *hours*, deep into the night. I felt like a real hippie.

When the festivities ended all these strung-out queens wanted rides back to the city. My Chevy was jammed with a lot of hung-over glitter.

54

Back at the house in St. Francis Wood, we greeted Christmas with indifference and irony. After all, that freaky buy-buy-buying was the epitome of bourgeois greed. Tina decided we should have an anti-Christmas. The three of us went to a Foster's on Market Street and enjoyed fried chicken off a tray.

Tina, Danny, and I were invited to a party for a young actor, Richard Spore, who was about to go on a national tour of *Dylan*, a play about poet Dylan Thomas. The party was at a flat on Dolores Street and Richard turned out to be the most singular individual I'd ever met. He was rail thin, incredibly high strung, with a truly striking face, jutting cheekbones, enormous deep-set pale blue eyes, and blond hair. Richard was in high spirits at the party, feeling his oats because he'd landed this Equity gig, carrying on like a star, declaiming about his destined fame.

Richard took a shine to me that night and for the next five years he pursued me. It's safe to say he was a bit obsessed. (Of course, Richard was an obsessive, so if it hadn't been me it would have been someone else.) After having my heart pulverized by Dale, I was ready to be shamelessly adored. I finally gave in. Like many a spurned lover, I may have overcorrected a bit, seeking the security of a relationship where I held most of the cards.

I quickly found out that Richard was a local legend in San Francisco, a fixture on Market Street. At about age 10 he started dressing like a dour old man in black slacks, white shirt with the top button done, black shoes, black raincoat—think a pre-adolescent William Burroughs. Richard had never been to school, he was deemed too odd, and the Board of Ed supplied home tutors. His mother Avis was a real Dust Bowl type, bosomy in thin cotton dresses and an Okie accent. She and Richard lived in a low-rent residential hotel.

Richard and I used to take long walks all over San Francisco, for four or five hours, sometimes until two or three in the morning. He was tremendously endearing, open-hearted, sincere, honest, out and proud. We acted in many plays together and on stage he was riveting.

People warned me he was crazy—nervous to the point of shaking, prone to outbursts—but that only made me feel more protective of him. Later he and I moved to New York together and for a while he had a good acting career going, until he had a nervous collapse and entered a severe depression, which sadly grips him still.

Over the wearying months the household in St. Francis Wood started to fall apart. The lack of money created a lot of tension. Danny was usually off hanging out with the Cockettes and when he was around, he was lazy and self-pitying. If it were his turn to do the dishes, he would fill the sink with soapy water and leave them to soak—for a day or two. Like a good '60s kid, he became a savvy scam artist. He got welfare under a couple of names, shoplifted constantly, walked out on restaurant checks, and knew a thousand ways to get free stuff. When Marlene Dietrich appeared at the exclusive supper club Top of the Mark, he found out there was a doctors' convention in town. He called the hotel's switchboard asking for Dr. Green, Dr. Smith, Dr. Katz, until he hit pay dirt and got a room number. Then he reserved a table at the club under the doctor's name, enjoyed dinner and Dietrich and signed for it with the room number. I'd pretty much stopped my thievery and I told him he was creating a lot of bad karma, but he brushed me off with anarchist bullshit. I believe Danny played a price for all his scams, that they stained his soul.

Danny eventually moved to Seattle, took up daytime drinking, and died of cirrhosis. His body wasn't found for days, until a neighbor looked in the front window of his house and saw him on the living room floor. A lonely end to a lonely life.

55

Back at State I'd fallen into some theater and writing classes I liked. Tina didn't drive and there was nowhere she could walk, except around the neighborhood to admire all the pretty houses. The isolation was unhealthy for her. She never found a therapist, and I didn't keep track of her meds. I felt guilty but I wanted to get more involved at college, not in the care and feeding of Tina. I missed the early signs of a relapse.

Tina grew increasingly remote and gloomy. I'd try and pull together dinners, spaghetti or an omelet, but after a few bites she'd push her plate away. She started spending most of her time alone in her room. Her behavior was a cry for help, but I didn't know what to do. Finally, she stopped eating altogether, unless you want to count Hostess cupcakes. She smoked incessantly and filled notebook after notebook with poems, scribbling, and diagrams, sentences that made no sense. She stopped coming out of her room. Then she never got off her bed. My anxiety spiked. One morning I went in to talk to her. Her room was chaotic—dirty clothes were mounded in corners, there were cups and saucers filled with cigarette and joint stubs, spiral notebooks, pill bottles. The air was thick with the smell of old sweat and rancid patchouli oil. Tina was lying on the bed corpse-like, staring up at the ceiling. I opened a window and sat on the floor.

"Tina, what's going on?" No response. "I'm worried about you." No response. "Are you getting sick again?"

She laughed, that crazy bitter laugh.

"Is there anything I can do to help you?"

That chilling laugh again. Her face was set, her jaw clenched, her eyes staring straight up at the ceiling.

She was hurtling away from me. I know now I should have taken her to a psych hospital emergency room, but it didn't occur to me at the time. I was confused and afraid and overwhelmed and pissed off. I was failing Tina again.

One afternoon our old friend Johnny Farrow showed up in St. Francis Wood. I have no idea how he found us. I was surprised to see him, and Tina actually emerged from her room. Johnny had been in the Sierras and he brought us some huge pinecones. He was smiling and made a big deal about how amazing the pinecones were. They were big. We sat around on the floor in the unfurnished living room with the ugly purplish curtains, and Tina didn't talk. Johnny was a very sweet guy, and he had a wonderful golden California energy that day, but I'm afraid we couldn't return the good vibes. It was a forlorn visit, especially in the late afternoon light.

I wrote a play for my writing class at State. One day I came home, and it wasn't on my desk. I went into Tina's room. She was on the bed staring at the ceiling. Her complexion matched the gray curling smoke of her cigarette.

"Have you seen my play?" I asked.

There was no response for a long time and then she said, in flat voice, "I burned it."

"You *what!?*"

"I burned it."

I felt like I'd been kicked in the gut. This was just unbelievable, an act of raw hostility. From Tina.

"Why?" Nothing. "Tina, why did you burn my play?" No response. "Well, fuck you, too." I'd never spoken to Tina like this, ever. But I was reeling.

A private little smile curled at the corners of her mouth. I recognized that smile. It was the same one she had when she spiked my soda with LSD that awful night at the Farrows.

I remembered what the kind man in the convertible had told me, that schizophrenics often turn on those closest to them. Today I understand Tina was angry at me for not saving her. And for not being sick myself. And underneath it all, of course, the cosmic choking sadness of her disease.

187

Tina got worse and worse in the pristine isolation of St. Francis Wood. She stopped smoking or even moving. All she did was lie on her bed and look up at the ceiling. I was at sea, barely keeping my own head afloat. One day the owner of the house dropped by and he was taken aback—no furniture and purplish curtains. I told him my wife was sick and that we were moving out.

In the week before the move I kept telling Tina we had to get ready to leave. It was like talking to a stone. I called Mom and Dad and told them what was happening.

Mom said, "I *knew* something was wrong. We never hear from either one of you."

The only advice or help they offered was a plane ticket home, which I didn't want.

On the bleak foggy morning of moving day, I walked into Tina's room and said, "We have to leave." There was no response. "Tina, this isn't our house, you can't stay here, the owner will call the police. *We have to get out!*" Still no response. I had no idea what to do and I still had my own packing to deal with.

About an hour later, when I was the living room filling a few boxes with books and clothes, Tina emerged from her room with nothing but the clothes on her back, no bags, no boxes.

"Tina ..."

She didn't answer or look at me. She just walked past me and out of the house. I froze for a moment and then followed her outside. She was heading down the street.

"Where are you going?" I called, racing after her.

She whirled around, her face contorted, and spit out through clenched teeth, "Leave me alone!"

I stopped dead, breathless and helpless, and watched as she disappeared down the street. Madness had claimed her again. As I went back into the house to finish packing, I realized that part of me felt liberated. Tina hadn't disappeared. *I had let her walk away*. The weight of her disease had lifted. I was free. Even if she never would be.

56

With Tina gone, Danny and I rented a sprawling flat on Haight Street, east of
Masonic, right in the beating, stoned heart of Haight-Ashbury. It was a relief to be
back in such a colorful crazy-quilt neighborhood.

But I felt like Tina had taken a part of me with her when she walked away in St.
Francis Wood. All my pumped-up hope deflated. The world was a fucking shithole
where wonderful people like Tina got sucked into hell by an incurable disease. I
was devastated by her rage and by my own inability to help. It all threw me into
a miasma of confusion and guilt. And on a strictly practical level I was frantic to
know where Tina was and whether she was safe.

I found out later from Tina herself that she had a friend from Staples High who
lived in San Francisco. Tina showed up on her doorstep and the friend gave her the
money for a plane ticket back East.

Then one day about two weeks after Tina left, I was in the kitchen of the flat
when Wanda called me. "I heard from a doctor at Hudson River State. Tina is
there." Wanda sounded relieved but also somewhat detached, as if Tina was her
niece, not her daughter. It felt like everyone else in the family had given up on
Tina. Where did that leave me?

"Did you speak to her?"

"They told me she was in a psychotic state," Wanda said. "But at least she's
safe and not on the streets somewhere."

"Do you have the number?"

Wanda sighed. I could hear her rummaging around. "Here it is."

I immediately called the hospital and got the dayroom. A woman answered.

"Hi!" she said with manic good cheer.

"Hi. I'm trying to reach Tina Montemora."

"*Teeeee-na!*" the woman shouted.

I waited. There was no response. "Could you possibly try and find her? Tell her *Sebastian* is on the phone."

I waited and waited. I knew by then to expect the wait to be filled with blaring TVs, occasional screams, and snatches of angry, excited, or slurred speech. It was like an audiobook of Dante's Inferno, a chilling soundtrack of the world Tina lived in.

The woman came back on, "I found Tina!"

"Well, can I speak to her please?"

"She doesn't want to talk to *you*! So there!" the woman said gleefully.

I hung up, feeling an itchy mix of pity and rage. Poor Tina. Fuck Tina.

The kitchen in the Haight Street flat was painted Depressing Yellow and overlooked backyards. I looked out at the hippie mishmash of clotheslines, macramé mandalas, wind chimes, makeshift altars, and dog shit. I could almost hear the doors slamming in my psyche. I was not going to let Tina take over my life. Even though I judged my parents and Wanda for pulling away from Tina, I vowed to detach. Tina was going down and I couldn't go with her. I felt a wave of guilt, but I balanced it out by reminding myself that I didn't make Tina sick and that I'd tried my best all along to be a good friend.

None of it stopped my imagining how awful it must be in that mental hospital. And what rough shape Tina must be in to refuse my call.

I made a pot of jasmine tea and rolled a joint. I sipped and toked and tried to pretend it was just another afternoon in the Haight.

57

The Drama department at State had some terrific teachers but the emphasis was on musical theater and my school chums and I wanted to tackle more serious material. So I dropped out of college and we formed a theater at a church in the Noe Valley. We put on a bunch of plays, old and new, and by the time I left San Francisco, I'd been in more than twenty shows. The most fun was *Dracula: The Erotic Necrotic*, a wild spoof on the Dracula legend. It was a hit and we performed it all over town and got gigs up in Point Reyes and around the Bay Area. I played Dracula as a slithering sex maniac—*not* type casting. In addition to putting on the shows, we created a really nice community and it was a happy time.

My feelings toward Tina softened. And on better meds and getting regular therapy, her psychosis lessened. We spoke on the phone occasionally, but I kept my emotional distance.

Mom came out to San Francisco because she was working on a *Life* story about Clint Eastwood and the director Don Siegel, who had helped make Eastwood a star with his film *Dirty Harry*. I hadn't seen Mom in more than a year. We'd arranged to meet at Siegel's hotel, the Huntington, atop Nob Hill. I was walking up the hill when I ran into Mom coming out of a parking garage. We both stopped in our tracks and looked at each other tentatively, as if we were friends who hadn't connected in a long time and weren't sure how each felt about the other. It was a strange moment. We didn't kiss or hug.

"Mom," I said, confused. I wanted her to show me some affection.

"Hi, Sebastian." Her tone was less than warm.

We walked to the Huntington in silence. Mom strode along with great confidence, as befitted her position in the show-biz firmament. I was one step behind. I felt like there was a thick wall of plate glass between us. Who was this woman? And how did I feel about her? And how did she feel about me?

I think one reason I embraced California so deeply was because the distance enabled me to escape my confused feelings toward Mom. I wanted her to love me. And she did, in her own way. But her love had always felt conditional—and I was never able to figure out what the conditions were.

That evening on Nob Hill we were on an exciting adventure with one of the biggest movie stars in the world. She was my entrée into this rarefied sphere, a powerhouse, and I loved that. But then her muted greeting doused a lot of my excitement. I felt no sense of shared anticipation or fun. Was she jealous of my starry childhood, a childhood she enabled? After all, her own childhood was one of sorrow and confusion.

Clint was a real gentleman—soft-spoken, friendly, and clearly enjoying his success. We went out to a fancy restaurant in the basement of the hotel and I got a first-hand look at movie star magic. The restaurant was filled with a well-heeled, sophisticated crowd and they all dropped their forks and their jaws and stared at Clint—I mean the whole place just *froze*.

Mom was at the peak of her powers—expansive and witty and knowing, dominating the table, asking questions, telling funny or fascinating celebrity anecdotes. Clint laughed and leaned toward her. I watched with awe as Mom worked her mojo.

After dinner we went to a screening of Clint's directorial debut, *Play Misty for Me*, at a theater on Market Street. I thought the movie was a nifty thriller, taut and well-acted. In the car afterward I was sitting in the front seat between Clint and his driver and he put his arm on the back of the seat, almost around me—*pitter-pat*. A fan came over and asked for an autograph. As Clint signed, I said, "It's lonely at the top." He turned and gave me a big grin.

A gaggle of Hollywood big shots had come up to San Francisco for the screening, and afterward we headed over to Ernie's, a venerable old SF steakhouse. Everyone was milling around outside. Mom was in a tete-a-tete with one of the honchos. I had a sudden attack of insecurity. I didn't belong with these high-powered people.

I walked over to Mom and said, "I'm going to head home."

She glanced at me and said, "Suit yourself." She flew down to LA the next day.

The next year I was accepted into the American Conservatory Theater's two-year acting program. William Ball, the head of ACT, was a wildly gifted actor and director, mercurial, crackling, lightning in a body. The program was immersive—9-to-5, five days a week. I liked it a lot and I did pretty well, but then at one point I acted out during a rehearsal, stomping loudly across the stage for some long-forgotten reason. The director frowned in dismissal. I wasn't asked back for the second year. I've often thought of that incident and cringed. It was stupid and pathetic and impulsive and self-destructive—and emblematic of all the blown opportunities and rash behaviors that litter my history.

There was a funny old music teacher at ACT—rotund, bald, with a perpetually enthusiastic yet harried manner. He reminded me of the chubby, officious, kinda-femmy character actors in those old Hollywood movies. He lived alone in the mansion he'd grown up in, in posh Presidio Heights. He took an interest in me and invited me over for an hour every Saturday for free singing lessons. He might as well have tried to teach a rock to fly, but I enjoyed his attention. We met in the ballroom, which had a fireplace that slept six. He would play scales on his grand piano and try to teach me life lessons as well as vocal ones: "Be punctual, be prepared, be polite." He told me he had great faith in me and that I was going to have a wonderful career.

One Saturday I arrived to find him on a settee in the vast foyer, very agitated. "I have these *urges*," he told me. "They get very intense late at night." His face grew red and he clenched his fists. "I resist them, oh, do I resist them! With my body, my mind, and my soul. I *pray*." Sweat broke out on his forehead.

I wasn't sure what to say. I wondered if he was a Christian Scientist or something. He was definitely *comme ça*. Today he'd probably just come out and get on with it.

"It's all right," I managed.

He exhaled with a huge sigh. "Thank God for music!" He leapt up and led me into the ballroom.

I finished up at ACT and then it was time to head back East to try and have a career. Whatever that was.

As soon as I left San Francisco I missed it with a physical yearning, a true ache in my body. I try to go back every few years and I always feel at home there. I still find it magical and captivating and I still remember my first night on Russian Hill, walking around agog, the twinkling lights of North Beach spread below me.

I wish I could say that the young man saying goodbye to the city was wiser and more emotionally stable than the boy who'd fallen under its spell seven years earlier. But that's not how things went down.

58

In the spring of 1974 Richard Spore and I travelled to the East Coast on the infamous Gray Rabbit, an old school bus with all the seats removed that charged something like forty bucks to haul your ass across country in glorious hippie filth. When we arrived in Manhattan, we checked into a moldy hotel just off Washington Square Park. Mom and Dad were living nearby in a charming brownstone apartment on West 12th Street, next to the New School. For some reason I will never understand–financial necessity?–they were sharing the apartment with Wanda. This arrangement caused Mom and Wanda's relationship to take its final trip south. Wanda had the bedroom behind the kitchen, which was quiet and looked out at gardens, and my folks had the front room, separated from the living room by pocket doors. Dad used to complain that Wanda took an hour-long bath every afternoon, tying up the one bathroom.

I hadn't seen Mom and Dad in at least a year and expected a warm welcome as Richard and I rushed over to West 12th Street, rang the buzzer and bounded upstairs. Instead their greeting was strangely muted, polite but distant, and they asked few questions about our plans. I sat there confused, at a loss, getting the sense that they were disappointed I'd come back East.

"I've always thought of San Francisco as *your city*," Mom said, grinding out a cigarette.

Richard and I didn't stay long and as we walked back to our hotel I felt deflated.

During the following months I realized that my folks had circled the wagons against their ungrateful children. We were all, to one extent or another, hostile to them and not shy about expressing it. I complained to them about having to work at crummy jobs, losing hours I could have dedicated to my career. Their riches-torags trajectory was an endless source of guilt for Dad—he knew he had raised us with unreal expectations and failed the woman he loved. We didn't hesitate to play on that guilt. The Stuarts had entered the tatty world of the have-nots. A sense of shock and loss hung over the family like a stiff itchy shroud. The vanished world of milk and honey and charge cards took on a mythical, Chekhovian cast. For us kids, bittersweet nostalgia warred with the fact that we were fucking pissed. Our entitlement had turned into a cruel joke.

Losing circulation and influence, *Life* magazine had folded in 1972. The family took another blow and Mom learned a hard lesson when people stopped returning her phone calls. I was still in San Francisco but heard from my siblings that she had some sort of nervous breakdown. It must have been tough to plummet from a position of real power to sharing an apartment with your less-than-beloved sister at age fifty-five.

Mom started freelancing at Walker Publishing, writing copy for large format softcover picture books. It was a long way from lunch with Liza. Dad had a serious affair and at least partly in retaliation, so did Mom. Like the rest of us she was devastated by our reduced circumstances and made cutting comments to Dad about how broke they were. They were facing a future very different from the one they'd imagined twenty-five years earlier in the Garden—that sylvan oasis just a few blocks south.

Today their detachment from me and my siblings makes sense. We were all disappointments in one way or another, and snooty and sarcastic to boot. But back then I was hurt by their distance, jostled by their wake as they pulled away.

As usual with me, it took a while for things to sink in. There would be no more checks from Dad, no more bills I could just send home, no more summers in Europe. The security blanket was ripped off and there I was, vulnerable and humiliated. I went into a kind of shock. It shouldn't have been so unexpected, Dad had tried to warn me that day on Noe Street, but the reality didn't hit home until I was broke—flat-ass, can't-pay-the-rent broke—and had nowhere to turn for help. Hardly adept at navigating the world to begin with, I felt dizzy and angry and lost, even less sure than who I was, what I wanted, or how to get it.

59

Richard and I found an apartment on West 69th between Columbus and Central Park West, just around the corner from my childhood home at 101 CPW. My first job was as a foot messenger. I picked up manila envelopes at one office and walked them across town to another. Most of the other messengers were retired old men who looked slightly dim-witted. At least I was young.

Richard was a dear heart, but he was also, well, *eccentric*. And *very* high-strung. When I was cast in an Off-Broadway show called *Women Behind Bars*, he tore the apartment apart in a fit of jealous rage, afraid I would become successful and leave him. This put a damper on my good news. A year later, when I was cast in a Broadway show, he had another fit, packing a suitcase, announcing he was going to the Port Authority to catch a bus to San Francisco, and storming out of the apartment. As I watched from the window as he raced down the street, I was flooded by an enormous sense of relief and exhilaration. I'm free! Half an hour later Richard, however, was back at the door, plaintively wondering if I was really going to let him go.

Women Behind Bars was a wild takeoff on women's prison movies, written by Tom Eyen, who went on to write *Dreamgirls*. I played the only man in the show (well, there was one drag queen). My wife is in jail and when I visit her the horny inmates attack me, rip my clothes off and start ravaging me as the lights go down. In a later scene, the dyke matron feeds my wife a Quaalude and when she's drugged up, she hallucinates that it's me humping her, when in fact it's the matron chowing down. Since I had to enter that scene naked I would warm up my willy backstage. One night it got a bit too warm and when I walked out the actress's eyes grew really round. At an uptown casting call about a week later I heard two actors gossiping that there was actual fucking in *Women Behind Bars*. Well, it was as close as I ever came.

The prison matron was played by Pat Ast, who was something of a mascot to the designer Halston and his crowd and was also part of Warhol's scene (she starred in his movie *Heat*). Pat, who died in 2001, was an over-the-top self-invention, a large girl with frizzy red hair and a motor mouth. She was originally from Flatbush but affected a grand plummy accent like she was minor royalty with a champagne jones. She told endless stories of her exploits among the rich and infamous, like the time she got her period on Halston's pristine white couch in the middle of a party. Pat was also prone to pronouncements. After I complimented her on her legs, she said, "Halston says my ankles *save* me."

Pat was in the Pothead Hall of Fame—she was basically stoned *all the time*. She thought nothing of lighting a morning doobie at rehearsal. When she got high it was like you flicked a switch. She would vamp around spouting delicious nonsense in that affected voice—you could see why the rich kept her around as a *divertissement*.

Because Pat and Tom Eyen were so well connected, everyone came to see the show, including Jack Nicholson and Angelica Huston. In the dressing room after the show Jack offered me a toke on his joint saying, "I'm jealous of you."

"*You're* jealous of *me*?"

"Yeah, you get to be with all these wild chicks."

The next night he sent the cast three bottles of champagne with a note thanking "All the women of *Women Behind Bars*. And the man, too."

One of the other actresses in the show was a downtown legend named Helen Hanft, who was Tom Eyen's muse. He'd written a hit one-woman play for her called *Why Hannah's Skirt Won't Stay Down*. Helen was short and busty and loudmouthed, with dye-pot orange hair and matching lipstick. She had amazing enunciation and spoke with a gun-moll New York accent, sometimes breaking into a mocking, upper-upper tone.

Helen and I hit it off and one day she said, "I'm going to give you the only acting lesson you'll ever need. Just look straight out at the audience and say your lines as loud and fast as you can." Very Actor's Studio.

Tina was back in Central Islip, and I called and asked her if she wanted to see the show. She asked for a pass and got it and we arranged to meet at a diner on Astor Place, just up from the theater. She'd sounded pretty solid, and I was hopeful.

As I approached the diner I saw Tina standing outside. It was a spring evening and she had on a simple belted shift dress with a sweater draped over her shoulders. Her hair was clean and brushed and she had on lipstick. She had clearly made an effort. I found it touching.

"Hey, stranger," I said. "You look great." The truth was that up close she looked sallow and troubled. And vulnerable. I felt my throat tighten. We hugged and her body tensed.

We sat down and ordered Greek salads.

I showed her the *New Yorker* review of the show, which had given me a nice mention.

She read it and said wistfully, "It's really happening for you, Sebastian."

I felt a wave of guilt. I was in a show that was getting some buzz and she would be returning to that awful mental hospital.

"I wouldn't go that far. How's everything out in Central Islip?"

"Oh, peachy-keen." She took a long sip of coffee. "It's horrible. But it could be worse. I like my doctor. He's cut back on my meds. I don't feel like a zombie."

"I'm proud of you."

Tina stopped eating and asked for a refill on her coffee. She lit a Winston. "Cigarettes become your best friend in the hospital."

"Have you made any non-nicotine friends there?"

"They're all crazy," she said, and we laughed. There was a pause. Then she looked down and said, "I'm sorry I burned your play." I could tell she was fighting back tears.

"You probably did me a favor."

"No, it was an awful thing to do. I'm sorry."

"Oh, sweetheart." I squeezed her hand. "I accept your apology." In fact, it meant a hell of a lot to me. Not only because it resolved a piece of unfinished business between us, but also because it showed me that Tina was working hard in therapy, was dealing with things, was getting better. We ate our salads and moved on to family gossip.

"I have to get going or I'll be late for my half-hour call. I'll see you after the show."

During the show I peeked out at the audience from backstage and saw Tina sitting near the back of the theater. She wasn't laughing. In fact, she was frowning and looking pained. When my scenes were over, I peeked again and she was gone. I was hurt.

She called a few days later. "I'm sorry I left. It reminded me of the hospital. All the screaming."

"That's okay. It doesn't matter. Just keep getting better."

The year after *Women Behind Bars,* I was cast in a Broadway show called *Legend,* a western written by Samuel Taylor. He was a courtly sort who'd had a few Broadway hits in the 1950's and had co-written Hitchcock's *Vertigo,* which earns him a place in my personal pantheon.

Legend starred Elizabeth Ashley, who took hip to a whole new level—that chick could make a sneeze sound ironic. Liz—as she freely admits in her rowdy memoir *Postcards from the Road*—loved her drugs. One day during rehearsal she led me to a backstage corner, handed me a small jade box and told me to push a tiny button. When I did a little drawer popped open. It was full of cocaine. "Help yourself!" she said and disappeared. On opening night, she gave everyone in the cast a lid of reefer.

Being in a Broadway show is a heady experience. You're invited to parties, you have cash in your pocket, producers and agents are nice to you and stage-door Johnnies show up and ask you out.

There were about a half dozen seasoned veterans in the show, playing the cowboys, and they gave me an education in the vagaries of the business. While they were appreciative to have a gig, most of them had a bitter brittle edge from years of show-biz ups and downs, and they treated me like the starry-eyed tenderfoot I was. One night in the dressing room I made an innocent remark about how much fun I was having, when one of them exploded at me, screaming, *"You don't know shit about shit!"*

We were all hoping for the best: a hit that would keep us gainfully employed for a year or so. Sadly, *Legend* got bad reviews and closed after about a week. It was set in a dusty Old West town and one of its conceits was that Liz was the only woman in the cast, although the town madam was mentioned in the script. On closing night one of the costumers—the one with a beard—got dressed up in drag and sashayed across stage as the madam.

It was fun being in both shows, and I got nice reviews, but I never parlayed it into getting an agent or another gig. The world of agents and grownups and casting directors in midtown office buildings seemed like a foreign land. I was so insecure that when I called an agent I would start to sweat, and if we met in person it was the same thing, I felt self-conscious and I'd either push too hard, which isn't my nature, or not push at all, which will get you nowhere. I went to the perfunctory open houses that agents were forced to hold under Equity rules and to the casting calls advertised in *Backstage*, both at the bottom of the food chain. I simply had no idea how the business worked. I know now that it's all about making a living really, you're looking for work, for a job, for a paycheck, not for a friend.

I just didn't have the chops to be an actor.

60

One day I decided to sit down and write a play about my early years in San Francisco. *Underbelly Blues* poured out of me in a fever. The play is set on a freeway on-ramp and the lead is a speed-crazed drag queen who, with her stud boyfriend, is trying to hitch a ride to a party. Various lowlifes join them, and then a square's car breaks down and violence ensues. It's intense, with brutal language and violent action. I submitted it to the Edward Albee Foundation. Albee read it and gave me a residency grant at his artists' colony out in Montauk, and the play was a finalist at the Eugene O'Neill Theater Center.

I managed to get a small theater to mount it for a couple of performances. About a week later I got a call from a producer who'd seen it, telling me he wanted to mount it Off Broadway. I thought *this is easy!*

The Off-Broadway production was a complete disaster. The director didn't know what he was doing, and my rewrites were terrible. A few years later the play was staged at Re-Cher-Chez, the Mabou Mines experimental space on St. Marks Place, and it developed a small following. José, one of the hitchhikers in the play, is a Mexican busboy who's deathly ill, delirious with a raging fever, and just wants to make it home to die. José was played by Michael Carmine, a beautiful and gifted actor whose artist boyfriend came to most performances. He was a quiet skinny guy with wire-rimmed glasses who always sat in the back row. In 1988, just as Michael's movie career was taking off, he got AIDS and died a year later. His skinny boyfriend was Keith Haring, who died of AIDS in 1990.

A few years later Helen Hanft—my pal from *Women Behind Bars*—starred in my play *Smoking Newports and Eating French Fries*. It was a raucous comedy set in a trailer in upstate New York. I directed it and Helen was hilarious. But she was a real old-fashioned drama queen—conflict was her oxygen—and she kept goading me during rehearsals, trying to pick a fight in front of the whole cast.

Finally, I exploded, "Helen, what the fuck do you want from me, *blood?*" She broke into a huge smile and said in her upper-upper voice, "Oh no, Sebastian, I can't *bear* the sight of blood."

Warhol superstar Jackie Curtis was a mad fan of Helen's and came to every performance. When Helen entered at the top of the show Jackie would start bouncing up and down in his seat like an excited kid. Jackie, who'd grown up in an East Village bar his grandmother owned, was a little ragged around the edges (heroin will do that), but he had an indelible girlish/boyish charm, was pixie-dusted, a real fallen angel, so touching. Jackie died of a heroin overdose eight months later. It was a cautionary tale to watch him fall. And there were many others, kids with blazing gifts but no ability to navigate the world. Drugs offer solace, or at least numbness, for tender romantics.

There was real camaraderie among the downtown "geniuses" and freaks, and I was finding an artistic home in the East Village. In the late '70s and early '80s, the 'hood was full of art galleries, music, theater, dance, drag, funky gay bars and sex clubs. Wild kids burning bright, turning rebellion into art (or an approximation thereof). It was an orgy of id, which led to some cringe-worthy stuff being put out there. But it was a blast, a joyous celebration and a fuck-you to the homophobic Reaganites and their lot in Washington.

Sex was a big part of that rebellion. Across town in the Meatpacking District the Mineshaft and the Anvil were incredible theater all on their own. Talk about pushing the limits. Pick a kink, any kink, and it went down at those clubs. Gay power! Sex power!

There was a bathtub downstairs at the Mineshaft and one night an incredibly hot masculine guy in his early twenties was sitting in it, naked, surrounded by an ever-changing group of men who were pissing on him. He kept repeating, over and over, like a mantra, in a deep working-class voice, "I'm not in private, I'm in public, I'm not in private, I'm in public." It was wicked erotic; I mean he was just so *into* it. But I also remember thinking: *This does not look healthy."* Then I felt like an uptight party pooper.

61

When I wasn't writing plays, most of my (limited) energy went into paying my bills. I had dozens of jobs:

Waiter (of course).

Cater-waiter for Day-Dean, *the* old money caterer. At the New York Botanical Garden's annual fundraiser, I had the Rockefeller table. I overheard the man sitting next to the first Mrs. Nelson Rockefeller (a bitter biddy who got dumped for Happy) say, "We don't *want* their oil, it's too *mucky.*"

Product demonstrator at department stores.

Medical transcriptionist for orthopedic surgeons, a soulless if brilliant bunch who viewed the human body as an erector set. Their bedside manner didn't include visits to the bedside, their egos ran rampant, and they barely acknowledged us underlings.

House painter and house cleaner.

Craft services (supplying food and drink) for commercial shoots, a totally fun gig that took me to cool locations in amazing old suburbs like Englewood, New Jersey.

Telephone sales (Boy, did I suck at that.).

World's worst escort, for a service called Adam's Athletes. Adam had a sophisticated mission statement: "Get it up, stick it in, pretend to cum."

Cab driver. It was a good job because once you had your license you could work whenever you wanted. If I needed cash I'd head down to the garage in the far West Fifties at 6 a.m. and pick up a cab. My favorite days to work were Saturday and Sunday because there was much less traffic. I'd head downtown and pick up guys coming out of the Mineshaft and the Anvil after a night of drugs and kink. A lot of them were bleary-eyed young guys who looked like they'd been dragged under a truck for a few blocks, but you could tell that with a little sleep, a hot shower, and a small fortune in grooming products, they'd be fine. Then there were the gnarly old bears, all hairy in leather. Many of them lived in fancy East Side buildings and were probably hotshot decorators by day. The working-class guys who lived in Mott Haven in the Bronx or Sheepshead Bay in Brooklyn were the sexiest. They were great fares because you ran up a lot of money and got to see the fascinating corners and ethnic enclaves of the outer boroughs.

After the sex-club crowd thinned out at sunrise, I'd go right to the churchgoers, pious middle-aged women who would get all beatific on me, saying "God bless you" as they handed me my dime tip. All in all, driving a cab was a lot of fun, full of surprises and exotic characters. New York, New York.

For two or three Christmases I worked at Sherry-Lehmann on Madison Avenue, the wine and spirits store to the carriage trade. The holiday rush was brutal so they hired a bunch of actor-types to help out. One day a tall distinguished man in a long overcoat came in with his wife. They sent gift orders to about a dozen people, including William Buckley, and told me it was a charge. A Rolodex in the back of the store listed the names of all the charge customers and we'd been instructed to confirm the name of anyone claiming to have an account. I asked the man his name and he said, "H.J. Heinz." It didn't register and I went and checked the Rolodex, and his name wasn't there. I returned to the front of the store and said, "I can't find you in our little wheelie thing." Mr. Heinz puffed up like a blowfish, like the might of empires, and turned to his wife and bellowed, "He can't find us in his *LITTLE WHEELIE THING!*" I felt myself turn the color of ketchup and shrink down to about six inches tall. I managed to squeak up at him, "I'll take your word for it."

The first year I was at Sherry-Lehmann, a well-dressed woman came in. She was on the older side, short, wearing a fur pillbox hat. She had an Austrian accent and radiated culture, sobriety, and kindness. I filled her gift orders and after she left someone told me that she was Viennese, had an apartment in the University Club on Fifth Avenue, and that she and her husband single-handedly bankrolled entire productions at the Metropolitan Opera. The next Christmas she came in again and asked for me.

"My husband has been sick," she told me. "I want to send his doctor the best cognac you have." I walked her over to the locked glass cabinet at the back of the store where the expensive cognacs were kept. The priciest was something like $600 and came in a beautiful cut crystal decanter. The next most expensive came in a perfectly nice bottle and was around $400. She asked for the latter, telling me, "I want to send him the best cognac, not the best bottle."

62

Mom and Dad finally moved out of the apartment they shared with Wanda and into a loft on Christopher Street, off Sixth Avenue. Mom was having a tough time adjusting to the loss of her lofty perch in show biz, and Dad was struggling for gigs. They were renting out their house in Amagansett every summer to cover expenses. They'd have me over for dinner now and then. Both sides were wary and muted but nice enough in a defeated sort of way. I had no money, and they had very little, and a pall just hung over everything.

In the middle of one of our desultory dinners Mom suddenly became frantic and had one of her mini fits. She went to a bookshelf and started hauling out scrapbooks filled with articles she'd worked on at *Life*. She flipped through the pages, rattling off insider anecdotes about the celebrities and photographers, about which shots she chose to use, their locations, and the editing she did. It would have been interesting except that she was so hyper and anxious and talking so fast that she was tripping over her words. I felt terrible for her, and terrified of her desperation. *Life* was revived at some point and she made a strong push to get rehired. She wasn't.

I had a set of keys to their loft and one day I was in the neighborhood with a couple of friends whom Mom and Dad knew. We decided to drop by to say hi, and I rang the buzzer. There was no answer, so I took them up. A little while later Mom and Dad arrived home and Mom said coolly, "What are *you* doing here?" I was hurt and embarrassed in front of my friends, who were barely acknowledged.

"We just thought we'd drop in and say hi."

Mom walked over to the open kitchen and put on water for her tea. "In the future please call first," she said.

I slunk out, friends in tow.

One afternoon my brother David and his (now ex-) wife were in town from Boston and staying at the loft. I went over to visit. Dad wasn't around. David, who was in his late twenties, was a Yale grad with a keen intellect, working on his doctorate. His wife was kind and supportive.

David said, "I want to write a book."

Mom's jaw tightened, her eyes flashed steel shards, she turned on David and seethed in a savage tone, "*You* can't write a book. You have no *credentials*. Who'd want to read anything *you* wrote? What would the book be *about?*" She kept at it, *rat-a-tat-tat*, tore into him from here to yesterday. "You don't have anything *to say*! Besides you have no *standing*, all you have is a BA for Christ's sake. *Write a book?! You? Ha!*"

David kept his cool and handled it well, reminding Mom that he had a Master of Divinity degree and firm ideas for a book topic. His wife added that David was an excellent writer. But they were no match for the Tasmanian devil in the camel cashmere sweater. It was so shocking and vicious. Maybe Mom's outburst wasn't quite as brutal as Wanda's wholesale destruction of Tina the night of the Ford Agency Christmas party. After all, David had a supportive family and a community in Boston, while Tina was pretty much alone in the world. But it was painful, revealing, horrible—two mothers slicing their kids to shreds.

Both times it happened, I was shocked and speechless. Why? *Why?* Where was it coming from, the Malinowski sisters' compulsion to eat their young? I remembered Tina's belief that their own mother—Elsie Masson—and her long and gruesome decline from multiple sclerosis had left them scarred, emotionally stunted, and enraged at the gods for striking Elsie down. I didn't dwell on this thesis, mainly because I was in the middle of my own struggle, but also because it seemed so abstract, all happened so very long ago. It was only when I started to research this book, and was in intensive therapy, that Elsie Masson came alive for me and the magnitude of her loss, and her daughters' loss, became obvious. And here again, with Mom eviscerating David, was evidence of the terrible multi-generational aftereffects.

63

In the early '80s, Tina was bouncing between public mental hospitals in the city, on Long Island, and upstate. She seesawed between relative stability and psychotic episodes.

Then Nicky called with some good news. "Tina has really stabilized and gone into remission. I saw her today and she's *so* much better. She's clean and alert and making sense."

My first thought was *I've been here before.* But truly hope springs eternal, especially when you love someone, and I felt a jolt of excitement, a familiar hunger to believe that Tina could get better and stay better. I pushed aside the past disappointments. "That's incredible news. What happened?"

"I met with her shrink. Who Tina loves. She said that it could be the beginning of her aging out."

"So, it's not temporary?"

"Maybe not."

"Can she keep seeing the doctor if she leaves the hospital?"

"That's the tricky part. The doctor is on staff there and doesn't see outside patients. But she said she'll make an exception and keep seeing Tina for several months and will help her find a good replacement."

In the silence that followed, our faint fragile hope hung unspoken in the air.

64

Tina was released and found an apartment in the East Village—a decent enough place in a tenement building. I visited her the day after she moved in, flowers and Italian cookies in hand. She opened the door and gave me a sheepish smile. She looked *so good.* Her hair was washed and brushed, she was wearing a clean black turtleneck and jeans, she smelled like lavender soap, and she'd even put on red lipstick. My throat tightened.

"Look at you, Wonder Woman!"

"More like Woolf Woman—as in Virginia."

I handed her the flowers.

"I don't have a vase."

"We'll cut them down and put them in a glass."

"I don't have scissors."

"We'll use a knife."

"You're a Boy Scout."

"Only on Christopher Street."

The apartment was a one bedroom with very little furniture—a small table, two chairs, and a mattress and dresser—but it was clean and ordered. "This is a cool little pad," I said.

"It looks like Shangri-la to me."

I cut the flowers down and put them into a tall glass.

"They're beautiful," Tina said in her heartfelt, soulful way. She was savoring her freedom, her privacy, her reprieve. "I'll make some coffee and we can have coffee and cookies."

"Sounds perfect."

Tina began the coffee-making ritual that had been a part of our friendship for years. She filled a small saucepan with water and set it on the stove to boil, took a bag of Bustelo out of the fridge, folded a paper towel on the diagonal, and put it in a plastic cone, which she set over a mug. When the water boiled, she poured one cup and then a second. We didn't speak, and Tina moved slowly, tenderly. I felt like we were in a state of grace, both of us sensing how tenuous the situation was, and trying to banish Tina's terrible history, at least for this interlude.

Tina put the cookies on a plate and we sat at the table.

"Mom bought me a couch, it's being delivered tomorrow," Tina said.

"That's nice."

"It's from the Salvation Army."

"The East Village Bloomie's."

We chatted about politics and poetry and cabbages and kings and laughed and shared gossip about family and friends. We were in our 30s now, not kids anymore, and we were searching for new common ground, someplace where we could plant our feet and move forward into a new phase of Tina's life and our friendship.

"You've been through hell," I said, wanting to face down my denial. I sensed Tina needed her nightmare acknowledged.

She looked down into her mug and said quietly, "I guess you could say that."

"But I think you're aging out, that good things are possible, that you may never have an acute episode again."

She ran her fingertips up the back of her neck and looked me in the eye and said wistfully, "That would be wonderful."

I put a hand over hers. "Let's try and make it happen."

I started to visit Tina once a week, often bringing the fixings for a spaghetti dinner. Sometimes Nicky would join us.

After my first visit to her apartment, Tina never brought up her illness and neither did I. But unlike in the past, this wasn't denial. It was what Tina wanted, for her pride and her hopes. She was going for long walks, writing poetry, seeing Nicky and her half-brother David and a couple of old pals who lived in the city, trying her best to stay on the beam.

Then I got very busy. One of my plays was being produced and I was working part time as a medical transcriptionist, barely making enough money to stay afloat. I skipped some of my weekly visits, but one night after rehearsal I headed over to Tina's, picking up her favorite cookies on the way.

The second Tina opened the door I knew that she was falling, falling ... her hair was dirty, she was wearing a too-big oxford shirt with greasy stains on it, there were dark circles under her eyes, she was sluggish, her mouth twisted down.

I hugged her. She just stood there, tense. She smelled funky.

The apartment reeked of pot and sweat. There were clothes and piles of notebooks on the floor, and multi-colored pills scattered on the kitchen counter. I put the box of cookies on the table.

"Tina, are you all right?"

"I'm groovy, baby." She cackled.

"You don't look all right."

"Don't judge me, you little fucker." She bit down and bared her teeth.

I took a step back, fear and dismay sweeping over me. "Tina, I think you need to call your psychiatrist. *Now.*"

"My free pass ran out, *Sebby baby*, I can't see her anymore, my free pass, my free pass!"

I was growing frantic. "We can find you another therapist. Or maybe we should go to an ER."

"*I'm not going into another fucking hospital!*"

She opened the box of cookies and started eating them, one after the other, quickly, as if they could be snatched away at any second.

"Anyway, I don't need a therapist. I need *them* to leave me alone."

"Who?"

"I just told you—*them!*"

"But who are *they*?"

"My landlord and his police force. If I go out, they come in and move things around and steal my food."

"You don't have any food."

"Of course I don't have any food, they stole it!"

By now she'd eaten the entire box of cookies. She washed them down with several pills and a glass of water. Then she started to screech. I shuddered. She lit a joint and a cigarette at the same time. I began to feel like she was putting on a performance for me. I felt disoriented, almost as if I was crazy, too. The universe was disordered, up was down, and the room started to spin.

"He wants to be my *boyfriend!* He wants to have SEX with me!"

"The landlord?"

"No, stupid silly Sebby, the man across the hall."

I was going to faint. I couldn't handle this. I had to get out of there. "Tina, I have to go."

"Get lost," she sneered. Then she cackled again. Then she frowned and looked dejected, just for a moment, like she might start crying, like a little kid who's just been slapped. Her sudden vulnerability broke my heart. I thought I would throw up. Or start weeping. I fled.

The next morning I called her psychiatrist at Hudson River State and filled her in. She was concerned but professional, "I'm very sorry, there's nothing I can do. Tina is no longer a patient here. I've haven't seen her for over a month."

"She didn't tell me that. No wonder she relapsed."

The therapist sighed. "I will tell you that she spoke of you often. You're very important to her."

"Is there *anything* I can do?"

"While she's in the middle of a grossly psychotic episode, very little. You could try and get her over to Bellevue. They're very good with acute psychosis."

"Thank you."

"Sebastian?"

"Yes?"

"Tina is a special person. She's gifted, and funny and kind. It's a tragedy when someone of her caliber gets this awful disease. I'm sorry."

The psychiatrist's words, along with Tina's flash of vulnerability, reignited both my guilt and the overwhelming sadness I felt about her fate.

I called Tina but she didn't answer, so I went over to her apartment. The door was open and a man was inside cleaning. All that was left of Tina's stuff was a ratty pile of clothes.

"Where's Tina?"

"I don't know Tina, I'm just here to clean."

"She lives here."

He laughed and gestured around. "Nobody lives here."

I walked down the stairs, numb. To some extent I blamed Tina for giving in to her madness, for not telling me that she wasn't seeing the shrink anymore, for getting drugged up on pot and pills. But she kept it a secret and I felt like an outsider and a failure. Why didn't she trust me? I could have helped her find a new shrink.

Today I think what happened was that Tina had begun to build a new life, and it was that progress, ironically, that caused her to grasp the magnitude of what she had lost. Her history, and the persistence of her disease, even in a less acute phase, pulled her down, and it was all unbearable.

About a week later I got a call from Wanda telling me that Tina was in Central Islip. I was disappointed, knowing how much she hated that place. But I was also almost indifferent. I remembered her disdain for me, her cackle. I had my own problems, and I didn't want to get sucked back into Tina's nightmare *again*. Over the next few months, my feelings softened, but I made no effort to get in touch.

About six months after Wanda's call, I got a call from Tina.

"I'm living in Woodstock, Sebastian." Her voice sounded older, but relatively sane.

"How did that happen?"

"I met a woman in the hospital who has a friend with a boarding house here. She had a room for me."

"I'll visit," I promised.

I didn't. Not right away anyway. I wasn't sure what the future held for me and Tina, but for now a little distance suited me fine.

65

After Richard Spore and I broke up, I found a charming aerie on the top floor of a brownstone on West 88th Street off Riverside Drive. To my mind the streets in that neighborhood are some of the loveliest in the city, quiet and free from through traffic, with fabulous old buildings, wonderful light coming off the river, the sweeping rise and curve of Riverside Park. The park was cruisey back then, especially after dark, and the neighborhood was safe.

My place was reached by a small private staircase. It had its own little tar "beach" out the back window and a tiny kitchen and bath right out of the 1940s. I loved it.

As a kid growing up in New York I'd always been attracted to working-class boys, especially Italian boys, especially skinny Italian boys who wore skinny black pants, their black hair greased up in a pompadour. I'd see them on the subway and swoon, especially if they saw me looking and smiled—or even better, sneered.

One night I was walking down Broadway near 79th Street when that very vision appeared walking toward me—not a boy, for sure, but that boy grown up. I thought: *That man is my perfect type.* We passed each other and I gave him the eye. I was pretty sure he was straight but then he turned down 80th Street, took out his dick and started to piss against a wall. (Try doing that on the Upper West Side today.)

I didn't need an engraved invitation to RSVP.

We talked for a minute and I asked him if he wanted to walk over to Riverside Park. He looked a little tough so I wasn't sure I wanted to bring him home. We went over to the park and started fooling around. He knew what he was doing. After a few minutes I invited him over.

Louie Ruggiero was unemployed and homeless, an ex-con, an orphan, and a high-school dropout. What a catch. He was also soulful, funny, charming, and I thought very sexy. He was thirty-nine, exactly ten years older than me, living with a friend and trying to pull his life together after an earlier relationship had imploded in an alcoholic blaze. The ex in question was Sarah Churchill, Sir Winston's wayward daughter, whom he'd met at a fancy Chinese restaurant, the Gold Coin, where he parked cars and she drank.

Louie had pretty much hit bottom when I met him that night. He was staying with his pal Jack, an older Armenian fellow who had once sung at the Met and now lived on the top floor of a tenement on 84th Street off Amsterdam. Sometimes when you were at Jack's he'd take a hit of poppers, burst into an aria, pull out his fat Armenian cock and wave it around as he wailed. Such precious memories.

Meeting Louie's other pals was to take a journey to *Boys in the Band*-land. Wendell, a wizened voice teacher who worked with opera singers, was a true ghoul. He talked in sepulchral tones, popped all sorts of exotic pills, and never opened the heavy wood shutters on his windows. He put on recitals, the guests a mix of threadbare but grand opera types, pill-popping homos, and hustlers who ranged from femmy to rough trade. He'd meet the hustlers through the "Traveling Companion" ads in the far back of the *New York Times* classifieds—a discreet way for hustlers and johns to meet that dated back to the 19th century.

Wendell was famous for the size of his endowment. He'd haunt the men's rooms at Lincoln Center and carry on long back-and-forth correspondence on scraps of paper with the guy in the next stall. Inevitably there were would be expressions of shock and awe at the size of Wendell's willy, which he'd briefly kneel down and present under the stall. He loved to share these missives, crowing over the words used to describe his dick: a flagpole, a kielbasa, a blue-ribbon-worthy cucumber.

Louie's other old friend, Ron, had been a promising actor. He was handsome in a Rock Hudson-ish way, and charming, but a complete lush. He told fun New York stories, like the time he and some boozy queen decided to start a caramel business in the queen's Upper East Side apartment. Somehow they got an order from Bloomingdale's and soon the kitchen was filled with bubbling pots of caramel, one of which spilled and they were so drunk they left it on the floor and Bloomie's never got its caramels and who gives a shit anyway? One day Ron disappeared, and no one ever heard from him again. New York was like that then.

Whoever Louie was or wasn't, I fell in love with him. The sex was hot, but my feelings went way beyond that. He triggered something deeply parental in me—a yearning to make things right for him, for me, for the world. I couldn't save Tina but maybe I could save Louie. When he was happy I had an intense feeling of satisfaction.

Louie wasn't overly bright—although he could get in a bon mot now and then—but his biggest drawbacks were his self-pity and his male-ego inability to admit when he fucked up. He had no family and that's what he wanted most, of course. He was a lost soul, going nowhere at thirty-nine, while I was getting my plays produced, feeling creative, meeting fun and talented people. After a stimulating rehearsal downtown, I'd take the train back to the Upper West Side where Louie, sweet as he was, would be waiting for me. He never asked how the rehearsal had gone, I think because he felt threatened by that world, feared it would take me away from him. I began to feel that he was holding me back.

One winter day in the early '80s, about a year after we met, I told him we needed to talk. We went out to a coffee shop.

"Lou, I don't think this is working for me."

I could see the hurt wash over him. "Okay. Why's that?"

"I just feel like we're in different worlds. You know I love you."

"Yeah right."

"I do. But I want more. I want to be a writer and be in the theater world."

"I'm not stopping you."

"I know you're not ..."

I felt rotten, like I might start crying.

"Go ahead. Just leave." He looked down.

"Don't you want to talk some more?"

"No, I don't. I want you to leave me alone." His bravado was like Tina's and like hers it broke my heart.

I left the coffee shop feeling hollowed out.

217

The next day, feeling *really* down, I went for a walk in Riverside Park. It was a truly bleak day—the sky low and gray, the paths icy and treacherous. There was no one else in sight, not a soul. And then, in the distance, coming toward me, I saw Louie, hunched in on himself, looking like the saddest person who had ever lived. I'd never seen a look of such abject loneliness. My resolve to end things melted away and I said to myself, in a voice I can still hear: *I will* never *abandon him*. He moved into my apartment soon after.

Louie had been born out of wedlock in Brooklyn and never knew who his father was. His mother, disgraced by the Catholic church, gave him up soon after he was born and he grew up in a series of orphanages and foster homes. He had a few snapshots of his mother and a single poignant letter from her, written in pencil, expressing her love. Every time I read that letter I cried. She was a poor Catholic girl, shamed by her pregnancy, pressured to give up the baby she loved.

I tried to keep my commitment to Louie, and we were a couple for about four years. We had some fun, took a trip to Key West, had a lot of laughs. Near the end of our romance I inherited $20,000 from Dad's stepfather and used it to buy a cottage upstate.

Although New York City was well into its resurgence and I loved the city, I'd developed a romantic obsession with the idea of living in the country. Like my yearning for California, it was inchoate, made up of fragmentary images—country lanes, endless evenings, cows in fields, the slow river of August.

I'd read an article in *New York* magazine that said you could still find cheap houses upstate. I looked at dozens and finally found one in funky West Saugerties, a hamlet seven miles west of the Hudson River village of Saugerties and seven miles north of the town of Woodstock (which needs no introduction).

I fell in love instantly. The small cottage had been built around 1840 to house the workers on the farm across the road. It sat at the base of the eastern escarpment of the Catskills, and the Plattekill, a major stream, ran through the yard. In addition to the cottage, there was a tiny one-room cabin next to the stream, a stone smokehouse, a garage, a chicken coop, and an outhouse. I made an offer and bought the place.

Louie had gotten a job driving a Good Humor truck over in Rockland County and decided to stay at my place in the city—an easy commute to the job—rather than coming upstate. So on a bright June day I packed up some clothes, my dog Sasha—an elegant pure-white borzoi mix that I adored—piled into my Chevy Vega (basically a plastic toy car blown up a few sizes), and drove up to my new home. I had no idea what I would do once I got there. Except, I guess, be peaceful and content as I ambled down bucolic country lanes.

The first night I had a panic attack triggered by *the bare windows!* I was sure there was someone out in the darkness looking in, probably a serial killer with an ax and a serious grudge. The next day I ran out to buy curtains. About a month later the *Times* ran an article about how the first thing city dwellers do when they move to the country is put up curtains because the bare windows spook them out. (See, someone *was* watching.)

I had enough money to see me through the summer and I spent those sweet months driving the back roads of Ulster and Greene counties, usually with a joint handy. The beauty of the area just blew me away—rushing streams, mountain roads, lush greenery, pastoral views, dreamy homesteads, great old architecture, quirky towns and villages.

These days the region has been discovered big-time, back then it had a time-out-of-mind quality that just sent me. There's a great swimming hole down the road from my cottage and I learned the joys of plunging into the crystal-clear water that comes tumbling down from the mountaintop.

I was in nirvana, and thoughts of the future didn't enter my deluded little head. And with my thirtieth birthday approaching, my ticket to Fantasyland was way past its expiration date.

66

At the end of the summer Louie moved into the cottage and I gave him half ownership, hoping that if he had a home that could never be taken away from him he'd feel safe and would thrive. In some ways he did okay upstate. He made friends and for a long stretch worked as a landscaper for a local artist. About fifteen years later I asked him to give back his share and he did. I gave him free lifetime tenancy.

I think my love for and commitment to Louie was exhibit A of my puny self-worth. I had suitors at least a bit further up the food chain but I cast my lot with a man quite literally with nothing. I now understand that I transferred many of my feelings for Tina onto Louie. Unlike schizophrenia, this was a pain I could lessen, assuage, soothe. I took on Louie's grief at being alone in the world and I made it my own.

Later on, I also understood that the grief I was taking on was far greater than Louie's.

67

Louie saved his money and bought a Good Humor truck of his own. I was proud of him. He kept his route in Rockland County and I loved going out with him because his rounds included a place called Letchworth Village. The hours I spent there remain some of the most vivid, heart wrenching, and spooky of my life.

Built in 1911 to house "the feeble-minded and insane," Letchworth Village sprawled over hundreds of rolling Rockland County acres. It was born of a progressive ideal—to give society's unwanted a home outside of the city, in the country air, in a setting more like a college campus than an asylum, with handsome stone cottages surrounding grassy quads. In its early years the Village had its own farm where the residents grew crops and cared for cows, pigs, and chickens.

By the early '80s, though, it had degenerated into a very different place, chipped and faded, the lawns patchy, the farm long gone. The sparse staff was lazy and bored; they mostly sat around outside and ate potato chips and smoked. The "villagers" were housed according to gender and affliction—one cottage would be for men with Down Syndrome, the next for schizophrenic women, the next for disabled girls.

Driving into Letchworth Village was like entering another world. There was a strange sense of disorientation because the insane, the afflicted, the outcasts were everywhere you looked. To me the place was overlaid with profound sorrow and loss, tinged with existential terror. The residents were forgotten souls, hidden away. They didn't seem to form friendships, and they had few visitors. Their loneliness was palpable.

A resident I called Jackie Kennedy lived in one of the cottages for schizophrenic women. She was tall and graceful, with a patrician face and impeccable carriage.

Jackie would walk down the path in front of her cottage like it was a Paris boulevard and demurely hand over a quarter for a Creamsicle. I always smiled at her and said hello, and she always returned my greeting in a demure near whisper.

We were warned not to go to one cottage up on a hill, set back by itself. So of course that's right where I headed first chance that I got. The yard—surrounded by a tall chain-link fence—was dotted with women wearing thin summer shifts, their faces and bodies contorted. Suddenly one of them ran toward me shrieking, yanking up her dress to expose her nakedness underneath. I can still hear that shriek—primal, part sex, part fear, part rage. I beat a fast retreat and never went back.

At a cottage for the developmentally disabled, Myra, an aggressive girl from Brooklyn, ruled the roost. She had more money than most of the villagers and she would rush up to the truck and buy a half-dozen ice cream pops, which she would wrap her arms around and devour with alarming speed. Another resident was a sweet middle-aged Black woman with an open, guileless face who followed Louie's truck around for hours, repeating endlessly, "How you do it? How you two get to be so cute? How you do it?"

The whole place felt like it was suspended in time, a slow-motion movie in the dripping summer heat. If I stop and listen, I can still hear the faint plaintive melody of the truck's song: *Pop Goes the Weasel.*

Letchworth Village was finally closed for good in the 1990s. Today its buildings are vine-choked and crumbling, but the melancholy spirits remain. It has earned a cultist afterlife on websites devoted to haunted places, the macabre, and the mad.

68

After I bought my cottage I began to see more of Tina, who was still living in a boarding house in Woodstock. I was happy she was in the country, where her life was easier and healthier. Her meds seemed to have hit the sweet spot, keeping her from full-blown psychotic episodes but not turning her into a zombie. She kept herself and her room clean. The corners of her mouth pulled down and her skin looked ashen, but she was still beautiful.

The house was a huge creaky old place owned by a beatnik woman and filled with ex-mental patients, recovering and relapsing alcoholics and druggies, and aging beatniks.

There wasn't much camaraderie, though. Everyone labeled their food and one day, when Tina and I were in the kitchen making coffee, a haggard old beatnik gal came in and opened the refrigerator. "Fuck you, Tina, you used my milk again!" Beatniks and hippies don't always age well. There's something vaguely tragic about a long gray braid and full-length denim skirt on a woman over fifty. Throw in sneakers and a peasant blouse and you're really in dangerous territory.

The woman huffed off.

"Next time I visit I'll bring a gallon of milk," I said.

"Make it skim. She hates skim."

"Still, this place seems pretty laid back."

"It beats a hospital, I'll tell you that. Those places are hell."

"What's the worst part?"

She was quiet for a minute. "There's no privacy. None. Even the toilet stalls have no doors."

"Well, let's try and keep you out of hospitals."

A few months later I opened the *Kingston Daily Freeman* and the Police Log reported that Tina had tried to hang herself from a tree in the Woodstock Artists Cemetery. I found out later that her suicide attempt was related to an obsession with a married man who she was stalking. He took out a restraining order against her and she was 86'ed from Woodstock by the police. She moved to Kingston.

Summer turned to fall, and my money ran out. Completely. I got a job driving an airport shuttle van up and down the Hudson Valley, taking people to Kennedy and LaGuardia and back. Then winter arrived and the landscape of my dreams turned into something closer to a nightmare—bare trees, dreary gray light, bitter cold, the ugly mini-malls and McDonalds. On bleak winter afternoons it got dark at four, and the rest of the day stretched in front of you like a black hole. Everyone I drove to the airport was going somewhere—often to places that were warm or exotic—and I was going back to Saugerties. The job turned into a real downer.

The worst part about country living is having to drive everywhere. I was a city kid and after one winter I came to my senses. Louie's old pal Jack, the mad operatic Armenian, told me there was an apartment available in his building on West 84th Street. I rented it.

But Louie loved the country and he decided to stay upstate. Our romantic relationship just gradually faded away. On my first night back in town, going to sleep to the sounds of the city was a balm. I still love the country, but not in the winter, thank you.

69

In 1990, I met my current partner, Stephen, and moved to Cambridge, MA. I spent less and less time in Saugerties. My long absences took their toll on Louie, exacerbating his core loneliness and making him angry. I arrived for one visit to find that he'd torn down the ancient outhouse, which he knew I'd loved.

In 2010, Louie was diagnosed with prostate cancer and then lung cancer, although it was a slow-growing kind. He also had a neurological disease, never definitively diagnosed, that affected his legs and his speech. His illness rekindled all the pathos I'd felt for him when we first met thirty years earlier. I was surprised and overwhelmed at the enduring depth of my feelings.

The fact that Louie had no biological family, that he barely knew mine, and that we had few mutual friends, made our relationship very self-contained—just the two of us and our history. This gave his struggle a frightening existential loneliness. As he grew sicker, I tried to visit more frequently and at times I would free-fall into a chasm of sorrow and yearning, driving around Kingston in tears after visiting him in the hospital.

People were always telling me that I was a good friend to Louie but as I looked back over his life I decided that he would have better off if he'd met someone able to commit to him in a way that I hadn't. After one trip to Saugerties, I returned to Cambridge and said to Stephen, "You know, the irony is that Louie would have been happier if he'd just met some dumb queen."

To which Stephen replied, "He did."

Louie turned out to be a tough old bird. He hung on for two years, growing more and more diminished, finally losing his ability to speak. I told him I loved him a thousand times. I had his power of attorney and his health care-proxy, and his doctors, nurses, aides, therapists, and social workers turned to me for decisions. He was a good patient, grateful and funny. All that was best in him came out. That was a beautiful thing to see, especially since he could be a cranky SOB. My favorite thing to do was pat his distended belly and ask, "Twins or triplets?"

Louie wanted to live to see Obama reelected, but he didn't quite make it. He died on August 31, 2012, one day shy of his 72nd birthday. He was in my life for thirty-three years, from my late twenties to my early sixties.

My therapist had told me I might feel like I'd been released from bondage when Louie died. I didn't. I still miss him and love him. To this day, when something big happens, I'll suddenly think: "I want to call Louie."

70

In the early '80s I got my first writing job, turning out what we scribes called "adult literature" (the rest of the world called it pornography). The outfit I worked for was laughingly named Corporate Design, and its office was located over a delicatessen in the East 30s. The "literary department" was housed up front, while the back rooms were devoted to a thriving mail-order business, including a large storeroom filled with porn magazines, dildos, and plastic vaginas with polyester pubes.

We writers would arrive on Monday morning and be given a subject, such as "incest in a suburban cul-de-sac" or "a teenage dyke in Harlem." We would sit down at a primitive computer and write the book in four days, off the top of our heads—which were often impaired by the joints passed around the office by our boss. There was *no* rewriting because our keystrokes went right onto a tape as 3-D dots—sort of like Braille—which was then fed into a printing machine. Presto, a book!

Not only was there no rewriting, there was also no editing. The manuscript went straight from the printer to a proofreader, a jovial old man who must have had an iron constitution because to keep ourselves amused we stuck some *kinky* shit in those books. The proofreader's corrections were then typed up, printed, and any spelling or other errors had to be stripped into the original manuscript. This was a painstaking process done with a single-edge razor on a light table.

Since we weren't paid for our time at the stripping table we had a powerful incentive to keep errors to a minimum. But sometimes they just happened. I once wrote an entire book in which I misspelled the protagonist's name, Brian, as Brain. The name appeared in the book hundreds of times and I would have had to pull an all-nighter to strip in the corrections. Instead, I wrote a short sentence that

I managed to strip in early in the book: "Brian was so dumb he was nicknamed Brain."

The business was owned by an Italian-American gay guy who had rumored Mafia connections. He was small and cute and neurotic and was forever being audited by the IRS. He did *a lot* of drugs. He and his WASP-y wannabe-actor boyfriend lived in a glamorous duplex around the corner from the office. They appeared now and then but left the day-to-day operation of the place to a large and unhappy gal named Mitzi, who was basically their slave/groupie. Like a funhouse Ed McMahon, Mitzi laughed at *everything* the bosses said. "Have you seen my pen?" would elicit gales of mirth. Mitzi smoked like a hound dog and broke down in tears at least once a day, although the rest of the time she tried to be tough. She was always ordering clothes through the mail to fit her full figure, but when they arrived and she didn't like the color she'd burst into tears again. (Luckily, she had a thriving side business selling her used panties.)

We writers were of course dignified types who read the *New York Review of Books* on our lunch break. Actually, we were all misfits who had a great time churning out the books. I liked to throw in celebrity cameos, like the one where my young hooker heroine was riding down Fifth Avenue in a limousine naked with her john between her legs, when the limo stops at a light and Jackie O peers in. I also threw in political screeds on topics like the environment or gay rights, usually as internal musings by a redneck lout. As long as there was a sex scene in every chapter you could pretty much do whatever you wanted.

Everyone had a signature scene. Most of us writers were men, but women did pass through. One had a nice clean kink. Every one of her books included a scene in which a woman was washing/pleasuring herself with a bar of soap in the bathtub, only to be surprised in the act by an interloper—at which point the soap would fly out of her pussy, zoom across the room, and bean the offender on the noggin. She had that scene in *every* book. I guess you could say it was her brand.

More than a few of the writers I worked with at the porn factory have gone on to good careers as editors, true-crime writers, and novelists. (I won't name names.) We had a lot of laughs, and there were always more applicants than jobs.

Some people came to write just one book, just so they could say they had. There's nothing like the thrill of holding your very own copy of *Judy Takes a Lady*.

71

I left and returned to the porn factory a few times. Once when I came back I heard that a new writer had just been hired. I remember the first moment I laid eyes on Steve Lott at the coffee machine. He was slight and shy and almost pretty, with enormous brown eyes, black hair, and pale skin.

"Hi," I said.

"Hi," he said in a soft voice that made you lean forward so you wouldn't miss a single word.

"You look about thirteen!"

"I graduated from Princeton last spring."

"What was your major?"

"Victorian literature. I wrote my thesis on Elizabeth Gaskell."

"I have a feeling I should know who that is ..."

"Not really, she's relatively unsung, especially compared to the Brontës, who I am *obsessed* with."

"Any other obsessions?" I asked.

"Hitchcock, animals, and sex, of course."

"*Everyone* is obsessed with sex.

"Especially the Catholic Church," Steve said.

"Confession is kinda hot. Not that I've ever been."

"You *know* the priests are jerking off on the other side of that partition."

"Religion in general sucks," I said.

"People need an imaginary friend."

And the conversation never stopped.

Steve was always carrying around a dog-eared Trollope, at least one of his sneakers was untied, and his cigarettes were at hand. He was a true intellectual with a fierce, restless mind. He was also rebellious, ironic, funny and gentlemanly, with a strong moral streak. I quickly fell in love with him. It was impossible not to. I simply couldn't get enough of his company.

Steve had grown-up all over Asia and the Middle East. His father was headmaster of a series of American schools abroad and this nomadic, exotic and spoiled childhood gave him precocity and sophistication. His "adult literature" was gothic, gorgeously written, dripping with atmosphere. But Steve was madly neurotic—insecure and arrogant, slutty and romantic. He used to quote a line from Woody Allen's *Interiors*: "I have all the neuroses of an artist but none of the talent." I would assure him he did have the talent—and he proved me right.

72

I'd written a few more plays by this point and managed to get them performed downtown at theaters like LaMama, the Kitchen, and Theater for the New City. I had the chance to work with some amazing talents like Marc Shaiman, Sam Rockwell, Penny Arcade, Everett Quinton (who directed my last two plays), Mabou Mines co-founder Ruth Maleczeck, drag superstar Linda Simpson, chanteuse Suzy Williams, puppeteer Theodora Skipitaris, actresses Charlayne Woodard, Mary Lou Wittmer, Bina Sharif, Penny Rockwell, Cynthia Hoppenfeld, and Crystal Field, actor Michael Lynch, multi-talented Michael Musto, creative whirlwind Jamie Leo, composer Tom Judson, actor/artist/producer Chris Tanner, and downtown legend and keeper of the flame Agosto Machado. I contributed material to several theatrical collages that Chris Tanner mounted at LaMama and my co-contributors included Edgar Oliver, Basil Twist, and the incomparable Taylor Mac.

I'd become good pals with the aforementioned Chris Tanner, who had played Glit, the speed-crazed Tenderloin drag queen hooker in my play *Underbelly Blues*. Chris was a California kid, wholesome and sleazy, charismatic with an untamed id, a lot of drive, and a wild sense of humor. He loved to have fun and loved to create it for others. He also loved to dress in drag because he transformed from a nice looking guy to a simply gorgeous gal, but he's also a total top—a fact he makes known within minutes of meeting him (even if you're his dry cleaner).

I had a hunch about Steve, so I called Chris and said, "I want you to meet this new kid I work with. I think you might like him."

Steve and Chris fell in love. Steve adored Chris's unbridled id, and Chris adored being adored. Like everyone else he was captivated by Steve's quirky brilliance. The two of them soon moved in together.

That began a happy, happy time for them, for me, and for the tight community they created. Chris and Steve's apartment on East 3rd Street was always filled with downtown actors, musicians, artists, dragformers, and assorted hangers-on, it was a party every night.

I wrote three plays inspired by the Hudson Valley/Catskills: *Smoking Newports and Eating French Fries; Four-Leaf Clover Cabins;* and *Beverly's Yard Sale.* Steve directed the last two and oh-boy did he have a gift. He would take each actor out to lunch, look at them with his infinite simpatico, and listen. He confided in me that it was partly manipulation, saying with a sly smile, "I just sit there and let them talk, nodding now and then." But it was much more than that. He loved actors and knew how to build trust, and his method worked, the actors gave themselves over to him. He delved deeply into the scripts, uncovering hidden meanings that I had no idea were there (and probably aren't).

I wrote a comedy called *Neon Tetra,* a satire on the culture of fame. It was about a girl who becomes an accidental lip-synching superstar, can't handle success, and falls into the gutter. Steve directed a production at Theater for the New City and it garnered a bit of interest. There were various readings with Marisa Tomei, Ricki Lake, and Kristen Johnson playing the lead. Then the play made it into Madonna's hands. She was interested and a reading was arranged at her bungalow on the Warner's lot in LA.

Of course I was thrilled, imagining fame and fortune. I wanted to get on the phone and tell all my friends, but I was sworn to secrecy, told that if I blabbed the deal would be off. So, I kept my lip zipped and flew out to LA.

Madonna's bungalow was an homage to guess who? Pictures of her lined every wall. I was the first to arrive and found her on her stomach on the floor, knees bent, ankles crossed, leafing through a huge scrapbook of clippings. "I'm not self-obsessed," she cracked.

Kevin Spacey, Debi Mazur, Lorraine Newman, and two other actors arrived. The romantic lead opposite Madonna was late and she was getting antsy. One of the actors was all over her.

"Oh, Madonna, I love you, you're amazing, incredible, I would do *anything* for you!"

Madonna smirked and asked, "Would you wipe my ass?"

"Of course."

"With your tongue?"

The room fell silent for a moment. Then someone changed the subject. The reading went okay, but there wasn't much chemistry between Madonna and her love interest. Madonna has a lot of talents. Acting isn't one of them.

A friend gave me the book *Shadowland*, which tells the chilling and tragic story of the actress Frances Farmer. Frances was beautiful and gifted and idealistic, but also—thanks to a gargoyle of a mother—angry, self-destructive and completely unable to play the Hollywood game. She worked with the left-wing Group Theater, had an affair with the playwright Clifford Odets, did some serious stage work, and starred in several movies. But her alcoholism, rage, and inability to dissemble landed her in a mental hospital. While there, she was allegedly lobotomized by Dr. Walter Freeman, a truly creepy man who was a great proponent of the awful operation, in which an ice pick is inserted into the eye socket and then jabbed into the prefrontal lobe of the brain.

I was riveted by Frances's story. She was brave and beautiful and doomed—like Tina. Working at Re-Cher-Chez, the Mabou Mines space on St. Mark's Place, I developed *The Frances Farmer Story* (this was several years before the movie starring Jessica Lange). The play did well at Re-Cher-Chez and was optioned and produced Off-Broadway by a neophyte producer.

I thought opening night went well, although the producer seemed very keyed up at the after party. The next morning, she called me. "Sebastian, I'm afraid I have some bad news."

My first thought was that someone in the cast had been hurt. I sat down.

"What's happened?" I managed.

"The play has to close. It's in an illegal theater."

"*What?*"

"It doesn't meet fire codes. I feel like such an idiot. I didn't have my lawyer check the contract. I'm so sorry."

I hung up and sat there for a moment in some sort of shock. *Doesn't meet fire codes?* I felt a wave of disappointment wash over me, which morphed into depression. I had made a terrible mistake: I had let myself grow hopeful.

I spent a dismal day on the phone commiserating with the cast and crew. The next morning I went to the theater to pick up my stuff. The set designer was there, striking the set.

I was cheerful, even whistling, and he gave me a funny look.

"At least the pressure is off," I cracked.

It was a bizarre reaction that I now see as part of my family legacy—the refusal and inability to acknowledge loss, grief, mistakes, a dying mother. You can't let your vulnerability in, not a drop. If you do it will swamp you and you'll drown.

But you can't turn off your emotions. You can willfully deny them, stuff them down, but at some point the bill comes due. With interest.

Luckily, I had other projects in the hamper. Steve Lott had written two plays of his own, *Charlotte in Wonderland* and *Macbeth in Hell.* Both were wildly inventive pastiches of the Brontës, *Alice in Wonderland*, Dostoevsky, Hitchcock, lounge music, and Shakespeare, with a touch of John Waters, and a lot of celebratory eroticism. They were produced at Theater for the New City and got terrific reviews and sold out.

Then, just as Steve was coming into his own, he got sick.

73

On July 3, 1981 that now famous one-column article appeared on the back page of the front section of the *New York Times*. It detailed a rare cancer of the blood vessels, Kaposi's sarcoma, that was appearing in gay men in New York and San Francisco. I clearly remember that morning and the jolt of foreboding that coursed through me as I read. I'd spent time at the sex clubs and the baths, I'd had bouts of herpes and gonorrhea, and I'd recently endured a series of really bad sore throats. Uh-oh.

Pretty soon we were hearing reports of so-and-so getting hit with some rare form of arthritis, or someone else in the hospital with a deadly pneumonia or a virulent stomach parasite that didn't respond to treatment. About a year before that article appeared in the Times, a friend had gotten really sick with something his doctors were never able to diagnose. He'd moved back to Buffalo so that his mother could take care of him, and he died shortly thereafter.

Now it all made sense. Terrifying sense.

As the months passed the fear on the streets grew palpable, you saw it in the faces, the eyes of the men rushing past, filled with a terrible unknowing. What was happening? *Who would be next?*

In early 1983, French scientists isolated and named the HIV virus. At least now we knew what we were dealing with. Testing became available in 1985. But there was still no treatment. A positive result was a death sentence.

I became something of a lay expert on the emerging epidemic, reading everything I could get my hands on, especially the *Times* and the *New York Native*, a gay weekly that was providing superb coverage. I knew all the early symptoms, had zero denial, and was pretty sure that I had it. I checked my mouth every day for thrush, the white coating that was an early symptom, I felt my lymph nodes obsessively, and I went to all sorts of ad-hoc meetings and groups.

ACT UP, which was founded in March of 1987, was thrilling because fear was turned into anger and action. But many of the pre-ACT UP meetings I went to were filled with panicked young men who had come to New York to make lives for themselves and were now facing a gruesome disease that killed you.

One warm spring evening in 1985 I made my way to the Gay and Lesbian Center for a meeting on HIV treatment options. The cavernous first-floor room was jammed with men of all ages and colors, and our women allies. The crowd was restless, urgent, desperate. There was a powerful sense of community and a willingness to fight for the development of drugs that could treat the infection.

I spotted an adorable young man, a boy almost—I think his name was George— whom I'd met several years earlier at Julius's, the venerable West Village gay bar. He was blond and bright and charming, newly arrived from Indiana, full of hope and promise. We didn't sleep together but I'd found him simpatico and we'd met for coffee a couple of times. Now he looked scared and lost, a look I'd come to recognize as a sign of a recently diagnosed infection.

We listened to presentations about macrobiotic diets, Reiki, floatation tanks, turmeric. George raised his hand, "Has anyone tried drinking their own urine?"

There was a low groan from some in the room, instantly met with a fierce "Shhh" from the rest. Dismissing or mocking someone's idea was verboten.

George was thrown but he went on. "It's an ancient remedy. Urine contains minerals, salts, hormones and enzymes."

The idea sounded crazy. You could feel the skepticism in the room. George seemed to deflate.

"Would you be willing to work up a presentation on it?" the moderator asked respectfully.

George nodded tentatively. The meeting grew increasingly somber as it became apparent that there was little hard science behind any of the treatments discussed. When it finally broke up, I wondered if I should say hi to George. He was surrounded by people eager to explore his idea, to show him support. I got close and waved to him. He looked at me blankly, as if he had no idea who I was. I ducked out into the night. I hope he was able to hold on until the treatments came along.

One night not long after that meeting Steve and I went to a movie at the 8th Street Playhouse. We were sitting on a stoop afterward when he started to scratch his legs really hard, telling me he'd had several bouts of intense itching lately. I knew this was an early symptom, but I didn't say anything. But I was worried.

A few weeks later we took the bus up to Woodstock. Louie was late to pick us up so we sat on a bench in the sun and within seconds large clear blisters appeared on Steve's exposed forearms. They came up so quickly that it was like science fiction. I felt a terrible dread pass over me, but since there was no treatment yet I saw no good reason to say anything. But I knew.

Whenever the disease was mentioned, Steve would get angry. He thought the sex police were trying to keep us from having fun, laying a big trip on gay people. I gingerly said something to Chris, who, with his California optimism, answered, "Oh, I don't think me or Steve or you will get it." The denial camp had quite a few followers, even as deaths mounted and their position grew untenable. The evidence was everywhere.

Who would be next?

The director and writer Andy Rees—so talented and so handsome—had an IV port inserted in his chest. He told me, "I wake up in the morning and for a minute I forget. Then I look down at my chest. It's like being in a horror movie."

Someone asked me to foster a young man's kitten and I went to pick it up. The man looked about nineteen and his hands shook as he handed over the little thing. He died about a month later. I found a permanent home for the kitten.

An old friend, with whom I'd appeared in my first New York show, came over to my apartment. He started talking in a falsetto and couldn't stop himself as his face contorted with helplessness and confusion. After several minutes he burst into tears and ran out of the apartment. I called him later and left a message, but he never called back. About a month later I heard from a mutual friend that he was in the hospital. He had gone blind.

Popular downtown playwright and actor George Osterman came to a reading of a play of mine at the Public Theater, his whole body trembling.

My dear friend Ken Ketwig got it and moved to San Francisco. I visited him there, where he was living in a group home, a dark, depressing flat. He'd constructed a makeshift altar in his bedroom, featuring totems from numerous faiths. Ken was both acerbic and cherubic, a writer who'd previously had no truck with religion.

When I was sixteen I'd picked up a criminally handsome actor, Noel Craig, on the AA train. I brought him up to our apartment at 101 CPW and we messed around in my bedroom. At the time Noel was playing Hamlet in *Rosencrantz and Guildenstern Are Dead* on Broadway. It was a New York tradition back then for older men to give beautiful newly arrived young men keys to their apartments, and Noel had keys to six pads. We had trysts in all of them. One of them was a West Village atelier with an immense mullioned skylight. It was pouring rain outside—and with the watery light, the lashing rain, and his kisses, it was one of the dreamiest afternoons of my life. Noel and I hadn't spoken in more than twenty years when one day he called me. I was surprised to hear from him and at first our chat was a friendly catch-up. I told him I was struggling financially and yearned for more recognition as a playwright. It became clear as we spoke that Noel had endured some similar disappointments, and our conversation became melancholy. He said, "I should have moved to Hollywood years ago and gotten into a series." Later in the call he boasted, "I've kept three cars in New York City." Then he told me he was sick. I remembered our luscious long-ago afternoons when I was just a kid and he was so gentle with me. I felt the passage of time, of growing up, of the uncertainty of life.

"Thanks for calling and for being so nice to me back then," I said.

"It was easy."

"Take care."

"Goodbye."

A man I'd met at the Mineshaft and gone home with called me from the hospital. He told me he had it and that I probably did too. He was kind of mean about it, but then he'd been kind of mean when we tricked. I'd told him I wrote plays and he said, "That's a nice *hobby*." I was hurt and pissed at the time, but now I just said, "I'm sorry you're sick." He started weeping.

The rich and sophisticated painter Vassiles Voglis held court in his loft, wrapped in a shawl, slowly shrivelling. Vas, a friend of my folks', was in the international set with houses in Amagansett, Positano and NYC. He was a great friend of Tennessee Williams and couple of years earlier I'd spent a weekend hanging out with them in Amagansett. World-weary doesn't begin to describe Williams' sad-eyed ennui and longing. At one point I performed a monologue from *Underbelly Blues* for them and he became momentarily animated, predicting, "It's going to happen for you." At dinner that night, he drawled, "I spend three grand a month keeping my sister Rose in a home." I said "Hell, she can live with me for *half* that." He laughed.

About a year before HIV was discovered I read in the *Native* that a doctor at Roosevelt Hospital was looking for one hundred gay men to enroll in a study of the emerging disease. At that time many scientists thought that cytomegalovirus, or CMV, caused AIDS. I was accepted into the study, which was run by Michael Lange, a warm and empathetic young doctor. He was up to date on all new treatment developments and saw us every six months to take our blood. For the first year no one in the study got sick, then people started to, one after another. I was home and had just taken a hit of pot when Dr. Lange called.

"I have some not-great news for you, Sebastian." A fear rat raced up my spine. "You've tested positive for cytomegalovirus."

I felt the blood drain from my head.

"Are you there, Sebastian?"

"Yes. Do you think I'll get AIDS?"

He hesitated. "There is no certainty of that. But I'm not going to sugarcoat this."

In the following days and weeks I lost my appetite and had trouble sleeping. I only told a few friends. I tried to just put one foot in front of the other, but each morning I woke up dreading the day.

As the number of the sick and dying continued to grow, we were all drowning in grief, bewilderment, exhaustion, horror. There were memorial services every week. And there were also good deeds by the billions—people were making hospital visits, cooking meals, taking care of pets, going along on doctor visits. The gay community learned how strong, ethical, and kind we were. Our unity and the fight for a cure changed us. In the years since, we have claimed our power and the closet seems like a relic from the Pleistocene Epoch. As for the attitude of young people (gay and straight), well, queer = yawn. I know we still have a long way to go and that there are exceptions—queer and trans kids trapped in right-wing families and towns, threatened and even attacked, homophobic preachers and pols, and married men carrying what for them is still a shameful secret. But to me and many of my generation, the speed of our acceptance and ascent—marriage, kids, legal protections, a serious presidential candidate — has been swift and deeply heartening.

Our community was taking care of our own, but we needed friends in high places to bring public attention to the disease and push for a cure. Elizabeth Taylor stepped forward, saying, "I am going to fight this disease every day of my life, for the rest of my life." She put her money, her time, her heart, and her soul into the cause, helping to found amfAR, the American Foundation for AIDS Research, and raising millions at benefits and auctions. She went to meetings and hearings and just never ever, *ever* shut up, forcing people to listen and act. Steve devoured every bit of Liz news because she brought strength and courage and light and hope. I will love Elizabeth Taylor, every day of my life, for the rest of my life.

Looking back at that time is difficult but I think it's important. It's our history, the foundation of our strength. And all those who suffered so terribly should be honored, their souls and spirits kept alive with our love.

74

At some point not long after HIV was discovered to be the cause of AIDS, the *New York Native* ran a piece about a new treatment that had been developed in Israel and supposedly killed the virus. It involved mixing lecithin kernels with water, freezing the mixture into ice cubes, and eating them. I ran to the health food store and bought a big jar of the kernels, the owner said he'd been selling a lot of it. The lecithin ice cubes tasted terrible but I choked them down for several months.

I was still in Dr. Lange's study, giving blood and getting examined every six months. One evening about a week after my latest visit with him, he held a large informational meeting at St. Luke's Hospital behind Columbia University. The hall was packed, and after the meeting I found Dr. Lange and told him about the lecithin I was taking. He said, "I apologize, I was going to call you tomorrow, I've been busy planning this forum. Why are you taking anything? You're HIV negative."

My relief was so overpowering I went into a kind of shock. My partner at the time—an art critic and poet—and I went out to dinner and I just sat there numb, mute, exhilarated, so light I felt like I was levitating. The survivor guilt came later, but that night I felt released from a death sentence.

Steve wasn't so lucky. He developed an anal fistula and was diagnosed with AIDS. His doctor was Brian Saltzman, an only-in-New-York character, elegant and adorable, a clotheshorse, social powerhouse, and a great doctor. He's one of my heroes. He moved mountains for Steve. When Steve had a drug reaction that burned his skin off, Brian immediately had a bed filled with undulating hot sand transported from a burn unit uptown—one of a few such beds in the city. We could reach him at all hours. He always knew the most up-to-date treatment and was always ready to laugh—but underneath Brian's wit, glamour and joie de vivre was one brave, kick-ass doctor.

One day I walked into Steve's hospital room at Beth Israel to find Brian sitting on the couch next to the bed, his hand resting lightly on Steve's forearm. The mood was somber. "We're having a serious talk," Brian said.

I kept quiet as Brian explained Steve's end-of-life options. Brian's tone was loving and compassionate, but it was tough stuff to hear. Steve listened, eyes wide, afraid. My throat tightened. When Brian was finished, Steve said, "I want to be kept alive by any means possible."

That was such a sad delicate important talk, and Brian handled it with such grace.

Amazing as Brian was, it was Chris who led the charge. He fought for his beloved Steve, this was life and death stuff and woe be to anyone who got in his way. He would bully and badger and scream and cajole and charm and threaten— whatever he had to do to obtain the best, fastest care. He went to every doctor appointment and fed and clothed and finally diapered Steve. Their apartment became even more of a hotbed of creativity, filled with friends and food and all love all the time. Because, you see, Steve was just this lovable little guy. To know him was to love him.

Steve adored long baths. He would sit on his shins in the tub, the bath tray in front of him holding his Trollope, his cigarettes, a joint, a pen and notebook, a Barbie doll or two, some caramels. Four or five of us would be in the bathroom with him, sitting on the floor, the toilet, a footstool—people would be coming and going, just hanging out, for hours and hours with naked Steve, his emaciated body scorched with lesions, as he held court with his warm smile and kind words and pithy observations, ever the gentleman, always eager to hear what everyone else was up to.

Steve had some interesting reactions to his mortality. He became obsessed with breeding mice. He named each one—with three names, quite grand—and kept meticulous records of their bloodlines, as if he were breeding thoroughbreds. Mice multiply quickly and soon one cage grew to a dozen. Finally, there were so many it became dicey medically to have them around. He agreed to give them up and he, Chris, and I made trip after trip to the beautiful old walled cemetery on 3rd Street between First and Second Avenues. We would kneel by the iron gate and release shoeboxes filled with mice. Maybe there are a few mice there today who can trace their lineage back to the House of Lott.

Steve's folks visited often. They were sweet brave stalwart people who loved their son, but they had met as Baptist missionaries in Asia and were unprepared for the disease, for New York, for Steve's bohemian friends, and for losing a child so young. Steve's dad would tell me stories of young Steve and his imaginary friend, whom Steve *insisted* was real, and how Steve loved to sit in a window seat and read all day long, his imaginary friend by his side.

Steve spent the last couple of months of his life in a private room at Beth Israel, which had a foldout couch. Chris slept there two nights in a row and I relieved him every third night. Sleeping in Steve's room was like sleeping on an airplane, the low lights and low hum, the uncomfortable bed, the sense of being suspended. Steve had a morphine pump that went into his stomach and delivered a dose on a set timetable. He became obsessed with that pump.

One-night Steve's voice woke me up at around 3 a.m.

"*Sebastian!*"

"What is it, sweetheart?"

"My pump isn't working, and I can't reach my doctor!" He looked frantic and terrified, holding the phone in his hand.

"It's three in the morning," I said.

"I don't care. My pump isn't working. *I need to see my doctor!*" He hung up and called another number from a bedside list. "… No, I don't want to leave a message, *I need to see my doctor. My morphine pump isn't working!*"

He called yet another number. He was so agitated, almost hysterical, bathed in the ghostly gray light, calling and calling. Finally, I said, "I'm sure someone will be here any minute."

Steve whirled on me and cried, "Don't you understand, Sebastian, I'm *fighting, I'M FIGHTING FOR MY LIFE!!*"

The fight went out of him slowly and he slumped down on the pillows and started to whimper.

75

Steve's memorial was a little weird. It was held at Theater for the New City, and because Steve's folks were religious we wanted to find a pastor to say a few words. But we had no idea where to look. We finally found one in the Yellow Pages. He was a boozy flea-bitten old freak who specialized in eulogizing prisoners and other "ne'er-do-wells" as he called them. Of course, he didn't know Steve from Adam and he gave a sermon about how even sinners and lowlifes were entitled to God's grace. It was all wrong. But it was also perfect. Steve would have gotten such a kick out of it.

I think of Steve less often these days, but when I do think of him it's more acute. Thoughts have been replaced by *feelings* of him. It's as if time has distilled him, through some alchemy of the heart, to his essence. He was kind and gifted and he touched me so deeply. I wonder what Steve would be like today if he'd lived. During his last months he wrote extraordinary poems in the middle of the night. About a decade after he died, Chris produced a show at LaMama, *Ravaged by Romance*, that was based on Steve's death poems. It was collage of poetry and song, gothic and glamorous, featuring a bevy of downtown stars, a theremin player, an opera singer, and a dying boy.

Steve's been gone for over thirty years now. Once or twice a year Chris and I talk about him. We share a history and talk in shorthand as old friends do, so we don't need to say much, just a few random remembrances. And then we let the silences between us be filled with Steve.

76

Upstate in Kingston, Tina had hooked up with an Indian psychiatrist who worked for the state. The woman took a great interest in her and had her draw up a family tree. The doctor sent me a copy, and I called her.

"Thank you for all the care you're giving Tina. She seems more grounded since she's been seeing you."

"It is just my job." She had a weary, compassionate voice with that sweet Indian lilt. "Tina is a lovely person."

"Do you think she'll ever age out?"

"I do not know. She certainly has periods when she is lucid. Then she has episodes where she is grossly psychotic."

"They're terrifying."

"If they are terrifying to you, imagine how terrifying they are to her. I asked her to draw the family tree to give her a sense of support and belonging. It would be very helpful if the family could get more involved."

"Most of the family has written her off," I said.

"Yes, that does happen. This is such a destructive disease. You in particular are very important to her."

I felt a stab of guilt. "I'll see if there's anything I can do. Tina tells me you hire her to do yard work." I found this so touching. "You're very good for her."

"Again, I get paid for it. I am just doing my job. But I am very fond of her." There was a pause and she said, "You know, it has not been a one-way street with Tina. She has been good for me. She has a wonderful sense of humor." There was another pause, and I could sense she had something else she wanted to say. When she spoke again her voice was soft and heartfelt. "My daughter was at medical school, in Dublin, at Trinity College. She was hit by a streetcar and killed."

"... I am so sorry."

"Yes, well ..." She sighed. "Such is life."

The implication was clear—she had transferred some of her grief, maternal feelings, and love onto Tina. "You've made Tina feel loved. Thank you."

About a year later the doctor got a better job and left Kingston. She broke the news to Tina slowly, but it was a terrible blow. Tina lost a mother figure who she trusted, even loved.

77

Over the years Tina's theory–about the effects that Elsie Masson Malinowski's long struggle with multiple sclerosis had on the family–lodged in a corner of my brain. I came to believe that Tina's schizophrenia existed within the context of the entire family, through at least three generations. I became obsessed with exploring this history. And with getting to know my grandmother.

In 1995 Routledge in London published *The Story of a Marriage,* two volumes of the letters between Bronio and Elsie, edited by my aunt Helena Wayne, the third and youngest Malinowski sister, who lived in London. When it first came out, I fibbed to Helena and told how much I enjoyed it, when all I'd done was look at the pictures. The letters themselves had seemed like ancient history. Now I saw them as an incredible resource for studying and understanding what had happened during Mom's childhood.

I knew we had a copy of *The Story of a Marriage* somewhere in our apartment, and Stephen and I hunted it down, finally finding the two books on the dusty hallway bookshelf. I took them into the living room, lay down on the couch and turned on the reading light.

Elsie's face graces the cover Volume Two and I studied it. She looks to be in her late twenties, so lovely, with enormous eyes dominating a beautiful, soulful face. But there's something sad in her eyes–it looks like both wisdom and almost a premonition of her terrible fate.

I opened the book and began to read. I didn't move for hours. It was like finding an old trunk in the attic, opening it and discovering the key to your family's psychosis inside. Everything that Mom had kept buried was revealed. It didn't take me long to realize that it was indeed Elsie, and not the exalted Bronio, who was the linchpin in our family story.

I began this book to honor Tina's memory and her life, and to understand the effects her disease had on me. As I read the letters, I realized that I wanted, *needed*, to also honor Elsie, my grandmother, and understand the effects *her* life had on the family and on me.

I devoured the two volumes. They brought Elsie Masson vividly to life. She was born in Melbourne in 1890. Her grandfather, David Masson, was a Scottish literary scholar best known for writing a sixteen-volume biography of the poet John Milton (sounds like a great beach read), and for a contentious interview he conducted with Elizabeth Barrett Browning, in which he challenged her admiration for Napoleon III. His son, Elsie's father, also David, chaired the Chemistry Department at the University of Melbourne and was knighted for his work promoting the sciences in Australia.

Elsie grew up in Melbourne, in an enormous house just off campus. It was a perk of her father's renown and came with a small staff. I imagine Elsie, all full of Aussie energy, bounding down the wide central staircase in the morning, eager to meet the day, racing into the dining room where the cook has put out a spread of eggs and rashers, toast and Vegemite and Weetabix—the perfect accompaniment to the morning papers and the intellectual ping-pong the latest news provokes.

When Elsie was sixteen, she, her sister Marnie and their mother took off for Europe for six months, studying music in Leipzig and art in Florence and exploring Paris. She prepared for the trip by learning French, German, and Italian.

In 1912, when she was twenty-two, she went on another great adventure, signing on to be an *au pair* for the family of the administrator of the Northern Territory, which had just become part of the Australian Commonwealth. The capital, Darwin, was remote, reachable only by a long sea journey around the Cape York Peninsula.

When Elsie arrived she found herself in a frontier town, the Aussie equivalent of the Wild West, dusty and ramshackle, populated by tough Australian settlers and Chinese and Malaysian laborers, surrounded by the endless bush that was home to the native Aborigines and their mystical culture.

Enthralled, Elsie wrote dispatches from Darwin that were published in

Australian newspapers and collected into a book published by MacMillan in London in 1915: *An Untamed Territory: The Northern Territory of Australia.*

I was surprised to learn of Elsie's book. Mom had *never* mentioned it. A Google search turned up a rare-book dealer in London who had a copy for sale for $140. When it arrived I opened the package gingerly. It was a bit frayed around the edges but otherwise fine, its deep green binding embossed with the title and author in gold. The book is filled with photographs of the Northern Australia of a century ago, a look into a lost world.

I inhaled *An Untamed Territory,* captivated by my grandmother's vivid descriptions. Here she writes about the arrival of the mail ship into Darwin harbor:

"Suddenly the full, deep roar of the mail steamer breaks upon the silence and she slowly sails into sight ... There is a period of restless suspense while the mail is being sorted. If it is night, the little twinkling lights of hurricane lamps can be seen hastening in from all directions towards the post office. At last a bell is rung from the post office steps to announce that the mail is sorted, and presently the crowd ... hastens away, bearing huge bundles of papers and letters. For an hour or so afterwards, everyone is reveling in the news of the distant world, revived by old interests, warmed by old battle cries. Then the savage cadence of a corroboree brings back the sharp realization that one is in Darwin, cut off by thousands of miles from the rest of civilization."

The book made me feel close to Elsie, proud of her and protective of her and angry for her. She was erased, swept away by Mom. Who paid such a terrible price—in a bill she passed on to her children.

Why did Mom freeze Elsie out of our family? I think it was because she froze her out of her *own* life. Denial is a powerful psychological tool that can shield us from the unbearable. And for Mom I imagine the slow loss of her mother was just that. Unbearable.

I, on the other hand, felt a growing need to resurrect my grandmother.

I keep her book by my bedside.

78

Back home in Melbourne from her Darwin adventure, with World War I raging, Elsie went to nursing college so she could help with the war effort. She found work at Melbourne Hospital. Nurses are my heroes and this alone makes me adore her. Then, at a dinner party at the Massons in the spring of 1916, she met a tall striking brilliant young anthropologist. Malinowski was on a break from his fieldwork in Papua, New Guinea. Sparks flew and over the coming months they fell in love.

After he returns to his fieldwork, Elsie writes him: "It is a delicious summer night. There is a strong sweet scent in the air. My thought is quick with you."

After being asked to join a committee at the hospital, she writes: "Oh, Bronio, I don't ever want to be a Committee woman, don't ever let me ... I couldn't go through life becoming aggressive and wily and political and calculating of effects."

And of her dream for their domestic life, she writes, "I want to have a nice untidy little house with you, a piano, lots of papers about, casual friends of congenial kinds and romantic walks."

These letters sealed my love for Elsie. Distaining petty politics, wanting a lively, warm home life, and engaged with her times. What a cool lady.

Elsie and Bronio married in March 1919. A year later they sailed to England. Elsie never saw Australia again.

Thus began happy times in Elsie's life. Bronio published books and gave lectures to growing renown, and she was his muse and informal editor, going over his work, making helpful suggestions. They traveled a lot. Mom was born in Edinburgh in 1920; Wanda in the South of France two years later.

Then ...

... one bright autumn day in Bloomsbury in 1924, Elsie is out running errands.

She moves quickly, eager, full of life, carrying a string bag filled with fruit and cheese and bread, her thick red hair tucked atop her head, strands hanging loose. She has two adored daughters and is pregnant with Helena, Bronio is teaching at the London School of Economics, they have pots of stimulating friends, dinners and plays and books, a comfy flat, a second house in the Dolomite mountains of northern Italy with a long veranda where she and Bronio love to sit and read.

Have two people ever been more perfectly matched, more in love?

Elsie smiles at her good fortune. Then she brushes aside the silly sentiment as she approaches the curb. London hums around her and she hums with it. She steps out into the street. And then she loses the vision in her right eye.

79

Elsie's vision slowly returned, but over the coming months and years she developed an ever-changing array of symptoms: more vision problems, pain, numbness and weakness in her limbs, tremor and fatigue.

Helena was born in Bolzano, Italy in the spring of 1925, Elsie worked hard to make a lively home for her three daughters and to shield them from her fear that whatever was attacking her body would be unrelenting and would eventually kill her. But with that radar kids have the girls must have known that something was very wrong.

Meanwhile, Bronio's career continued to soar. The Rockefeller Institute offered to sponsor him on an extended American tour. On hearing the news, Elsie, who was too frail to accompany him, writes: "I am very proud of your success, my darling, but very, very sad ... that what are still the best years of our lives seem to be going to be passed alone, getting used to being without each other. We didn't marry for this."

In OB with the children, Elsie writes: "Towards evening I walked up and down the veranda and the whole place seemed saturated with the happy and even unhappy times we have had there."

I imagine Mom on that day, peering out the window as Elsie paced, feeling her mother's loneliness and foreboding. Was she quiet, or did she play with her two sisters? I imagine their nascent denial taking hold, I see them escaping on a hike to get away from something that they only vaguely understand but feel and fear deeply.

In January 1928 in London, Elsie was finally diagnosed with multiple sclerosis. She understood the bleak prognosis. In growing desperation, she underwent all kinds of treatments, some of them experimental. She had fluid extracted from her spine and turned into some kind of vaccine, which was then re-injected it into her spine. She had chemotherapy injections and ultraviolet ray treatments. She had surgery to open her sinus membranes. She spent time in numerous spas across Europe. No treatment provided more than temporary relief.

Elsie didn't tell Mom and her sisters about her diagnosis but they no doubt sensed her new fatalism. She writes to Bronio: "I feel so sadly how inadequate I have been lately as a mother. All the things that children prize ... I have not been able to do. Children grow accustomed to this, but it spoils their attitude towards their mother. They leave her out of things, just as she seems to leave them out. And yet I feel that Jozefa loves me really, deep down, more than anyone and has to struggle with a certain disappointment herself."

I read this line over and over: "... *Jozefa loves me really, deep down, more than anyone* ..."

Battling her disease, her marriage growing tenuous, wanting to shield her daughters from witnessing her painful decline, Elsie simply couldn't return Mom's love in kind, though she tried. A lack of parental attention and affection, for whatever reason, can lead to a child turning inward for validation of self. This is a classic template for narcissism. Mom fits it perfectly.

I also believe Mom was enraged by Elsie's sickness. How fucking unfair it was! I think of grown-up Mom, her clenched teeth and temper tantrums, her bitter trashing of friends, her nasty asides to her children, her haughtiness and condescension. All her life Mom had been raging at the gods about her mother's fate. And her own. If only she could have exposed her broken heart and vulnerability. Instead her rage ate her alive from within.

80

At one-point Elsie finds the strength to go to OB alone. A terrific storm hits, bouncing around the mountains. Lightning strikes the house, the lamps dance, and then there is darkness.

Elsie writes words that just send me: "It was so touching in between crashes to hear the little storm bell in Maria Himmelfahrt tolling away, utterly impotent and yet comforting just because so human and so very *un*divine."

Dear Grandmum—I can see you on that night, bundled up on the mountainside, alone and awed in the candle-lit darkness, maybe forgetting your illness for a precious little while.

Oh, Grandmum, I hope you did, I hope it so much.

All love – your grandson Sebastian.

At times Elsie is overwhelmed by grief. In one letter she writes: "… in the night I wake up quite in a panic about what I don't quite know myself. When I hear music, I feel such a rush of longing to be alone with you, which I see now we have not been for a long, long time. When you come back, we must try to bring it about sometime. We have so much separation still ahead.

Goodbye, my dear, dear love of bygone days.

Your Elsie"

Bronio starts sleeping with other women and is consumed with his career. His ego swelled alongside his accolades. In his 2020 book *Gods of the Upper Air*, Charles King quotes the anthropologist Ruth Benedict, who described Malinowski to Margaret Mead as being "vain as a peacock and as cheap as a saloon story." Mead said she felt "an undercurrent of disregard whenever Malinowski entered a room." King also alleges that Bronio once slipped money into the stocking of author and anthropologist Zora Neale Hurston as an invitation to go to bed with him.

Clearly Bronio's wife and daughters weren't his priority. His early letters are filled with passionate declarations of love and ardor, but these diminish as the years go on and Elsie's health continues to deteriorate. Then he writes mostly of his career. His growing detachment from his family was no doubt confusing, even devastating, to Mom and her sisters, who were left to admire him from afar. One more facet of a childhood defined by trauma, loss and sorrow.

In one letter Bronio expresses guilt at his absences, and Elsie replies:

"I hate to think of you depressed about me, dear ... I quite understand if you act entirely on your own judgment, and I want you also mainly to consider your own work and life.

Ever and ever so much love, my darling boy.

Don't be sad about your

Elsie."

When I first read these words, I cried. She gives him permission to move on. And he takes it.

In 1934, Elsie and her companion Rosa Decell moved to Natters, a village outside Innsbruck. Her decline accelerated. Bronio rarely visited. Mom and her sisters were off at English boarding schools.

Elsie's last months were cruel indeed. She lost the ability to speak and swallow and was wracked with unbearable pain. She died in Natters on September 18, 1935. She was forty-four years old. Mom was fifteen.

Of her three daughters, only Mom came from London for the funeral.

Bronio brought his mistress.

Elsie is buried in the Western Cemetery in Innsbruck.

81

One summer when I was ten or eleven years old, Mom took us to Innsbruck to meet Rosa Decell, Elsie's faithful caregiver and companion. Rosa was elderly, living in a house for retired women. The place was cozy in a funeral parlor-y way, with wide hallways, thick carpets, and velvet curtains. Rosa's room was large and dark and filled with boxes of chocolates. She was anxious and fidgety and not eager to share her chocolates. Mom was anxious too and we didn't stay long. Seeing Rosa may have been more painful for Mom than she'd anticipated.

Later that same summer we visited anthropologist Audrey Richards in the English village where she lived. She'd been Bronio's star pupil and went on to become well-known in her own right. She'd also been a dear friend of Elsie's. It was a quiet, lazy English afternoon. Audrey had a set of rooms in a large stucco house. The setting was cozy but not sedate, Barbara Pym-ish. We toured the yard and met a bearded young scholar who was hanging out his laundry.

"Doesn't he look just like Jesus Christ?" Audrey chuckled.

We went for a walk to the top of a hill from which a dirt road descended through green fields, bucolic and inviting. It called to me and I took off down the hill, running and running and running. Finally, out of breath, I slowed and stopped, exhilarated.

I turned and saw Mom and Audrey in the distance. I was proud of myself for my run and was sure Mom would be, too. I chugged back up to them, expecting her praise. She and Audrey were chatting and Mom ignored me. I waited and waited. Finally, almost desperate, I asked, "Did you see me run?"

"I saw you," Mom said over her shoulder, in a nasty tone, in dismissal.

I felt like I'd been slapped for no reason. Had I done something wrong? Over the years that scene has become emblematic to me of Mom's erratic responses and the insecurity I felt around her. Running down the hillside had felt like a thrilling rush of independence, away from her. Maybe she saw it that way, too, and found it threatening.

Later that afternoon we had tea on a stone patio at Audrey's. I sensed a growing discomfort between Mom and Audrey, something unsaid, words unsaid, Elsie unsaid. Their conversation trailed off and we left soon after. The unsettling end was just like our visit to Rosa, and for the same reason.

Mom never saw Rosa or Audrey again.

Reliving all this history today, I believe that the grief and loss felt by Elsie and Mom and her sisters became woven into the fabric of our family's emotional legacy, our shared soul, and that I've carried that heritage all my life. And that it's shaped many of my behaviors and choices, often in a self-destructive way. But up until my early thirties I didn't understand any of this. It was just all bottled up inside me, ready to be shaken until the cap flew off. Or the bottle exploded.

I needed help.

82

I visited my first therapist in San Francisco when I was around nineteen. There was a large poster of Freud over his desk. I sat down and asked him, "Are you gay?" He practically jumped out of his chair, before answering a weak, "No." I never went back. The last thing I wanted was a closeted shrink.

Therapy was not popular in our family. A friend once asked Mom if she'd ever been to a therapist. She answered, "I wouldn't touch therapy with a ten-foot pole!" (A Freudian twofer—both phallic and paternal.) Years later a family member was floundering, and I offered to pay half the cost of therapy. The reply: "I went to see a therapist once and realized after twenty minutes that I was smarter than him, so why waste my time?"

"*Smarter than him.*" If my family had a coat of arms, that would be our motto. In Latin, of course.

When I hit my thirties I began to feel a real need to talk to someone. I was crazy with worry about my health and tangled up with Louie. I knew the relationship was doomed but I still loved and pitied him, felt this bottomless pathos for him, and I was stuck with him forever. Tina was always on my mind and in my heart. Career and money issues were causing me a lot of anxiety and frustration.

I'd been going to yoga classes at the Integral Yoga Institute on West 13th Street and I saw a card for a gay therapist named Peter Hendrickson tacked on a bulletin board. I started to see him. Peter was a tall lanky guy with enormous brown eyes, a little older than me, earnest, bright, and helpful.

I took to Peter and therapy immediately. Everything poured out, all of my insecurities and self-loathing and guilt and shame, my queerness, Mom and Dad, my wild days in SF, Tina, Louie, AIDS, work and art and money. I sat there yakking and little by little my demons seemed less daunting and had less power over me. They were being dragged out of the darkness and into the light of day, where they began to wilt in the sunshine.

The more I talked, the more I understood. I stepped back and looked at my behaviors and saw that maybe I wasn't such an awful person. Maybe I was a decent guy. For the first time I saw my parents as complicated people with rich, conflicted emotional and intellectual lives. I was one of their four kids, an important part of their lives for sure, but hardly the be-all and end-all. As I gained a deeper understanding of the role my folks played in my problems, I stopped blaming them.

I talked about why Mom was so harsh and angry. Peter agreed that it stemmed from watching her own mother die a slow hideous death while her father was gone for long stretches, and when he was around had little time for his daughters. Bronio was condescending, especially to women, an intellectual as well as social snob. In an attempt to curry his favor, whip-smart Mom mimicked this disdain.

Talking to Peter I grasped that Mom had a *compulsion* to feel superior to other people and that she had passed it down to me. If I met someone better looking, more talented, or richer than I was, well, I probably wasn't going to spend much time in their company. (No wonder I was alone a lot.) I always looked for a way to feel superior: if he was better looking, I was more talented; if he was more talented, he was also going bald; if he had more dough, well, money is crass and shallow. I realized that this was exactly how Mom reacted to people, that it explained her perpetual put-downs, the one-upmanship, the friendships lost, and the whole family's default posture of condescension.

One day writer-performer-mensch-amigo Robert Rubinsky and I were working on a screenplay at my apartment when Robert said, "You know, Sebastian, sometimes you scoff at my ideas so strongly that I feel inhibited or like an idiot or something."

I was devastated, but—cliché alert—Robert's honesty was a gift. It showed me how obnoxious I could be. All I can say in my defense is that I hadn't understood how insufferable I was.

I became obsessed with the condescension in my family. I began to see how self-destructive and unearned it all was. What right did I have to condescend? Underneath my flashes of arrogance, I was a roiling mass of insecurity and self-loathing. To the world, I was just one more asshole.

It took me years to get control of my knee-jerk, in-bred reaction to people. I trained myself to pause before I opened my mouth, to cut off my condescension at the pass. By and by, it withered. Of course, it was an artificial response to begin with—a reflex to protect myself from my true doormat feelings.

A couple of months later Robert arrived for a screenwriting session with flowers and said, "You know, Sebastian, you're *much* easier to work with these days."

All this led me to question my family's core collective myth: that we were all so damn smart. Sure, some of us were quick and articulate, facile, brilliant at playing *gotcha!* at our dinner table condescendathons, but why didn't we have more of what we wanted from life—success, money, love, accomplishment? Why did we make lousy decisions and squander opportunities? Why was our rage kept at a continuous simmer, ready to boil over at the slightest provocation? Why did we alienate people with our arrogance?

Maybe, in spite of our agile tongues, we weren't so clever after all. In fact, in some ways we were fools—particularly in thinking we were so smart. I stopped denying that I was insecure, vulnerable, hapless, and limited. My relief was the world's deepest exhale. The seismic plates shifted. I'd earned the right to humility. And it felt right, it just fit. I know that confidence is appealing and reassuring, but it's just not me.

Mom always acted like we were above money, going on about Europe's intellectual aristocracy (guess who was a charter member?), so superior to one created by wealth or title. To crave money for its own sake, to be motivated by money, was crass, beneath us. We heard "nice people don't talk about money" on an endless loop. But the truth was that Mom had money on her mind big time and judged people by how much they had. She idolized and envied her rich friends. I looked around and it hit me—nice people not only talk about money, but it also drives a lot of them to create wonderful things. Many gifted artists, writers and musicians are motivated to some extent by money. Many great inventions were born with an eye on the dollar sign.

Dad burned through his dough paying for our schools, trips, clothes, dentists, camps, etc. He tried to help Tina. Sure, I wish he'd had a better financial head, but he paid a big price. Aside from having to live low himself, he felt he'd failed Mom and his kids, and I'm sure his guilt was brutal. He was a great guy and I loved him. As I talked about it in therapy, my regret and anger about money slowly melted away. Once I stopped condescending to money, I even made a couple of decent investments.

One day I came into Peter's office and started to talk about Louie. Within minutes I just broke down, wept and wept describing his life, the lonely letter from his mother, the way he looked that miserable winter day in Riverside Park. Peter just sat there wide-eyed, handing me tissues. The next week he told me that I'd almost gone into convulsions.

Today I believe that torrent of grief was part of the family legacy. On some unconscious level I was expressing Elsie's grief at losing her life and Mom's grief at losing her mother and my grief about losing Tina to madness.

Something astounding happened after that Louie session. My pity and sadness for him lifted, if not completely, greatly, and stopped being so painful—at least, until he got sick thirty years later. That day in Peter's office the plates shifted yet again. It proved to me the alchemy, the magic of therapy. Talking, spewing, crying, raging, mourning—as I let them rip, the bindings of my neuroses loosened.

I was hooked.

What drove me to therapy in the first place was anxiety about my health. I was seeing Peter when I found out I was HIV-negative, and when I told him the news, his response was curiously subdued. He said something about how one's status changed everything. Later I realized, of course, that he was positive. At the time I was so elated and self-absorbed that I didn't pick up on it.

I stopped going to see Peter once my anxiety had shrunk to a manageable level. I was grateful for all his help and I sent him a thank you note. He'd bought a little place up in Woodstock and one day as I was walking across the green, I heard "Sebastian!" I turned to see Peter leap out of his car. We hugged.

A year later I saw an announcement at Integral Yoga that Peter had died of AIDS.

83

With Tina more or less settled in Woodstock, Wanda began to come upstate more often. At this point in her life Wanda seemed to really care about Tina. Like Mom, I think she felt some guilt over her mothering sins. Her amends felt sincere and touching. She and Tina would go out to lunch or dinner, sometimes with Tina's psychiatrist, and then Wanda would spend the night at my cottage. She and Louie became pals. Nicky was always a dear sister to Tina and regularly sent her packages of clothes and shampoo and food. I always visited her when I was upstate.

One weekend I read an article in the *Kingston Daily Freeman* about a drive along a canal overhung with graceful branches, evocative of the French countryside. It sounded lovely. I called Tina. "Want to go on a mystery drive tomorrow?"

"That sounds like fun."

"Great, we can have a long leisurely meander and stop for lunch. I'll pick you up at ten."

Tina seemed in pretty good shape the next morning, happy about our outing.

"Could you stop at my drugstore first? I need to pick up a prescription."

I waited while she went inside. When she got back in the car, she took a couple of pills.

"What are those?" She didn't answer. It was annoying, but ... whatever. I didn't want it to cast a pall on our outing.

The canal road was enchanting, and we drove in a comfortable silence, but then Tina's eyes grew lidded, her speech slurred.

"Tina, what were those pills?"

"Mother's little helpers."

She turned and looked out the passenger window, nodding, struggling to keep her eyes open. I was hurt, betrayed. "I thought we were going to have a nice time together."

"Boo-hoo."

"I think you're being a selfish bitch."

For just a second a look of hurt washed over her, but then she reverted to what I thought of as her "hipster face," lips pursed, all cool and distant and knowing.

"Deal with it," she said.

I drove her straight home in silence.

One summer weekend Nicky came to visit. We picked up Tina for another drive. It was late afternoon, just turning to dusk, the air was warm, we were riding through the hilly section of Kingston that spills down to the Rondout Canal. The route took us along curvy streets, past ramshackle houses with wooden staircases and side alleys. The world was still and we were moving through it.

Nicky said, "It's a nice evening."

And Tina replied with a heartfelt, "Yes, it is."

We drove in love-filled silence and ended up at an ice-cream stand. We bought cones of soft-serve and sat on a bench slowly enjoying them in the thick Hudson Valley evening.

That's my fondest memory of Tina's later years.

84

My last memory of Tina isn't so sweet. It was Christmas 1986 and Chris, Steve Lott, our friend Mary Lou, her boyfriend Nick, and I were spending the holiday together, jammed into my tiny cottage with Louie and his pet rabbit.

I wanted everyone to meet Tina, whom they'd heard me talk about for years. And Nicky, a NYC public school teacher, had given me about a dozen small, wrapped presents that she'd gotten from her students, to give to Tina.

Tina was living on Pinegrove Avenue in midtown Kingston, in the upper unit of a nondescript two-family house. I called to tell her we were coming and when I knocked, we heard footfalls. Tina had cleaned herself up for our visit and was wearing a black turtleneck and jeans, her favorite outfit. A hopeful sign.

I handed her a box of cookies I'd brought.

"It's a party," she said, both sweet and ironic.

We all laughed.

"You look nice," I said.

"Ya gotta maintain."

She led us upstairs. The apartment was decent, but it was barely furnished, with just a mattress on the floor and a small table with a few chairs. The kitchen had a box of cereal on the counter and a coffee machine that looked like it got a lot of use.

"I'm just settling in," Tina said. She'd been there for months.

I made the introductions. My friends smiled, but I could tell they felt awkward. Although Tina was in relatively good shape, she was anxious and wary and self-conscious. She opened the box of cookies, took one, and then passed them around. They weren't very good.

"I'm sorry I don't have anything else to offer you. Water maybe. But I only have two glasses."

"That's okay," I said. "I have some presents for you. From Nicky." I handed her the bag.

"Oh."

There was a pause. The living room opened onto a wood-paneled sunroom that looked more appealing.

"Should we go out there?" I said.

"Okay," Tina said.

The sunroom had no furniture in it, just an awful green Astroturf carpet that was bunched up in places. We sat in a circle.

"Do you want to open your presents?" I said. That was a stupid thing to say because it set up this dynamic of all of us watching Tina, who was growing more self-conscious by the second. The room was heated but chilly, uncozy.

Tina took out a present and unwrapped it. It was a small box of Russell Stover candy. Then she unwrapped a pair of socks with Santa on them. "Ding-a-ling," I said, and my friends let out strained laughs. Then came a pink plastic hair clip. Everything looked cheap and useless, the kinds of things parents with little money would give their kid's teacher.

Tina looked morose. I could tell she was falling. I didn't want our visit to be like this. I wanted everyone to get along and to have a nice time. Tina unwrapped a small ceramic duck.

"I've been telling these guys about you," I said. "What a wonderful poet you are."

"Do you still write poetry?" Mary Lou asked.

Tina scrunched up her face and then said, "Not right now. I used to be pretty."

Kind Mary Lou said, "You still are."

Tina seemed sad beyond sad and the mood grew more strained. There was some chitchat, but Tina had checked out.

Everything was going wrong.

"I guess we should go," I said finally. Why the fuck didn't I invite Tina to come with us, to be one of the gang, just paling around? Instead she might as well have been on display at Hubert's Freak Museum: *Tina, the Crazy Lady.*

We stood up; Tina stayed seated. There was an outdoor staircase and my friends filed out. I was last and I turned to Tina, sitting there surrounded by Russell Stover chocolates and a pink hair clip.

I gave her a lame smile. "I'll come back soon, okay?"

"Sure thing, Sirbasketball," she said.

Then she tried to smile. She wanted to leave me with a smile.

85

On the afternoon of November 23, 1987, eleven months after that last awful visit, I got a call from Wanda, her voice electric: "*Tina's dead! I found her body, I just found her! There are police cars and an ambulance! Lights, sirens!*"

I froze, going into some kind of shock. "She's dead?"

"*Yes!*"

I felt a wave of nausea. "Where was she?" I managed.

"On the floor! Her body was all swollen and dark! The police are here! They want to ask me questions! Her body! It was horrible! *I found her!*"

I hung up stunned, dizzy.

Tina was dead. At thirty-eight. I guess I shouldn't have been surprised, considering her life for the past twenty-plus years. Was it really only that long? It felt like a lifetime of madness and sorrow. It was over now. For Tina. And for me. For my hope that we would someday, somehow, get back what we'd had as children. That she would finally age out of the disease and we would have summer afternoons filled with long walks, talk about books and politics, mystery drives, laughs and more laughs.

I called Nicky. "Tina's dead," I said, fighting down tears.

"I know. Mom called me." Nicky said in a monotone.

"Do you want to go for a walk?"

"Okay."

I headed down to the East Village where Nicky lived. We started to walk downtown. It was a mild November night. We made our way to Little Italy. The streets were teeming with tourists and festive colored lights were strung across Mulberry Street, but I felt like I was looking at the scene from inside a bubble.

"I can't believe Tina is dead," Nicky said quietly.

"I can't either. There's a hole in the world."

"Tina will never get better now. I'll never have my sister back."

"She was so unhappy. Did Wanda tell you how she died?"

"No. They're going to do an autopsy."

"Maybe her heart gave out," I said. "Do you want to get something to eat?"

"I'm not hungry."

I wanted to cry and Nicky did, too. But no tears came. The shock was too great. Tears would come later.

I walked Nicky home. It was a hard, horrible night but I was thankful we could share it.

Wanda arranged a memorial service at St. Joseph's Catholic Church on Sixth Avenue in the Village, and had memorial cards printed up. It wasn't a special service, it was part of the church's lunchtime Mass. There were about a dozen people there for Tina, and about the same number of regulars. Mom and Dad came, and they were solemn if detached. Wanda had asked me to speak. I planned to talk about our childhood adventures, to conjure up those long-ago days and what a great friend Tina was. I walked to the front of the church, feeling relatively composed.

"Tina and I were best friends ..." I said.

And then I lost it, just totally broke down, shaking and blubbery and sucking air—*"Oh Tina poor Tina poor dear sweet Tina."* I fought to pull myself together. It took a while. I hadn't felt my outburst coming and it consumed me. Finally, I was able to go on, ending with, "Goodbye, my friend."

I cried a lot that day but it was years before I really understood how much Tina meant to me, how very close we'd been as kids, and how her sickness unhinged me, confused me, and left me forever feeling sad, angry, guilty.

Because Tina's illness was so dramatic, even violent—burned plays, suicide attempts, surprise acid trips, stalking, arrests, remissions, false hopes—and caused so much collateral damage, it was easy to focus on the symptoms and not delve deeper.

And she was sick for so long. Over the wearying years I lost sight of young Tina, of the girl I fell in love with, whose company I adored, my other half, always and forever.

I dreamed I went on a ferry boat
a ferry boat that would float and float ...

It's been painful and beautiful to summon up all this history, to remember Tina before she got sick—her wit, her poetry, beauty, athleticism, moral core, sweet sly smile, self-conscious laugh. I thought she would be with me forever—but she was snatched away, sucked into a crazy cackling kaleidoscope.

I know now that my heart broke when Tina got sick—and that I raced out into the world bereft, shattered and suffering, desperate for obliterating sensation.

86

Several years after Tina's death I visited Wanda at her apartment in the West Village. She led me to a small room with a view of the Empire State building. She lay on a daybed. There was a box of chocolates on the bedside table and she ate one.

"This is my favorite place to read."

We sat in silence for a moment.

"I miss Tina," I said softly.

"So do I, I miss her so much. I wish I could have done more for her. But I had no money, you see."

"You were good to her in her last years."

"I was, wasn't I?" Wanda said, both wistful and proud. "I'm going to scatter her ashes in OB, in the churchyard."

"I think she would like that."

Wanda ate another chocolate. "You know, when I first came to New York, I lived in the Village. One night I had a dinner party. Kirk Douglas and his wife came. After dinner, Kirk came into the kitchen and said, 'I wish my wife could cook like that.'" She tilted her head, "You know what he meant, don't you?"

"No, what did he mean?"

"He meant that he wished that he had married me."

My feelings about my beautiful aunt are so mixed. I have sympathy and affection for her, yet I hate her for how she treated Tina. I adored her when I was a kid—she was so glamorous, witty and open-minded and kind, a refreshing contrast to Mom.

I think at heart Wanda was a lovely and romantic person but that the trauma of her childhood deformed her character, just as it did Mom's. Instead of powering forward like Mom, Wanda chose the opposite, retreat, soft edges, days of wine and more wine, seductive oblivion.

I also believe Wanda resented, even hated, her first three children. Michael was born when she was twenty-three, capricious and oh-so fetching, a hot ticket in jazzy post-war Manhattan. She had no interest in motherhood. Then Nicky came along, then Tina, and by then her marriage was crumbling. Broke, her modeling money gambled away by Monty, she took the children and retreated to OB, from which she often fled for long stretches to party in Rome or Cortina d'Ampezzo, leaving her children up on the isolated mountaintop with the housekeeper Hilda.

After Wanda died, Nicky found a letter she had written to her mother—who was off in Rome—when she was four or five years old: "Mommy, please come home soon. We have no money."

87

In 1998, my folks decided to give up their apartment in the city, sell their house in Amagansett, and move to Boston. They wanted to be close to me and Stephen, and to my brother and his family, including their three grandchildren. By this time my feelings for them were mostly affectionate. They sold the place in Amagansett for many times more than they'd paid for it. Suddenly, in their mid-seventies, they were, if not rich, comfortable again. They made no secret of the fact that having some money was a relief, and they bought a condo in a former church in Boston's hip South End.

I don't know if it was the move, the infusion of cash, or age, but Mom mellowed out. She stopped ranking people all the time and I rarely heard a critical word about any of my siblings. Both of my sisters endured bouts of cancer and my folks spent time in Mendocino and Berlin helping them out.

Although she never said it, I believe Mom came to understand that she'd been a harsh undermining mother and was trying to make amends. It's a cliché but I think it was true for Mom: getting old meant a lot of shit that once seemed important fell away. She wasn't out in the world, in competition with everyone she met. She could finally exhale. Yeah, she could still be a condescending bitch at times—lifelong reflexes die hard—but she was a lot easier to be around.

My folks never talked about their health and each of them suffered slings and arrows. Because they didn't talk about it and remained so lively and engaged with the world, they didn't really seem old. It was a powerful example. I was proud of them. They loved each other, and with friends and family around they were gliding into a nice old age.

And then ...

88

On a slush-gray October morning in 2002 I was in the kitsch-cluttered (I've outgrown it, I promise) kitchen of our Cambridge apartment, drinking my first cup of Irish Breakfast tea and reading the *Times*—my daily procrastination routine, delaying my dive into the giddy delights of ghostwriting a business book. Stephen was off at a yoga class. The phone rang. It was Mom.

"I have some news, Sebastian," she said, speaking slowly and deliberately, which immediately alerted me that something was up. "I have lung cancer."

I was surprised but not shocked. Mom was eighty-two and still puff-puffing away. Then I felt a rush of sympathy—and secret excitement. "Mom, I'm so sorry. When did you find out?"

"Yesterday. I start chemotherapy next week." Now she sounded more like herself: she had a plan, a way forward. "So, there it is," she said with finality.

"Is there anything I can do?"

"Please don't call your siblings. I want to tell them myself."

I hung up and stood still. The world was quiet. I waited for waves of emotion to sweep over me. They didn't. I mostly felt numb—with that secret undercurrent of excitement. So, Mom, scary blazing Mom, is going to die. *This* should be interesting.

Old memories welled up. The first image that came to mind was of Mom's pursed lips and put-downs; her cigarettes, the fierce way she stubbed them out in her large glass ashtrays; how terrified I was of her. In my mid-twenties I chipped a bit of wood from the corner of her dining room table and cowered in apology, so abject and sweaty that she said mildly, "It's all right"—before re-igniting my guilt by telling me she'd bought the table thirty-five years earlier in B. Altman's antiques department.

I remembered her vivacity and charisma and strong opinions. Never dull, she was always ready with a quip or an interesting insight. She read like mad and could talk about Russian history and African geography and how "Theodore Dreiser writes with a sledgehammer."

I thought of her smug sanctity, like the time she found a wad of cash in the Rome train station and turned it into the Lost and Found, knowing the odds of its being returned to its owner were slim. But, at least, she said, puffed up and proud, "*I* did the right thing."

Finally I thought of her rare flashes of warmth and concern, of the time she came into my room when I was a teenager and said, "If there's ever anything you want to talk about, please come to me." I tensed up, taken aback and mistrustful of this out-of-the-blue offer.

"I don't think there is," I'd said.

And there hadn't been—then.

But now, when it's too late, there is.

89

Mom decided to get a second opinion and she, Dad, and I went to visit an oncologist at Mass General. As we sat in a cramped exam room and waited for the doctor, Dad tried to be cheery, chatting about my siblings and the latest movies and cracking a few forced jokes, but Mom was unusually quiet. She sat there, wearing beige as usual, her still-shapely legs crossed, her white hair well-cut, looking oddly resigned and passive and a bit dazed.

The doctor came in holding Mom's x-ray. He clipped it to a light board, looked at it and said, "It's possible it could be an infection." I could tell by his tone that he was just being kind. He asked, "Are you a smoker?"

Then it happened, striking and odd: Mom folded her hands in her lap, her eyes grew large, she tilted her head and said in a plaintive good-little-girl voice, "I'm trying to cut down." I was thrown by her wide eyes and wistful tone—but couldn't quite get a handle on why it was so jarring.

The three of us went out for pizza afterward, to a simple Italian place on Charles Street that serves square slices of pizza baked in a tray. We each got a slice. Mom didn't touch hers and at one point she said vaguely, "He did say it could be an infection."

The seismic plates had shifted yet again. Mom was the alpha dog in our family pack, but her power was diminishing in front of my eyes. She would be gone, and I would be free. Free of the anxious shadow she cast over the family with the sheer force of her intellect, condescension, and rage. Free of the cowering she had always ignited in me, often with a simple withering look. Free of the echoes:

"What the hell is wrong with you?"

"Are you ever going to learn how to think?"

Or an almost casual, *"I'm disappointed in you."*

Free of the fear of the monster within her that came spewing out that day in their loft on Christopher Street when she attacked David.

Free of all of it. It was hard to grasp.

I felt more emotion for Dad, who was so clearly broken up. He loved Mom so much. I squeezed his hand. "How about we split a cannoli?" I asked. Dad loved cannolis.

I walked up to the counter and got the pastry, cut it into three messy pieces. Again, Mom didn't touch it. Dad ate slowly. Everything seemed to be happening in half time.

After all, what was the hurry now?

Out on the street, in the cool October air, we said goodbye. Mom looked oddly blank and Dad just looked stricken.

It was only that evening when I was back home in Cambridge telling Stephen about the doctor's visit, that I realized what had been so striking about Mom's demeanor when she told the doctor she was trying to cut down on her smoking: it was the first time in my life that I had seen her display simple vulnerability. Beneath the years, the sophistication, the education, the snobbery, and the anger I glimpsed the little girl she had once been, a girl who grew up in the midst of a terrible, life-defining trauma.

Mom had a couple of chemo treatments, which she weathered well. She never talked about dying and showed nothing but resolve, determination to "beat this." She was in Mass General for a week and I spent a lot of time with her there. Family and friends dropped in, there was the too-bright chatter of hospital visits, flowers and chocolates. Mom put on her game face, sat up straight in bed, and took on all subjects except her health.

I welcomed the activity because when we were alone, I was at a loss. I loved Mom. Didn't I? I kissed her and told her I loved her when I arrived and left, but I'm not sure I meant it. There was no outpouring of affection from either of us, no checklist of final things to say and share, no summing up, no unburdening, no goodbye. There were just a lot of silences filled with a vague mistrust, some sympathy, but mostly distance.

It was simply too late to catch up.

I admired how stalwart she was, yet each new x-ray held more bad news.

Dad was a wreck. He tried to put up a brave front for Mom, but he was unable to disguise his fear and grief. At times, out in the corridor or walking to our cars, he would start weeping. Even when it was brutally clear that Mom was headed in one direction, he would ask the doctors what more could be done. I felt powerless to ease his pain. The best I could do was tell him I loved him a thousand times.

Mom lived for six weeks after her diagnosis and during her last month I felt suspended. The outside world fell away and I was in a tunnel, holding my breath till I got out at the other end. It was intense, surreal—making a cup of tea, running a bath, eating a sandwich—everything took on freighted meaning because Mom's days were dwindling and the enormity of her death threw life's everyday actions and demands into stark relief. In those final days I took nothing for granted. But there was that seductive light at the end of the tunnel: life without her.

90

During those strange days I often thought of Tina, who'd been dead for fifteen years. I missed her with an urgency that surprised me. It wasn't the Tina of her last years, lost and ravaged, that I imagined. It was the two of us as teens before she got sick, knocking about, yakking away, laughing, touching.

In my daydreams Tina is alive and we're sitting in a cozy coffee-scented Cambridge café, leaning into each other, talking about Mom's coming death and the family and a thousand other things. We've quit smoking, of course, but now and then we duck outside and share a Players (which doesn't really count because they're English). And it starts to rain, and Tina says, "I feel like we're in an Anita Brookner novel."

And the afternoon never ends.

91

October turned to November, the New England dark coming earlier each day.

Mom moved from Mass General to a hospital not far from us in Cambridge. She went downhill quickly and before long she was too sick for chemo. The family came to see her one last time: Diana from Mendocino, Rebecca from Berlin, David from Brooklyn, Helena came over from England and stayed with me and Stephen in Cambridge. Mom and Wanda were still bitterly estranged, and Wanda didn't come.

Helena, who died in 2018 at the age of ninety-two, was very English, with a round face and pale skin, a bit fluttery and vague, proper but touching, "terribly bright" in that Malinowski way that let you know she knew it. She'd worked as an editor and writer, raised two wonderful children, and didn't have that bitter, rage-filled edge that Mom and Wanda had. I was curious as to why.

One afternoon, between hospital visits, Helena and I were sitting in the kitchen having tea and biscuits. It was just the two of us in the apartment and I'd put on some Brahms because I found it soothing. It felt like we were sharing a moment of respite from all the emotion and activity surrounding Mom's death.

"May I ask you a question?" I said.

Helena looked at me warily over the rim of her cup. "Now is not the time to get inquisitive, Sebastian."

"I'm sorry. It's just that I'm interested in my grandmother, your mother."

"Mummy," Helena said, and her eyes got a faraway look.

"I got a copy of her book about her time in Darwin."

Helena smiled a soft smile. "Did you? Did you really? Wasn't she a marvelous writer?"

"Terrific."

"Did you know she wrote a play? It was a comedy about an African anthropologist who travels to Europe to study the natives."

We both laughed. Then Helena grew serious. "Who knows what Mummy might have gone on to accomplish?"

"Do you have any favorite memories of her?"

Helena tiled her head, listening to the music, still and wistful. Then she leaned forward and in voice full of emotion said, "What you must understand, Sebastian, is that I never knew Mummy when she *wasn't* sick. I never saw her walk unaided. I'm afraid it was much more difficult for Wanda and Jozefa. They saw Mummy's entire decline. I think their hearts just broke."

We sat in silence for a moment. Finally, I said, "Still, it must have been hard for you?"

There was a pause and then Helena straightened her shoulders and lifted her chin, as if she was an actress and the curtain was about to rise. "Tell me, Sebastian, are there any more biscuits to be found?"

About two weeks before Mom died, Stephen and I went to visit her at the hospital. He asked her how she was. "Feeling sorry for myself," she answered with a sheepish smile. Stephen always brought out the best in her.

Mom had started reading a new book about Berlin during World War II, and he asked her how it was. "I can't read," she said, exasperated and sour, looking at the book on the bedside table as if her loss were its fault.

A little while later, Stephen left, and Mom and I were alone.

Instead of the bland back-and-forth I expected, her face grew hard and she clenched her teeth, an expression I knew oh-so-well.

"You know, your father and I set up annuities when we sold Amagansett."

"Yes, I did know that."

Then she spit out, "*When I die, you'll each get a quarter of my annuity!*"

I was dumbstruck. Was this the time to wallow in that dark trough? After all, for the past five years they'd been relatively flush. Yet Mom was so angry, so late in the game, so very late, enraged that her kids were going to inherit some of her money.

Two days before Mom died, I arrived at the hospital to find her thrashing around on her bed, moaning and screaming, trying to get up, in a fit, a frenzy really. A nurse was at her bedside, trying to get her to take a sedative.

"Mom, try and relax, please try and relax," I said over and over.

Finally, she turned on me in a fury and hissed, "I don't *want* to relax!"

Those were her last words.

92

Now Mom is actively dying, her eyes closed, her breathing slow. Dad is beside her bed, touching her, smoothing her face, her arm, her shoulder, saying over and over, through his tears, "Everyone who loves you is here, everyone who loves you, we're all here, Jozefa, it's okay to let go, it's okay, I'm here, I'm here with you, I love you, my darling, I love you ..."

And Mom finally does let go. There's a large picture window in her room that frames the view of a tree—and at the moment she stops breathing a gust of wind blows up, rattling the leafless branches. Without a word, all of us in the room —— her husband, children, sister, daughter-in-law, Stephen—exchange hugs, one after the other. It's pure instinct, marking the end of Mom. All the demons and woes fall away in the pure finality of the moment. There are no more chances, no more hopes. Dead. Gone.

93

In the summer of 2003, we all gathered in OB to scatter Mom's ashes around a tree she'd planted in the yard many years earlier. It was my first visit to the house in almost forty years and the cars that jammed the town jarred with my childhood memories of a timeless, car-less Brigadoon.

For the scattering ceremony the whole family—including several cousins and family friends—formed a circle around the tree, holding hands. Dad was crying. David said a few words and spread the ashes around the tree trunk. It was nice. Later, in the tiny chapel down the lane from the house, the family and various townsfolk, some of whom had known Mom since she was a little girl, attended a small service.

There's a traveling flower vendor on the mountainside, a robust old fellow who goes door-to-door with a small wooden cart pulled by a donkey. He appeared in our front yard one morning, we bought some flowers, and then he asked about "the nice lady of the house." When we told him that she had died, he took off his cap and looked down for a moment.

Then he continued on his way.

94

Dad lived for another four years. He was awful lonely, poor guy, but all-in-all they were decent years for him. We had him for dinner every week and he saw other family members and friends. Like Mom, he died of lung cancer. Also like her, he lived six weeks after his diagnosis, and his last hours were equally as gut-wrenching and heartbreaking as Mom's.

But his final weeks had one great difference: there was an outpouring of pure love between the two of us. It was intense and beautiful. I thanked him for everything he'd done for me and told him I loved him again and again. I would spend hours in his hospital room, even as he slept, just wanting him to know that I was there, and that I would carry his spirit with me always.

Dad never lost his sense of humor. In his last week, after he'd been discharged from the hospital and moved in with me and Stephen, our friend Lesli Gordon came over. She and Dad liked to share jokes. She told one and he laughed and then said, "Stop it, you're killing me."

95

The distance I felt from Mom as she was dying hasn't diminished much over the years. I understand her better than I did but I still don't feel the instinctive abiding love for her that I do for Dad. It's sad, because I know she loved me. I remember her reading *Charlotte's Web* to Rebecca, her voice filled with tenderness, while I lay under the bed crying.

I imagine Mom as a child, in her bed at night, frightened and bewildered and determined, alone in the dark. Trying to make sense of a world gone wrong, turning to herself for answers, solace, courage.

In the end, after all the memories and images have washed over me, I feel regret, regret that we couldn't have been closer, couldn't have been friends. I feel respect for her work ethic and integrity. And I feel sympathy for that little girl who, when getting a second opinion on her lung cancer, plaintively told the doctor that she was "trying to cut down."

96

After Tina died, Wanda told me and Nicky that the autopsy showed that her death was caused by a seizure. We believed this for many years. Then, when I was working on this book, I wrote to the registrar in Kingston and got a copy of Tina's death certificate.

The cause of death is listed as "Suicide by multiple drug overdose."

My heart split open all over again. I suppose I shouldn't have been a surprised, since I knew that Tina was often anguished. But suicide? It can be a brave act, and a merciful one. I hope it was for her. I wish she had left a note. Something. Anything. *For me.* I want to claim Tina for my own. Nobody in this world loved her like I did. Like I do.

I often flash back to that awful last Christmas visit with her, friends in tow, on the Astroturfed sun porch, with the box of Russell Stover chocolates and the pink hair clip, how badly I handled it. And her smile at me when we left. Her brave smile. I smiled back. That counts for something, doesn't it? Our last smile. I tried my best, didn't I?

I wish I hadn't requested the death certificate. I can't stop imagining Tina's last hours. Alone in that awful apartment. Alone with her madness. The depth of her loss and despair. Did she think of me?

If she did, I hope she forgave me.

And I hope she knew how much I loved her.

EPILOGUE

I'm in my 70s now and I guess you could say things have worked out for me. I live in a nice apartment in a beautiful neighborhood of old trees and big houses, in a town I love, filled with people who gave Trump seven percent of their votes, a place urban enough to keep existential terror at bay. I can hear the soothing whoosh of the tires on Mass Ave.

I've been with Stephen, just about the man of my dreams, for over thirty years.

I still have my little cottage by the stream.

My writing career has chugged along and I'm proud of (most of) my work.

I've developed some social anxiety and a few garden-variety phobias—subways, elevators, bridges, tunnels, leaving the house, waking up. But I can usually handle them and rise to the occasion.

I've had skin cancer on my face and chest. A hip replacement. At age 66 I was diagnosed with hepatitis C. I took the cure and my liver is functioning fine.

I live a quiet life, which suits me. I love to read and walk and swim. Watch TV. See friends. I'm content enough of the time.

And grateful. I realize what a privilege it is to be a neurotic old man with skin cancer and a titanium hip. So many of my tribe didn't have that privilege. All the brave beautiful boys cut down on the cusp of their futures.

Memories of what has gone by, thoughts of my family, of loss, make me sad.

I remember Dad and Steve Lott and Elsie.

And Tina.

ACKNOWLEDGMENTS

This book never would have seen the light of day if it weren't for a lot of generous and talented people who helped me wrestle it into something vaguely resembling coherence.

My deepest gratitude to my editor Don Weise, whose insights, suggestions and nudges always paid off. I'm indebted to Amy Hoffman for her terrific copyediting, and to Patricia Bull for eagle-eyed proofreading that went above and beyond. Also to Linda Kosarin for the terrific cover design. And Raymond Luczak for his excellent typesetting. And to the dynamic Michele Karlsberg for helping me launch it into the world. And to Chuck Forester for his great generosity.

The following people, in no particular order, helped me immeasurably with their support and most excellent notes: Meredith Hall; Michael Lowenthal; Dan Doyle and Jenny Ross; Lesli Gordon; Ann Fitch and Stona Fitch; Mary Lou Wittmer; Mark Bruce Rosin; Jonathan Strong and Scott Elledge; Robert Rubinsky; Penny Rockwell; Chris Tanner and Anthony Rocanello; Michael Borum and Chris Castellani; David Hirsch; Brian DeFiore; and Dr. David Dolittle. My apologies to anyone I may have missed.

I worked on this book in Grub Street's Memoir Incubator, and my gratitude to my fellow incubees is enormous: Tina Dolan, Haley Hamilton, Denise Frame Harlan, Diane Fraser, Britta Kelly, Sara Orozco, Melanie Smith, and Tara Sullivan. Spending time with you was inspiring (and so much fun). Leading the Incubator was Alysia Abbott (whose memoir *Fairyland* is one of the most moving books I've ever read). Thank you, Alysia.

My admiration and gratitude to Grub Street itself, and to its founders Eve Bridburg and Christopher Castellani, is boundless.

I owe a deep debt of gratitude to my lovely, late aunt Helena (Malinowski) Wayne. Her brilliant and moving book, *The Story of a Marriage*, on Elsie and Bronio was an invaluable resource in writing this book. Thank you, Helena.

To my dear siblings David and Rebecca (Diana died in 2019)—thank you for putting up with me. And love to my cousins Nicky Montemora, Patrick Burke, Lucy Burke, David Allen and his wife Gerry Griffin, and to my nephews Zach Stuart and Dan Stuart, Dan's wife Mari Stuart, and to my niece Jessie Hollister. And to Kippy Dewey, my ex-sister-in-law.

As for Stephen McCauley, well, there aren't words. Should I use an emoji?

ABOUT THE AUTHOR

Sebastian Stuart has published nine novels, four under his own name, four co-written, and one ghostwritten. The list includes a national bestseller published in eight languages, a *New York Times* bestseller and a Book of the Month Club selection. His own novel *The Hour Between* was an NPR "Season's Readings" selection and won the Ferro-Grumley Award as best LGBT novel of the year. As a playwright, he was dubbed "the poet laureate of the East Village" by Michael Musto in the *Village Voice*. His work has been seen at La Mama, the Public Theater, the Kitchen, Theater for the New City, and other venues, and he has won grants from the Edward Albee Foundation, the Jerome Foundation, Theater for the New City, as well as two play commissions. His screenplays have been optioned by Lee Grant, Sondra Locke and others. He has written over a dozen original e-books, including biographies of Michelle Obama and Lady Gaga, travel guides, business books, and a cookbook. He lives in Cambridge, Massachusetts.

CPSIA information can be obtained
at www.ICGtesting.com
Printed in the USA
BVHW072030060721
611232BV00007B/213

9 781637 603635